# ANSWER ME THIS

# Answer Me This

by
The Rev. Claude Beaufort Moss, D.D.

LONGMANS, GREEN AND CO., INC.
NEW YORK · LONDON · TORONTO
1959

LONGMANS, GREEN AND CO., INC.
119 WEST 40TH STREET, NEW YORK 18

LONGMANS, GREEN AND CO., LTD.
6 & 7 CLIFFORD STREET, LONDON W 1

LONGMANS, GREEN AND CO.
20 CRANFIELD ROAD, TORONTO 16

ANSWER ME THIS

COPYRIGHT © 1959

BY THE REV. C. B. MOSS, D.D.

ALL RIGHTS RESERVED, INCLUDING THE RIGHT TO REPRODUCE
THIS BOOK, OR ANY PORTION THEREOF, IN ANY FORM

PUBLISHED SIMULTANEOUSLY IN THE DOMINION OF CANADA BY
LONGMANS, GREEN AND CO., TORONTO

FIRST EDITION

LIBRARY OF CONGRESS CATALOG CARD NUMBER 59–13546

Printed in the United States of America

230.3
M853a
7802106

# PREFACE

I have written this book because I was invited to do so. My commission was to answer all the questions that were asked in as plain, brief, and forthright a manner as possible. I know nothing about the askers, except that they are Americans; I have been constantly conscious that I am writing for them as a foreigner and that my firsthand knowledge of America is limited by a week's visit in the United States many years ago. I have also been aware that the faith of the Church is not limited or changed by accidents of race, color, or location: it is the same everywhere, for all men and for all time. Nonessential customs and practices do vary, however, and for helping me to speak intelligently to those of the American Church I am grateful to the Reverend Harris T. Hall, who has gone over my book with a careful eye and a willing hand.

Because I cannot expect all my readers to have access to theological libraries, I have seldom given references, except to the Bible and the Book of Common Prayer (English or American).

Some of the questions are about facts, others about the teaching of the Bible and of the Church; but others are about matters of opinion, in which cases I have given my opinion, right or wrong. If the reader does not agree with me, he must ask himself why he doesn't. I am prepared, of course, to give reasons for everything I have said, and many, but not all, of my opinions (for no one can have sufficient knowledge about so many things) are the result of long and careful study. If, therefore, I seem to anyone to write too dogmatically, it is not because I set any great value on my own opinions, but because I was required to give, as far as possible, a plain and definite answer to every question.

Should anyone read this book who does not belong to a Church of the Anglican Communion, let him bear in mind that it was not written especially for him and that at first he cannot be expected to agree with everything I have said. I hope that I have not been guilty of want of charity or of courtesy toward fellow Christians of any allegiance. I am sure, however, that it is a mistake, which has often been committed, to conceal what one really believes for fear of hurting people's feelings. I have never had any doubt that the Catholic religion as understood by the Anglican Churches is true and I can see no reason whatever for concealing the truth which I have been commissioned to preach.

C. B. Moss

# CONTENTS

# ANSWER ME THIS

## Chapter One

# GOD

**1. What is God?**

God is not "what"; He is "who."

God is a spirit, which means He is necessarily a personal being. God is self-conscious—He thinks, knows, chooses. He is pure spirit: He has no body, and therefore cannot be seen by human physical eyes (St. John 1:18). If God were not personal He could not be the cause of personality, nor could He have designed the universe, nor could He be morally good.

God is not limited by space or time. He is present everywhere. He is eternal; that is, He always has been and always will be, or, more correctly, He always is, for there is no past or future for Him. God can do everything that is not contrary to His own nature. Thus "it is impossible for God to lie" (Titus 1:2, Heb. 6:18). He cannot do what is contrary to reason or contrary to love. But God has chosen to set limits to His own power, by giving us free will. Having once decided to do this, He will not change His purpose (James 1:17, etc.).

God does not depend upon anyone or anything outside Himself. God made out of nothing all things that exist and He keeps all things in being; if He did not, they would immediately cease to exist. He knows everything that has been, is now, or will be. He is perfectly holy, just, wise, and merciful. He is love (I John 4:8). He made all things good; He did not create evil, but evil is believed to be not something but the absence of something (see Question 6).

God is one, and only one. But He is three "persons" (see Question 10). God is revealed as fully as possible in Jesus Christ (St. John 1:1–18). His love, which is the most profound thing we know about Him, is shown in the life and death which Jesus Christ, God the Son, experienced for us.

**2. What reasons can or does the Church give for an intellectual belief in God?**

There are five traditional proofs of the existence of God:

(1) From the agreement of all nations. All races of men feel and have felt the need to worship. This need would not exist if there were no real object of worship which would satisfy the need. (It is true that there are today many who seem to feel no such need, but the absence of a felt need to worship has arisen only in modern times; no race or tribe has ever been discovered which had no religion whatever.) Therefore the general opinion of mankind is opposed to those who deny that there is a God; the burden of proof thus rests upon those who think there is no God.

(2) From the necessity of a First Cause (the Cosmological Argument). There is only one way in which we can understand what is meant by a cause, and that is a personal will. The very idea of cause requires such a will. All causes are the result, direct or indirect, of the Will of God.

(3) From the necessity for a Designer of the universe (the Teleological Argument). The universe is a vast and complicated system in which all the parts are fitted to one another. This system must have been designed by Someone; machines don't come into existence without a mind to design them. The evolution of the universe requires that there must have been a Designer not only to have made it but to continue to guide its development.

(4) From the fact that the human power of reasoning requires the idea of God (the Ontological Argument). This point is too difficult to explain here, for it cannot be understood without some training in philosophy.

(5) From the existence of our human belief in morality and our acknowledgment of conscience. As far as we know there is no such thing in nonhuman nature. Morality and conscience must be either accidental products of life on this planet or they must correspond to something outside mankind. We cannot believe the former; the latter can only mean that the Maker of the universe is a moral Being.

To these proofs may be added a further proof from the existence of beauty in the natural world, that its Maker is the supreme Artist, and the proof from the necessity of an unmoved source of motion.[1]

None of these proofs depends upon revelation. The revelation

[1] J. H. Beibitz, *Belief, Faith, and Proof.*

of God, first to the Hebrews under the Old Covenant and then in Jesus Christ, has given rise to an enormous part of human history, for which there is ample evidence, but the proof of God's existence does not rest entirely upon this revelation.

These intellectual proofs are cumulative, that is, they confirm one another by leading to the same conclusion, that there is a God, but they cannot do more than produce a very high degree of probability. But we need something more than proof; it is not enough to believe that there is a God; the devils also believe and tremble (James 2:19). We have to surrender ourselves to Him: to believe in Him, to fear Him, and to love Him, with all our heart and mind and soul and strength. For this we need the gift of Faith which He alone can give.

### 3. We all worship the same God, don't we?

Christians, Jews, and Moslems nominally worship the same God, the God Who made a covenant with Abraham, though many of them hold false or defective beliefs about Him. But in reality many Christians (it is not for me to speak of the others) worship money, or power, or pleasure, or popularity, or their nation, or their children, since these are valued more highly than God. Whoever makes any person, thing, or cause the object of his life, rather than to serve and glorify God, is worshiping an idol. God has said, "Thou shalt have no other gods before me" (Ex. 20:3).

Christians believe that God may be worshiped, or prayed to, only through Jesus Christ. For this reason we are forbidden to join in worship, even of the true God, with those who cannot pray through Jesus Christ, because they do not believe in His Godhead. Christians may pray and worship God only with other Christians; that is, with those who recognize Jesus Christ as God.

### 4. In this modern age, how do we know God's Will? Through pure intelligence, reason, feeling, etc.? How can I be sure that I am doing God's Will?

We learn God's Will by praying for His help and making use of the means of discovering His Will which He Himself has given us. First, there is Holy Scripture: we need to steep ourselves in Scripture, especially the New Testament, with the aid of all the best advice we can get for understanding it. Secondly, there is the teaching of the Church in its widest sense; especially of the

Episcopal Church if we belong to it, and of the best and wisest teachers we can find within it. Thirdly, there is our reason, with which we judge between truth and falsehood, and our conscience, with which we judge between right and wrong. Sometimes we may also see God's Will in the events and circumstances of life. For instance, a man had been offered a certain position quite unexpectedly and without any effort on his part. After considering it carefully he concluded that it was God's Will that he should accept it, and this has turned out to be true, so far as one may dare to say that anything of this kind is God's Will.

**5. Why am I here?**

"To glorify God, and enjoy Him for ever." The reason for my existence is to serve and love God, to praise and thank Him for all His goodness, and for His sake to love my neighbor as myself: to take my share in bringing all human beings into union with God.

**6. Did God create evil?**

No, for all things that He made are good (Gen. 1:31). Even the Devil was created good.

St. Augustine taught that the only evil thing is an evil will and that evil is not something but the absence of something, the absence of love; just as a hole is not something but the absence of something, as darkness is not a thing but the absence of light. In Isaiah 45:7 God says, "I make peace and create evil," but "evil" here, as often in the Old Testament, means not sin but misfortune.

**7. What is revelation? How is it to be interpreted?**

Revelation is the message of God, given to mankind through the Hebrew prophets, and more fully in His Son Jesus Christ. "God, who at sundry times and in divers manners spake in time past unto the fathers by the prophets, hath in these last days spoken unto us by his Son, whom he hath appointed heir of all things, by whom also he made the worlds" (Heb. 1:1, 2).

God's revelation was recorded by the writers of the Bible, who were given for that purpose the special guidance which is called "inspiration." The most important part of these records is the story of the life, death, and resurrection of our Lord Jesus Christ, which is found in the four books, the Gospels According to St. Matthew, St. Mark, St. Luke, and St. John. But the writers of the Bible were men, limited by the language in which they wrote and by the ignorance of the age in which they lived. They were not free from the danger of making mistakes; the earlier writers especially had most imperfect notions about God's nature and purpose. The Hebrews were a primitive people, and they were not taught everything at once. Their ideas about history, geography, astronomy, etc., were those of their age and country, and are not to be regarded as revealed by God, even though we find them in the Bible. But the Bible, under the inspiration of God, tells us all that we need to know in order that we may have eternal life and union with Him.

We cannot hope to understand the Bible without long and careful study and without the help of the best commentaries written by those who have read the biblical books in the original languages. Some of the books are extremely difficult. Each book should be read as a separate volume. To read the Bible "from cover to cover" is foolish and has little value. Begin with the New Testament, especially the Gospels. The beginner is advised to avoid the Revelation of St. John, a book which is not meant to be understood literally but requires the aid of a good commentary (those by H. B. Swete and Martin Kiddle are recommended); some people, with matter-of-fact minds, cannot hope to understand it at all. Much of the Bible, especially the Old Testament, is poetry, and nearly all of it was written by Hebrews, who thought in pictures, not in concepts as most of us do.

## 8. What is Trinity?

The New Testament teaches clearly that there is and can be only one God; that Jesus Christ is God, though distinct from God the Father; that the Holy Spirit is equal to the Father and the Son, though distinct from both (St. John 14:25, 15:26; Rom. 8:16; II Cor. 13:14). From these and other passages the Church has worked out the doctrine of the Trinity. The doctrine cannot be better expressed than in the ancient doctrinal hymn, the Quicunque Vult, which has unhappily been omitted from the American Prayer Book but is found in all other Anglican Prayer Books. It is held to be binding upon their members by the Eastern Orthodox and Roman Catholic Communions, and by all Lutherans; thus it is found, translated into Finnish and Swedish, in the new catechism of the Lutheran Church of Finland, which is taught in all Finnish schools.

The Quicunque Vult says: "The Catholic Faith is this: that we worship one God in Trinity, and Trinity in Unity; neither confounding the Persons, nor dividing the Substance. For there is one Person of the Father, another of the Son, and another of the Holy Ghost: but the Godhead of the Father, of the Son, and of the Holy Ghost is all one: the glory equal, the majesty coeternal. Such as the Father is, such is the Son, and such is the Holy Ghost. . . . The Father is God, the Son is God, and the Holy Ghost is God, and yet they are not three Gods, but one God. So likewise the Father is Lord, the Son is Lord, and the Holy Ghost is Lord; and yet not three Lords, but one Lord. For like as we are compelled by the Christian verity to acknowledge every Person by Himself to be God and Lord; so we are forbidden by the Catholic Religion to say, there be three Gods, or three Lords. . . . And in this Trinity none is afore or after other; none is greater or less than another, but the whole three Persons are coeternal together, and coequal. So that in all things, as is aforesaid, the Trinity in Unity and the Unity in Trinity is to be worshiped. He, therefore, that wishes to be in a state of salvation [*quicunque vult salvus esse*] must thus think of the Trinity."

In the English and most other Anglican Articles of Religion the Quicunque Vult, otherwise known as the Athanasian Creed (though it was not written by St. Athanasius) appears beside the Apostles' and Nicene Creeds in Article 8. "They ought most thoroughly to be received and believed, for they may be proved by most certain warrants of Holy Scripture."

**9. Explain the Trinity so that a child can understand it.**

**10. Explain the Trinity in simple layman's language.**

It is impossible to explain the doctrine of the Trinity. There is a legend that St. Augustine, one of the greatest Christian thinkers who have ever lived, was thinking out his book on the Trinity when he saw a boy pouring water out of a bucket into a hole in the seashore. On being asked what he was doing the boy said, "I am emptying the sea into this hole." "How can you expect," asked St. Augustine, "to empty the sea?" "And how can you," said the boy, "with your human mind, expect to understand the mystery of the Trinity?"

The best way to teach the doctrine of the Trinity is this: God is love, He must therefore have someone to love. Before the world was made, before angels and men were created, who was there for Him to love? The revealed doctrine of the Trinity, which we could never have discovered for ourselves, gives the answer. God has an object of love within His own being: from all eternity, the Father, the Son, and the Holy Spirit have loved one another.

But we must not think that the Father, the Son, and the Holy Spirit are three separate individuals. There is one God, not three Gods. They have one Essence, one Nature, one Character. The word "person," which is a bad translation of the Greek word "*hypostasis*," is perhaps best interpreted as "center of consciousness." God the Father created us through His Word. That Word, or Son, took human nature as Jesus Christ. The Holy Spirit was sent to guide the Church, and it is He with Whom we have now to do.

**11. Are there occasions for prayer to God the Father and others for prayer to our Lord Jesus Christ? Or, as there is but one God, does it make no difference?**

Liturgical or public prayer is usually, but not always, to the Father through the Son. Prayer to the Son or to the Holy Spirit, or to the Holy Trinity, is right also. See the first four petitions in the Litany of the Prayer Book and the lesser Litany—"Lord have mercy, Christ have mercy, Lord have mercy"—addressed respectively to the Three Persons. In private prayer, any one Person may be addressed, or all Three together. If prayer is directed to the Father or to the Holy Spirit, it must be "through Jesus Christ." We may not pray to God without mentioning Jesus Christ, but we must take care not to pray *exclusively* to Jesus Christ and not to neglect the Holy Spirit, Who is equal to the other Two. We must never address our prayers to anyone but God; the Father, the Son, and the Holy Spirit.

**12. How much can the Church know about the Holy Trinity? Can the Trinity be defined?**

The Church can only know what God has revealed about Himself, as recorded in Holy Scripture, and deduced from Scripture by the Church, with universal agreement. The definitions in the Creeds and the decrees of the Councils are intended to warn us against one-sided conceptions of the Holy Trinity which represent falsely what has been revealed.

**13. How does free will operate in the face of omnipotence?**

This is a mystery about which speculation is futile. Milton describes the devils in hell as engaged in endless and useless arguments about it (*Paradise Lost*, Book II, lines 557–65).

> Others apart sat on a Hill retir'd,
> In thoughts more elevate, and reason'd high
> Of Providence, Foreknowledge, Will, and Fate,
> Fixed fate, free will, foreknowledge absolute,
> And found no end, in wand'ring mazes lost.
>
> .   .   .   .   .   .   .   .   .   .
>
> Vain wisdom all, and false philosophy.

All we can say is that God has limited His omnipotence by giving us free will, because He wished that we should love and serve Him freely and should become partakers of the Divine nature (II Peter 1:4).

**14. How do you tell your close friends who are pagans that God is worth worshiping?**

I assume that by "pagans" is meant "post-Christians" rather than worshipers of false gods (such as Hindus and others), which is the proper meaning of "pagans." I suppose that the best way is to follow our Lord's example and teaching as closely as possible, to show that all that is attractive or lovable in you comes from God and from your worship of Him, and to be ready, when opportunity occurs, to explain (without arguing, which is worse than useless) in whom you believe and why.

**15. Discuss the difficulty of believing in a personal devil even if one believes in a personal God.**

To me there is no difficulty at all. God created the devil, as He created men, good. The devil, like men, rebelled against God. He is simply a wicked spirit with no body, as a bad man is a wicked spirit in a body. God permits the devil to continue to exist just as He permits wicked men to continue to exist. We do not know why, but we suppose that if there were no devils and no wicked men we should not have to endure the temptations which are necessary for the building up of our character. Anyone who has all his life been carefully shielded from all temptations cannot exercise the heroic virtues which God desires to see developed in all of us.

**16. Isn't Christianity a form of self-hypnotism, something you want to believe?**

Perhaps it is possible to hypnotize oneself into believing that the Christian religion is true, but such cases must be rare. In any case, such self-hypnotism would lead to believing for the wrong reason, and would not in any way affect the true reasons for believing in Jesus Christ. An American might hypnotize himself into believing that the United States is the greatest, richest, and noblest country in the world. Hypnotism or no hypnotism, the belief might be true all the same.

Great numbers of Christians have not wished to believe. If to be a Christian meant that you were extremely likely to be crucified, torn to pieces by lions, roasted alive, or made to suffer some other form of agonizing death, would you hypnotize yourself into being a Christian? But that has been the fate of many Christians in all ages, from St. Stephen the first Christian martyr to the modern martyrs of Uganda and those murdered by the Mau Mau in our own time. St. Paul certainly had no wish to be a Christian, and when he became one his life was such as few men would envy: "five times received I thirty-nine stripes. Thrice was I beaten with rods, once was I stoned, thrice I suffered shipwreck . . ." (II Cor. 11:24–25).

### 17. What are the promises of Christianity?

These are some of them: "My sheep hear my voice, and I know them, and they follow me: and I give unto them eternal life; and they shall never perish, neither shall any man pluck them out of my hand" (St. John 10:27–28). "Verily I say unto you, There is no man that hath left house, or brethren, or sisters, or father, or mother, or wife, or children, or lands, for my sake, and the gospel's, but he shall receive an hundredfold now in this time, houses, and brethren, and sisters, and mothers, and children, and lands, with persecutions; and in the world to come eternal life" (St. Mark 10:29–30). "Come ye after me, and I will make you to become fishers of men" (St. Mark 1:17). "He that believeth on me, the works that I do shall he do also; and greater works than these shall he do . . . If ye shall ask any thing in my name, I will do it" (St. John 14:12, 14). "Eye hath not seen, nor ear heard, neither have entered into the heart of man, the things which God hath prepared for them that love him" (I Cor. 2:9).

### 18. Why is Christianity the best and truest religion, as compared with other great religions?

What are the other great religions? Judaism, Islam, Hinduism, Buddhism, and possibly communism.

Judaism is true as far as it goes, but it needs the revelation in

Jesus Christ to complete it, as St. Paul discovered. Men found it impossible to keep fully the Law of the Jews; but Christ by His death and resurrection delivered them from the heavy burden of the Law and gave them grace to enable them to keep the even higher standard laid down in His Sermon on the Mount. He gave them the means of reconciliation with God, something that the Old Covenant lacked.

Islam is the religion of the Arab prophet Mohammed, and it teaches that God is an Almighty Sultan, Who destines some men to heaven (a very sensual heaven) and some to hell. This religion sanctions war, slavery, and polygamy. No one rightly trained in the Christian tradition could prefer Mohammed to Christ.

Hinduism is not so much a religion as a vast collection of Indian traditions, many of which are barbarous. It divides men by a system of rigid castes; it requires no definite belief in a personal God, but permits the idolatrous worship of such demons as the lustful Krishna and the murderous Kali; and it offers not eternal life but a series of reincarnations ending in the destruction of personality.

Buddhism is, strictly speaking, not a religion but a philosophy, a way of escape from life, which is regarded as evil. The complete Buddhist must be a monk or a nun; the prize offered to the Buddhist is not eternal life but absorption in an impersonal deity.

Communism, the teaching of Karl Marx based on an obsolete philosophy, is a doctrine of hatred and class war, without God or a future life. In practice this system of thought promotes intolerable tyranny.

The religion of Christ is not just the best religion, it is the only true religion. All that is good and true in the other religions comes from the only true God and is completely fulfilled in Jesus Christ. No founder of any other religion has even claimed to be more than a man or to have risen from the dead; but Jesus Christ is the eternal Word of God, Who became man and died and rose again to save us. "Neither is there salvation in any other: for there is none other name under heaven given among men, whereby we must be saved" (Acts 4:12).

Every religion must be able to answer three questions: What am I to believe about God? How can I overcome sin? What will become of me after death? The Christian religion gives the only true answers. For the answer to the first question see Question

1. The answer to the second question is: Believe in Jesus Christ, repent of your sins, be united with Him in His Church by Baptism, and with the help of the Holy Spirit you will be able to resist all temptation. The answer to the third question is: Our Saviour has promised to them that love Him and are members of His Church, the resurrection of the body and eternal life (St. John 10:28, 11:25; I Cor. 15:13).

**19. When, where, and by what authority was the Nicene Creed issued?**

The Nicene Creed was issued, in its original form, by the First General Council of Nicaea (now Isnik) on the Asiatic side of the Bosporus, in the year 325. It ended with the words: "And in the Holy Ghost." It was an old baptismal creed except for the word translated by: "Being of one substance with the Father." The new word was used in order to assert clearly that Jesus Christ is God, equal to the Father.

In its present form the Creed was issued by the Fourth General Council of Chalcedon, opposite Constantinople, in 451, except the words "and the Son" ("Who proceedeth from the Father and the Son") which were added later in Spain, were accepted at Rome in 1014, but have never been recognized by the Eastern Churches. Except for these words, the Nicene Creed is accepted by all parts of the Church.

**20. Why may not we Episcopalians believe in reincarnation?**

Because there is no evidence for it. To believe that for which there is no evidence is gross superstition. We are told (St. Luke 16:22; Heb. 9:27) that immediately after death judgment is passed upon our actions in this life and we are then sent to wait for the final judgment. We shall not return to this life, and there is no place for reincarnation. For this reason also, no Christian ought to believe in it.

Reincarnation is a theory invented by the ancient Indians, and by Pythagoras in Greece, to account for the fact that good and bad deeds do not always receive their due reward in this life. It was supposed that the good are rewarded and the bad punished by a series of fresh lives on earth. The theory is connected with the Indian belief in karma, the inevitable automatic destiny, which is inconsistent with belief in the sovereign power and love of God. When the disciples of our Saviour asked, "Who did sin, this man or his parents, that he was born blind?" He rejected the notion that blindness was the punishment for a sin committed in a previous life (St. John 9:3). Indeed it would be contrary to the justice of God to banish a man for a sin which he could not remember and which he could not be shown to have committed. No part of the Church nor any group within the Church has ever taught or permitted the doctrine of reincarnation.

21. I pay my pledge, attend church regularly, and really try; yet illness and financial trouble befall me. It does not seem fair.

22. If God were good and loving, He would not let my child die.

23. What are we to say to the parents of a child who dies by accident, when they ask, "Why did God do this to me?"

24. Why does such a good man have to suffer like that?

25. Why does not God always reward the good and punish the wicked? Why do evil people seem to escape the consequences of their sins?

The problem lying behind all these questions is the subject of the Old Testament Book of Job (which is not history but a problem drama like *Hamlet* and *Lear*, though not intended for the stage). Job is a pious, wealthy, popular Arab chief. Satan sneers, "Does Job serve God for nought?" suggesting that Job is pious for what he can get out of it. Job loses all his ten children, all his property and his health; his friends conclude that he must have done something very wicked to be treated in this way. Job insists that he is guiltless; like the asker of Question 21, he does not think it at all fair. He says, "Behold, I cry out of wrong, but I am not heard: I cry aloud, but there is no judgment" (Job 19:7). At last the Lord speaks out of the whirlwind and says, "Who are you to criticize the justice of the Creator?" (Job 40:8) As I read the story, Job is satisfied: he has seen the vision of God and nothing else matters. "I have uttered that I understood not . . . I have heard of thee by the hearing of the ear: but now mine eye seeth thee. Wherefore I abhor myself, and repent in dust and ashes" (Job 42:3, 5, 6).

But we Christians know more than the writer of the Book of Job knew. He had no clear belief in a future life, but we have been promised eternal life and perfect joy. The wicked are punished and the good are rewarded: if not in this life, then hereafter. "Remember that thou in thy lifetime receivedst thy good things, and likewise Lazarus evil things: but now he is comforted, and thou art tormented" (St. Luke 16:25). The bereaved are to remember that God knows the future and that their loved ones may be taken away from the evil to come (I Kings 14:13; II Kings 22:20); in any case, God knows what is best for their children better than they do. Besides, at a deeper level, we who follow Jesus Christ must expect to share His sufferings and carry our cross after Him (St. Matthew 10:38).

**26. Why should seventeen people perish in a blizzard and all others survive? Why should a woman suffer for months from cancer, instead of being allowed to die of a heart attack?**

Our Lord was asked a similar question (St. Luke 13:1–5) and He refused to answer it. We do not know about our real needs as God does. All such questions take for granted that pain and death are the worst misfortunes but they are not. The worst misfortune, the only permanent injury, is separation from God and the sin that leads to this. Pain and death are to be avoided, for ourselves and for one another. Our Lord healed the sick and raised Lazarus from the dead, but both pain and death may bring us to God. "Nearer, my God, to Thee, e'en though it be a cross that raiseth me." Our Lord Himself, as Man, learned "obedience by the things which he suffered" (Heb. 5:8); and no human being is complete without suffering of some kind, as our own experience shows. A long painful illness has sometimes brought to God people who had never thought about Him before.

Death is often a blessed release. St. Paul wrote, "For to me to live is Christ, and to die is gain" (Phil. 1:21), when his death by the sword of the executioner was drawing near. "For I am now ready to be offered, and the time of my departure is at hand. . . . Henceforth there is laid up for me a crown of righteousness, which the Lord, the righteous judge, shall give me at that day: and not to me only, but unto all them also that love his appearing" (II Tim. 4:6–8). The poet Tennyson, when in old age he was told by the doctor that he was soon going to die, answered, "Death, that's good."

**26a. What about death being predestined? Is it true that "he won't die till his time's up"?**

It is true that God has appointed the time of our death, but it is also true that He has given us free will, by which we can, to a limited degree, interfere with His purpose. If I were so foolish and wicked as to kill myself, or if someone were to murder me, I might die before God intended me to die. Nevertheless, He overrules man's wickedness for good, as He overruled the treason of Judas Iscariot for the salvation of mankind.

**27. Are not all religions going in the same direction? What difference does it make what God you worship?**

All religions are not going in the same direction (see Question 18). The inquirer seems to be suffering from the common delusion that the chief purpose of religion is to help us to be good. The chief purpose of religion is worship and glorify God. We cannot do this unless, by His help, we are trying to be good, but being good is the means, not the end. Different religions teach very different notions of what being good is, and they have quite different moral ideals.

But if, as we believe, the God Who revealed Himself to the writers of the Bible is the true God, He has laid down as His first commandment, "I am the Lord thy God . . . Thou shalt have no other gods before me" (Ex. 20:2, 3). To disobey this commandment is one of the greatest of sins, and will certainly lead to disaster sooner or later. Conduct depends largely on belief, even in earthly affairs. The American Civil War, for instance, was caused by a difference of belief about the relation of the states to the Union, and about slavery. It cannot be too strongly emphasized that what we do and how we behave depend very largely on what we really believe (though not necessarily on what we say, or even think, we believe). If you worship a devil you will behave like a devil. If you worship the God Who is revealed in Jesus Christ you will try to obey Jesus Christ and be like Him. The difference will be immediately observed by all your neighbors.

*Chapter Two*

# JESUS CHRIST

**28. Was Jesus really Divine?**

Yes. He is "God of God, Light of Light, Very God of very God; Begotten, not made; Being of one substance with the Father;

by [that is, through] whom all things were made" [Nicene Creed]. "The right faith is, that our Lord Jesus Christ, the Son of God, is God and Man: God, of the substance of His Father, begotten before the worlds; and Man, of the substance of His mother, born in the world; perfect God and perfect Man, of a reasonable soul and human flesh subsisting; equal to the Father, as touching His Godhead, and inferior to the Father as touching His Manhood. Who, although He be God and Man, yet He is not two, but one Christ: One, not by conversion of the Godhead into flesh, but by taking of the Manhood into God" (Quicunque Vult, or Athanasian Creed).

Every part of the New Testament bears witness to this doctrine. Among many passages that might be cited are the following: "God sent forth his Son" (Gal. 4:4). "If thou shalt confess with thy mouth the Lord [that is, the God of Israel] Jesus . . . thou shalt be saved" (Rom: 10:9). "There is . . . one Lord Jesus Christ, by whom are all things, and we by him" (I Cor. 8:6). "Who is the image of the invisible God, the firstborn of every creature: for through him were all things created" (Col. 1:15, 16). "All things are delivered to me by my Father: and no man knoweth who the Son is, but the Father; neither knoweth any man who the Father is, but the Son, and he to whom the Son willeth to reveal him" (St. Matthew 11:27; St. Luke 10:22). "The beginning of the gospel of Jesus Christ, the Son of God" (St. Mark 1:1). "The high priest . . . said unto Him, Art thou the Christ, the Son of the Blessed? [i.e., God] And Jesus said, I am" (St. Mark 14:61, 62). "The Word was God" (St. John 1:1). "The Word became flesh' (St. John 1:14). "Before Abraham was, I am" (St. John 8:58). "I and my Father are one" (St. John 10:30). "Thomas answered and said unto him, My Lord and my God. Jesus answered, Thomas, because thou hast seen me, thou hast believed" (St. John 20:28, 29). "Feed the church of God, which He purchased with His own blood" (Acts 20:28—this is the true reading). "Unto the Son he saith, Thy throne, O God, is for ever and ever (Heb. 1:8—see the whole chapter). "Jesus Christ . . . is on the right hand of God" (I Peter 3:22). "A servant of God and of the Lord Jesus Christ" (James 1:1). "I am the first and the last: I am he that liveth and was dead; and, behold, I am alive for evermore, and have the keys of hell and of death" (Rev.

1:17, 18). "The Lord God Almighty and the Lamb are the temple of it" (Rev. 21:22).

**29. Christ was one of the finest men that ever lived, but how can you prove such a weird statement as that He was the Son of God?**

It is more than "weird"; it is the most astounding thing that ever happened. If you believe the New Testament when it tells us what sort of man He was, you must also believe it when it tells us that He was more than man. If He had been only a man, even though He had been a great prophet, He would not have been our Saviour; yet that is what Christians have always believed, and it is impossible to explain the Christian religion apart from this belief.

It must be understood that the word "son" is not used here in a physical sense. God is pure spirit—He has no body. We have to use human language when speaking about Divine things, and our words must not be pressed literally. The son of a man is a man—he has the nature of his father. The Son of God is God—He has the nature of His Father; He was not created but was eternally begotten. This is a mystery which we, being finite beings, cannot expect to understand. We have to believe God's revealed word.

No mere man, however great and good, could have said, "Take my yoke upon you, and learn of me; for I am meek and lowly of heart" (St. Matthew 11:29), without showing that he was not humble and that he was making false claims. No man, who was only man, would claim to be the future judge of all nations (St. Matthew 25:31–46) unless he was mad. And it is quite certain that Jesus Christ was not mad. No man, if he had been only man, could have risen from the dead or even claimed to have done so, and yet the central point of the Apostles' preaching was that Jesus is the Christ, because He has risen from the dead, and they claim to have seen Him after He had risen (Acts 2:32, 3:15, 4:10, 10:41, 13:30, 17:31, 26:23; I Cor. 15:4, 17, etc.). No such claim has been made for any other man. If He did not rise from the dead, it is impossible to explain the empty tomb, the rise of the Christian Church, or the observance of the Lord's Day (Sunday, not Friday, the day of His death).

No other man has claimed to be without sin. Jesus Christ did make this claim, and His disciples, who knew Him well, accepted His claim (St. John 8:7, 46; Heb. 4:15). Even if His claim had been true and He had been only a man, it would not have been modest to make it; a mere man who claimed to be sinless would refute his own claim just by making it. The whole description of our Lord in the New Testament makes no sense unless His claim to be God is true. This is the fundamental doctrine of the Christian religion. Unless a man believes that Jesus Christ is God he cannot properly be called a Christian.

> Worth while a thousand years of woe
>   To speak one little word,
> If by that "I believe" I own
>   The Godhead of my Lord.
>                     (F. W. Faber)

**30. How could Jesus Christ be God on earth, and then refer to God as His Father and an entirely different person?**

See Question 8. Jesus Christ is not an "entirely different person" (in the ordinary, not the technical sense) from the Father. There is only one God. But within the being of the One God there are three distinct "Persons" or centers of consciousness, the Father, the Son (Who became man as Jesus Christ), and the Holy Spirit. Jesus Christ said, "I and the Father are one." He allowed St. Thomas to address Him as "My Lord and my God" (St. John 20:28).

**31. Is Jesus Christ still existing in His Manhood? Where? How? What does "never to be divided" (Article 2 of the Articles of Religion) mean?**

Jesus Christ is still, and forever will be, Man. He ascended into heaven as Man; He is at the right hand of the Father (the position of supreme honor and power—Acts 8:56).[1] It is because Man is on the throne of heaven (Heb. 8:1) that we have such confidence in His sympathy (Heb. 4:15).

> Our fellow sufferer still retains
> A fellow-feeling of our pains
> And still remembers in the skies
> His tears, His agonies, and cries.
> With boldness therefore at the throne
> Let us make all our sorrows known,
> And ask the aid of heavenly power
> To help us in the evil hour.
>                     (Michael Bruce)

[1] God has no body and, therefore, in the ordinary sense, no hand.

"Never to be divided" means that our Lord's Divine nature and His human nature will remain united in one Person to all eternity.

**32. Explain the difference between the Incarnate God-Man and Jesus Christ the Son-God.**

There is no difference. God the Son, the Second Person of the Trinity, became Man, that is, He became incarnate. His human name is Jesus; His human title is Christ. He is "God, of the Substance of the Father, begotten before the worlds; and Man, of the substance of His mother, born in the world; perfect God and perfect Man; not two but one Christ" (Athanasian Creed).

**33. Is my reasoning correct regarding the Father-Son relationship of God and Jesus?** (A long confused statement follows, which it would be unkind to reproduce.)

God the Father and God the Son are one God. God the Son was eternally begotten by the Father: "He was in the beginning with God" (St. John 1:2). He did not become the Son when He became Man; He was always the Son. He took human nature, which was created by His Father. His Divine nature was uncreated. He is one Person with two natures. We are God's children by adoption, whereas He is the Son of God by nature. Therefore He said, "I ascend unto my God and your God." In the Lord's Prayer Jesus Christ tells His disciples to say "Our Father" because they are disciples. He never joins Himself with them in saying "Our Father": for He is God's Son in one sense and the disciples are God's children in another sense. We are created by God, not begotten by Him; when we were baptized we became His children by adoption. Thus our Catechism says, "My Baptism wherein I was made . . . the child of God." St. Paul says that we are adopted as sons of God because of Jesus Christ (Gal. 4:6; Eph. 1:5). The only place in the New Testament where men as men are called the offspring of God is Acts 17:28, where St. Paul is quoting a heathen poet in order to persuade the philosophers of Athens to listen to the gospel.

**34. How do we reconcile the statement that Jesus is our only Mediator and Advocate with the fact that the Father and the Son are one? How can God intercede with Himself?**

See Question 8. The Father and the Son are one in Being (Substance), but they are personally distinct. We find our Lord constantly praying to His Father; He tells us that the Father loves the Son. The Father is not Man; He did not take to Himself human nature. The Son is Man; He was born and suffered and died. He is therefore the Mediator between God and man because He is perfect God and perfect man.

**35. If Christ died to save sinners, what of all those who died before He became man?**

He died for them as well as for us—for Abraham, Isaac, and Jacob as well as for the Apostles. He said, "Your father Abraham rejoiced to see my day: and he saw it, and was glad" (St. John 8:56). He died also for the heathen. In St. Matthew 25:31–46 He foretells that He will judge all nations, most of which have never known anything about Him; and will say to those who have acted according to the light they had, "Come, ye blessed of my Father, inherit the kingdom prepared for you from the foundation of the world." But no one can obtain salvation by any other means than by the death and resurrection of Jesus Christ, for there is "none other name under heaven given among men, whereby we must be saved" (Acts 4:12).

**36. What is the answer to the comment, Islam, Buddhism, etc., also have very high moral and ethical standards, therefore why should we try to convert Moslems or Buddhists to Christ?**

The assumption made by this comment (it is found in many other questions too) is that the purpose of religion, perhaps its only purpose, is to produce a high moral standard. This assumption (called "moralism") is false and pernicious. The purpose of our religion is to do the will of God and promote His glory. We cannot do His will or promote His glory unless we are trying with His help to obey His command "Be ye perfect as your Father in heaven is perfect" (St. Matthew 5:48). Only those who are pure in heart will see God. But morality is the means, not the end. We can only come to God, to do His will or promote His glory, through Jesus Christ. It is only the Holy Spirit sent forth by the Father through the Son Who gives us the power to resist the Devil and to serve God. No other religion even claims to do so.

The moral standard of Islam, laid down once and for all in the Koran, which was an advance for the heathen Arabs in the seventh century, cannot be regarded by Christians as a satisfactory substi-

tute for the teaching of our Lord. Mohammed believed in God
as the almighty Creator, not as a loving Father. He also believed
that God sends some men to heaven and others to hell simply because He chooses to do so. Moslems are commanded to make war
on all non-Moslems: to kill those who worship idols, and to offer
to those who believe in one God and have a sacred book the
choice between death, conversion to Islam, and total submission
to Moslem overlords. Each Moslem may have four wives, whom
he may divorce (on certain conditions) at his pleasure, and as
many concubines as he wishes. There is no equality between men
and women, or between Moslems and non-Moslems. No non-Moslem man may marry a Moslem wife, but a Moslem man may
marry non-Moslem wives. No Moslem may reject the Moslem
religion on pain of death. Islam is a religion very well suited to
the wishes of fallen man, especially in Asia and Africa; but it
has not, and does not claim to have, Divine grace to enable the
believer to overcome all temptation.

Buddhism, strictly speaking, is a philosophy rather than a religion. The Buddha regarded life as misery because it was full of
desire. He claimed to have discovered the Noble Path by which
men could overcome desire and get rid of life. Buddhism does not
include any belief in God or in human personality. The really
good Buddhist must be, or become, a monk or a nun; only by
following the prescribed moral course (which has many admirable features, it is true) may he at last attain to Nirvana,
which means absorption into the Infinite. There are several different kinds of Buddhism, some of which include features that
have probably been derived from Asiatic Christianity. But in
general the Buddha claimed to deliver men from life, while Jesus
Christ came that men might have more abundant life (St. John
10:10).

Neither Islam nor Buddhism provides any satisfactory substitute for Christian morals or any means by which their followers
may be helped to attain their ideal. But we do not merely preach
Christianity as a system; we preach Jesus Christ as the Saviour
of all mankind, for whom there cannot be any substitute.

**37. What doctrine of the Atonement does the Anglican Com-
munion celebrate?**

The Anglican Communion has no doctrine peculiar to itself on this or, for that matter, on any other subject. The Catholic Church, of which the Anglican Communion is a part, has never defined the doctrine of the Atonement nor does Holy Scripture appear to provide the means for doing so. The Church and the Bible alike teach that the death and resurrection of Jesus Christ deliver us from sin and its consequences and reconcile us to God, but they do not say how. Many theories have been put forward, but they cannot be discussed here.

38. What is the Atonement? How can we explain, in twentieth-century language, the meaning of the Atonement?

Atonement is at-one-ment, reconciliation of man to God. God made man "very good" (Gen. 1:31): why, then, does man need to be reconciled to God? Because of the Fall. Unless we accept the doctrine of the Fall with all our hearts we cannot believe the doctrine of the Atonement, which is the heart of the Christian gospel.

God gave the human race a limited power of free will. If He had not given us this power of choosing between right and wrong, there would be no morality nor virtue. Man used the power to disobey God. How or when this happened we do not know, and probably never shall know. The story in Genesis 3 about Adam and Eve and the serpent describes the Fall in the form of an allegory or myth. This story is not history and was never intended to be taken as history.

There is no suggestion in Genesis that the serpent which tempted Eve was the Devil. It was a snake, the first snake. The Hebrews knew as well as we do that snakes cannot speak like men. Of course God could, by a miracle, make a snake speak; but would He do so in order to destroy His own work? The tree of the knowledge of good and evil is not to be found in the garden or in a book of botany; it is an allegorical tree. The story is an origin-myth, the sort of story found among all primitive peoples. The inspired biblical writer has made of it a story which conveys the profound truth of the Fall of Man. There is no more striking case of Divine inspiration, and no chapter in the Old Testament is more important or more necessary than this third chapter of Genesis.

St. Paul tells us that man not only disobeyed God but passed on to his descendants a tendency to prefer evil to good. This is not only revealed biblical truth but a fact of experience. We all know that from our earliest childhood we find it easier to do evil than good, to disobey God rather than to obey Him. This tendency to evil is called by theologians "original sin." It is common to all races of men, the civilized and the savage alike. It produces, unless it is checked by Divine grace, actual sin, which is the chief source of all the troubles of mankind. Disobedience, selfishness, lack of love, these are found in all men, both as individuals and as societies.

This doctrine is particularly hard for people nowadays to accept because, for two hundred years, liberals and "progressive" people have been telling us that there is nothing wrong with human nature, that the troubles of man come not from him but from his environment, and that this doctrine of original sin is a fiction. Our Lord Himself taugth us that what defiles a man is not what goes into him, not his environment, but what comes out of him, that is, the evil in his will (St. Matthew 15:17, 18). Reinhold Niebuhr has given us in our generation the lesson so loudly proclaimed by St. Paul and revived by Luther: that our nature is corrupt and that we are saved by Divine grace alone. "By grace are ye saved through faith; and that not of yourselves: it is the gift of God" (Eph. 2:8).

God made man for union with Himself; but man cannot be united to God as long as he is sinful. Therefore man needs to be reconciled to God. But man does not usually even want to be reconciled to God; he is so corrupt that by himself, without Divine grace, he does not want to be holy. God will not take away man's power of choice, for then he would cease to be man and would become only a thing. If man is to be united with God he must be changed. He cannot change himself and, if he could, he would not want to change.

What, then, did God do? In spite of everything God still loved His human creatures, corrupt as they were. (How corrupt, you have only to read the story of the Greeks, or the Romans, or even the Jews in the time of Herod—peoples that were on the whole better than the Babylonians, the Carthaginians, and other nations, to get some slight idea.)

God the Son, the Second Person of the Trinity, took human nature, was born as a baby, and lived as a man. He suffered the

most cruel of deaths then known, and He rose from the dead. By
rising from the dead He broke the power of the Devil over mankind; He won a great and final victory in the unseen world. Men
had by their own fault placed themselves under the power of the
Devil; how strong that power is, even now, any missionary with
experience in a heathen country will tell you. The first thing, then,
that our Saviour did, out of sheer love and at a terrible cost to
Himself, was to break the power of the Devil. The final victory
was won on the first Easter Day; all that followed may be described as "mopping-up operations." That is why every sermon
of St. Peter and of St. Paul led up to the good news of the Resurrection (Acts 2:24, 3:15, 5:31, 10:40, 13:30, 17:31, 26:23); that
is why St. Paul wrote, "If Christ be not raised, your faith is vain
(I Cor. 15:14, 17); that is why Easter Day is the greatest festival
of the year, and why the Church keeps the Lord's Day every
week as a memorial of the Resurrection.

But men still had to be told the *good news*, which is what the
word "gospel" means. The disciples, therefore, were commanded
to proclaim it to all nations (St. Matthew 28:19; Acts 26:23).
Since not all men will believe the good news (or even that it is
good), but prefer to remain bound by pride and hatred, covet-
ousness and lust, the Church is commissioned to persuade men to
accept the Gospel.

Even when a man has accepted the Gospel he still has to be
restored to spiritual health. Therefore our Saviour allows each
one of us to share in His risen life by means of Baptism, which
makes us members of His Body the Church. The new risen life,
what St. Paul calls "the new man," gradually takes the place of
the old corrupt life which we had before. This process begins at
our Baptism. God the Holy Spirit, Whom our Saviour has sent
into the world, is the Agent of this process. It is He Who, through
the sacraments and other means of grace, builds us up in the new
life both here and hereafter, until at last we shall be fit to come
into the presence of God. All this is part of the Atonement.

There are other aspects of the Atonement which we cannot
discuss here. There is the cosmic aspect—our Saviour died and
rose again to free not only mankind but the whole material universe. There is His function as High Priest, to offer His sacrifice
of perfect obedience to the Father. There is His function as the

Second Adam, the Head and representation of all humanity. And there are other aspects.

But there are two beliefs about the Atonement which we must firmly reject. Some people think that our Lord died merely to set us a good example and to move us to follow that example. He certainly did this, but it is by no means the whole of what He did. Those who think that this is all the Atonement means ignore most of the New Testament, such as St. Mark 10:45; Gal. 1:4; I Cor. 15:3; or Heb. 5:9, and cut the heart out of the gospel. Other people think that Jesus Christ died as a substitute for us; that someone had to be punished, and God the Father was willing to punish Him, Who was innocent, in place of us who were guilty. There is no basis in the New Testament for this doctrine, which would make God out to be a monster of cruelty and injustice. There is no difference in character between the Father and the Son. They are one God, one in character, and God is love. God did not need to be reconciled to man; it was man who had to be reconciled to God, and the Atonement is wholly the work of Divine Love.

**39. What do doubts about the historic Person of Jesus say to our faith in Him as our Saviour?**

There are no historic doubts about Jesus Christ that need be taken seriously. The theory that He never existed, for example, has been entirely discredited. If He really had never existed, the Christian religion would be false, for it is a historic religion like the religion of Israel out of which it sprang; it rests on certain historic facts and a certain interpretation of them. Jesus of Nazareth was the Son of God: He was born of a Virgin, was crucified, rose from the dead, and ascended into heaven. If we did not believe this we could not trust in Him as our Saviour.

**40. Is belief in the Virgin Birth of Jesus necessary to salvation according to the teaching of the Episcopal Church?**

Yes; and not only of the Episcopal Church but of the whole Catholic Church of which it is a part. The doctrine of the Virgin Birth is an article of the Creed. Every person who is baptized or confirmed has to affirm (if an infant, through sponsors): "I believe all the Articles of the Christian Faith, as contained in the Apostles' Creed." When we go to the Holy Communion we are required to recite the Nicene Creed, of which this article is a part.

The Virgin Birth may be proved by most certain warrants of Holy Scripture (St. Matthew 1:20; St. Luke 1:35), as Article 8 of the Articles of Religion says. This belief has always been held by all parts of the Church. The two passages mentioned are both extremely early, for they were written while the Church was still Jewish, which it ceased to be within one generation. As Archbishop William Temple wrote, the difficulties which some people find in accepting the Virgin Birth are not put forward on historical grounds, but because of a materialistic philosophy. The historical evidence is sufficient and it is supported by theological considerations. Those who deny that God can work a miracle cannot accept the Virgin Birth, which was a miracle, and unique. Only once did God take human nature. Jesus Christ, unlike all other men, had existed from all eternity in heaven. He was free from the tendency to sin which the rest of us inherit, for otherwise He could not have saved us from sin. Therefore His birth had to be unique. Those who have adopted a philosophy which conflicts with the revealed Christian Faith must change their philosophy if they wish to be Christians.

**41. How can the Church permit the clergy to believe or not believe in the Virgin Birth?**

The Church does not permit this. The Virgin Birth of our Lord Jesus Christ is an article of the Creed and is proved by most certain warrants of Holy Scripture. Every priest at his ordination solemnly promises "to banish and drive away all erroneous and strange doctrines contrary to God's Word." Denial of the Virgin Birth is certainly such an erroneous doctrine. The priest is further bound to recite the Apostles' Creed on Sundays in public; to require of everybody whom he baptizes, or presents for Confirmation, to say of the Creed, "I believe all the Articles of the Christian Faith, as contained in the Apostles' Creed"; to "minister the doctrine and sacraments and the discipline of Christ," and to "teach the people committed to his cure and charge with all diligence to keep and observe the same." These are the conditions on which he was ordained; these are a necessary part of what he is paid to do. (The English clergy are bound to recite the offices of Morning and Evening Prayer daily; for the American clergy this is a moral rather than a legal obligation.)

It is a dishonest quibble to pretend that "born of the Virgin

Mary" does not mean what it says. That our Lord was born of a woman does not need to be stated in the Creed; this article is placed there to protect the doctrine that His mother was a virgin, that He had no human father. The priest who doubts or denies the Virgin Birth cannot honestly or wholeheartedly teach it to his people, as he is bound by his ordination vows to do. He should consider the grounds on which he denies it and whether he really thinks that he is wiser than the Universal Church with all its saints and scholars, past and present. If he still cannot in conscience say that he accepts the Virgin Birth, the only honest course for him is to give up his office as a teacher in the Church and retire into lay communion (if his conscience will permit it) and seek some other means of earning his living. (I do not think that he ought to seek a position in the ministry of some sect that does not require its ministers to accept the doctrine of the Virgin Birth. To do so would only be adding schism to heresy.)

If a disbelieving priest refuses to take this course he renders himself liable to prosecution for heresy. In English-speaking countries such trials do much more harm than good, partly because of the publicity they receive in the public press and partly because the majority of the people (as these questions show) think that religion is entirely the concern of the individual and therefore that heresy is meaningless, while a man deprived of his post for heresy is regarded as a hero and a martyr. For these reasons bishops avoid at almost any cost prosecuting anyone for heresy. Still, we can only regard with disgust and abhorrence a priest who refuses to observe the conditions on which he was ordained and to fulfill the duties of a teacher commissioned by the Church to teach, not his own opinions but the doctrine and practice which the Church sent him to teach in its name. The faithful should, as far as they can, refuse to attend his ministrations.

**42. How do you reconcile the Virgin Birth with the references to St. Joseph as the father of Jesus?**

The Jews had no surnames—a man was known by his own name and his father's name. Officially our Lord was "Jesus the son of Joseph," just as St. Peter was "Simon the son of Jonas." The true story of our Lord's birth must have been concealed, during His own lifetime on earth and during His mother's lifetime, from all those who did not know that He was the Son of God. If any of these had known about it they would not have been able to believe it. Even His stepbrothers, the sons of St. Joseph by a previous wife, can hardly have known it, for "even his brethren did not believe on him" (St. John 7:5) (see Question 97).

The genealogy in St. Matthew (1:16) reads: "Joseph the husband of Mary, of whom was born Jesus, who is called Christ." Our Lord was not physically the son of David, but He was legally a member of the house of David because in Jewish, as in English, law the son of a married woman was legally the son of her husband, unless the husband formally declared that he was not the father, which St. Joseph clearly did not do. The genealogy in St. Luke (3:23) reads: "Jesus . . . being (as was supposed) the son of Joseph." In St. Luke 2:33, 48, St. Joseph is spoken of as His father, that is, stepfather, which was a common usage then as it is now. In the latter passage our Lord, referring to God as His Father, reminds His mother and St. Joseph that His real and only Father was God.

In St. Luke 4:22 the people of Nazareth ask, "Is not this the son of Joseph?" That was the title by which they had known Him from boyhood; the secret of the Virgin Birth was kept hidden from the neighbors. St. Matthew 13:55 ("Is not this the carpenter's son?" or "the carpenter") and St. John 6:42 ("Is not this Jesus, the son of Joseph, whose father and mother we know?") are to be explained in the same way, the latter with a touch of the irony characteristic of St. John. In St. John 1:45, St. Philip says, "We have found him, of whom Moses in the law, and the prophets, did write, Jesus of Nazareth, the son of Joseph." This was the only way in which he could have described our Lord; he had only just joined the band of disciples and cannot have known the secret of the Virgin Birth.

**43. What is the teaching of the Church on the Virgin Birth? The report of the Archbishops Committee on Christian Doctrines seems ambiguous.**

Archbishop Davidson, who was not a theologian, appointed the Committee entirely on his own authority. It contained at least one member who was notoriously unorthodox on the subject. The report was never accepted by the English Provincial Synods or by the authority of any other part of the Church. Some of its conclusions are valuable, but on this subject it carries no weight at all. The teaching of the Church is, as it has always been, that when our Lord was born His mother was a virgin and that this is an article of faith, to be thoroughly received by all members of the Church as a condition of their membership.

**44. Is not the doctrine of the Virgin Birth of the Deity common to several religions?**

This subject was examined thoroughly by a German scholar named Lobstein, who did not himself believe in the Virgin Birth. In his book, which I have read, he searches all the religions of the world, ancient and modern, for parallels to the Virgin Birth. There are plenty of stories, some of them very unpleasant, of heroes who were the offspring of a god in human shape and a mortal woman. But the only case of a hero who was said to be born of a virgin occurs in a very late legend about the Buddha, a legend which is almost certainly due to Christian influence. In the original story of Sakyamuni, the Buddha (an Indian prince of the sixth century before Christ), he was born of two human parents in the ordinary manner.

The story of the Virgin Birth as told in the Gospels, if it were not true, could only have come from a Jewish or a Gentile source. The Jews did not admire virginity; they regarded it as a misfortune, not as worthy of honor. The Gentiles had no stories of virgin births, and if they had had any, the pious Jews from whom the story in the Gospels came would have regarded such tales as heathen abominations.

**45. Was the Transfiguration necessary for our Lord as well as for the Apostles?**

We do not know. Our Lord's human nature had the same weakness as ours, as far as it was not caused by sin. Perhaps His human nature needed to be strengthened before His passion. However, such a thing is not even suggested in the Gospels.

**46. What is the best answer to give to those who deny our Lord's resurrection?**

That depends upon the grounds on which they deny it. If they deny it on historical grounds, and are capable of weighing historical evidence (few people are), they should be shown that there are four independent contemporary accounts, St. Paul's, St. Mark's (on which St. Matthew's is based), St. Luke's, and St. John's; that it is impossible on any other assumption to explain why the tomb was empty; that St. Paul writes of more than 500 persons, at the time he wrote, who had seen the risen Lord (I Cor. 15:6); that we cannot explain why the group of terrified or despairing disciples, after their Master's crucifixion, should have defied the Jewish Sanhedrin and grown into a world-wide Church, unless something very extraordinary had occurred; that if the story of the Resurrection had been a fiction or a mistake, the disciples would not have continued to proclaim it publicly at the risk of losing their lives, a loss that actually took place in many cases; that we cannot even account for the universal Christian observance of the first instead of the sixth day of the week, except as the commemoration of the Resurrection. Such an objector should be asked to read Morison's book, *Who Moved the Stone?*

If, however, the objection is that miracles do not happen, the objector should be asked how he knows that. The theory that miracles cannot occur is overthrown by sufficient evidence for even one miracle. If he believes in God he must believe that God created the universe; if God created the universe He could raise a man from the dead. If the objector does not believe in God, it is useless to try to persuade him to believe in the Resurrection. Something more than argument is needed:

> He that complies against his will
> Is of his own opinion still.
> (Samuel Butler)

If Jesus Christ really rose from the dead, the Christian religion is true, with consequences for the objector to which he may not be willing to submit. As a great and holy man once wrote: "It was not God's Will to save His people by argument." The objector also needs the will to believe, and faith in Jesus Christ; this is a gift which only God can give, and without which the most overwhelming evidence will not convince.


*Chapter Three*

# THE HOLY SPIRIT

**47. Our priest says we should always pray for the guidance of the Holy Spirit. I don't know what he is talking about. What is the Holy Spirit?**

### 48. What is the relation of the Holy Spirit to the Trinity and to the Church?

The Holy Spirit, the Holy Ghost, the Giver of Life, the Paraclete (Advocate or Comforter)—these are some of His titles —is God, the Third Person of the Trinity; He is equal to the Father and the Son, and with Them is worshiped and glorified. From all eternity He proceedeth from the Father through the Son. He inspired the prophets and all other writers of Holy Scripture. He gave to the Blessed Virgin Mary the power to bear her Son, the Word of God. He descended upon that Son at His baptism, giving to His human nature the strength needed for His ministry on earth. After our Lord's ascension into heaven, the Holy Spirit was sent forth to the Apostles and the other disciples, and He has directed the Church ever since as the true Vicar or Representative of Christ on earth. That is why the Church is more than a human society, why it is the principal means by which the Holy Spirit works among men. He guides the Church into all truth (St. John 16:13), especially when councils of bishops meet and are willing (though they are not always willing) to listen to His voice. He dwells in the body of every baptized Christian as in a temple (I Cor. 3:16) unless He is driven away by sin. Our Catechism says, "I learn to believe in God the Father, Who hath made me and all the world; and in God the Son, Who hath redeemed me and all mankind; and in God the Holy Ghost, Who sanctifieth me and all the people of God."

Thus it is God the Holy Spirit with Whom we have direct contact now; Who guides our will, our reason, and our conscience, if we are willing to let Him; Who has provided us with light through the Bible and the Church, and with power through the sacraments. It is He Who gives us the New Birth at our baptism and the sevenfold gift at our confirmation; it is He Who changes the bread and wine that they may become the Body and Blood of Christ, after a heavenly and spiritual manner, for the strengthening and refreshing of our souls. It is the same Holy Spirit Who is given to bishops, priests, and deacons at their ordination to the ministry (St. John 20:22) when the words "Receive the Holy Ghost" are spoken to them. It is He Who conveys Divine power to the bridal couple in Holy Matrimony, to the sinner in Absolution, to the sick in Unction. Whenever we say, "Lord have mercy,

Christ have mercy, Lord have mercy," the second "Lord have mercy" is addressed to Him.

> Our blest Redeemer, ere He breathed
>   His tender last farewell,
> A guide, a comforter bequeathed
>   With us to dwell.
>
> He came in tongues of living flame [Acts 2:3]
>   To teach, convince, subdue;
> All powerful as the wind He came,
>   As viewless too
>
> He came sweet influence to impart,
>   A gracious willing Guest,
> Where He can find one humble heart
>   Wherein to rest.
>
> And every virtue we possess,
>   And every conquest won,
> And every thought of holiness,
>   Are His alone.

(Harriet Auber)

### 49. Why is the Holy Ghost not the Father of Jesus?

The Father of Jesus Christ is the First Person of the Holy Trinity, not the Third, Who is never given that title. The Holy Ghost gave to the Blessed Virgin power to bear her Son, but not in a physical sense. He did not take a human body as the gods did in the filthy legends of the heathen. The power which He gave was entirely spiritual and miraculous. That is the meaning of the words "conceived by the Holy Ghost." "The Holy Ghost shall come upon thee, and the power of the Highest shall overshadow thee: therefore also that holy thing which shall be born of thee shall be called the Son of God" (St. Luke 1:35).

### 50. Is the Spirit that brooded over the face of the waters the same as the Holy Spirit?

Yes, although the writers of the Old Testament did not yet know that the Spirit of God was personal. In the Old Testament "the Spirit of God," like "the angel of the Lord," often simply meant "God"; and certainly did not, in the mind of the writer, mean the Third Person of the Trinity, for that doctrine had not yet been revealed. However, when we Christians read the Old Testament we can see meanings there which the writers of it could not perceive. That is part of the meaning of inspiration. Tertullian, a famous Christian writer of the second century, writing about Genesis 1:2, says that the "Spirit of God" that brooded over the waters at Creation now broods over the water at baptism, which is a new creation; water is the car or chariot of the Holy Ghost.

**51. What is the unforgivable sin against the Holy Ghost?**

**52. I have heard three priests give three different definitions of the unforgivable sin.**

"He that shall blaspheme against the Holy Ghost hath never forgiveness, but is in danger of eternal damnation: because they said, He hath an unclean spirit" (St. Mark 3:29, 30).

The one thing that can be said with confidence about this difficult passage is that anybody who is disturbed because he thinks he may have committed the unforgivable sin has certainly *not* committed it. If he had he would not worry; he would be perfectly sure that he was right.

Commentators of different schools seem to agree that the sin which has no forgiveness is deliberately to destroy one's own knowledge of the difference between right and wrong. The Son of God performed works of mercy, which everyone who saw them ought to have known were good and of God; yet some of His critics said that He had a devil and by this means did these works. The unforgivable sin is the sin of those who refuse to admit that their political or religious opponents can be sincere or can do anything right. As long as anyone remains in this state of mind, which may easily harden into a habit, he cannot be forgiven because he cannot repent. Such a man has stifled his conscience and deprived himself of the means of distinguishing right from wrong. A man may be mistaken about the claims of Jesus Christ through ignorance or prejudice, and may still be forgiven, but if he thinks that acts of mercy are really the work of the devil, because they are performed by someone whom he does not like, he is blaspheming against the Holy Ghost. So Isaiah (5:20) says, "Woe unto them that call evil good, and good evil; that put darkness for light, and light for darkness; that put bitter for sweet, and sweet for bitter!"

*Chapter Four*

# HOLY SCRIPTURE

**53. What historical proof have we that no further revelation is necessary, and therefore no addition to the Bible?**

There cannot be historical evidence of a negative statement about the future, for historical proof refers only to the past and it is seldom possible to prove a negative.

Since the list, or "canon," of the books of Scripture was finally closed, about fifteen hundred years ago, it has been agreed by all Christians that nothing can be added to it. The alleged revelations that have appeared, such as the Book of Mormon and *Science and Health*, cannot be taken seriously and are, in any case, contrary to the existing Scriptures. We cannot say with certainty that God will not make a fresh revelation; but it is so unlikely that He will that for practical purposes we may ignore the possibility. The full revelation of God was given in Jesus Christ and recorded in the New Testament. From time to time prophets arise who proclaim fresh or forgotten aspects of that revelation. We may well believe that God has yet more light to bring forth from His Word.

**54. Are the Holy Scriptures the infallible word of God? If so, how should Church tradition be followed when it conflicts with Scripture? (St. Mark 7:1–13)**

Only God is infallible. The books of Scripture were produced by human minds and make use of human words; therefore they are not infallible, for nothing human is free from the possibility of mistake. But they are a sufficient guide to God's revelation (II Peter 1:21). No tradition is to be accepted which is contrary to Scripture and no doctrine is to be regarded as necessary to salvation which cannot be proved from Scripture (see Articles of Religion 20 and 34). It is, however, for the Church, and not for the individual, to decide when a tradition is contrary to Scripture. The traditions of the Church, when they are ancient and widespread, are to be treated with respect (Article 34). No one should judge hastily that such a tradition is contrary to Scripture.

**55. How can we reconcile the Christian tradition of the first day of the week as the Sabbath with the Fourth Commandment?**

There is no such tradition. The first day of the week is the Lord's Day, which never had anything to do with the Sabbath. Christians are bound by the moral law of the Hebrews but not by their ceremonial or civil laws (Article 7). This position was decided by the Apostolic Council (Acts 15).

The Ten Commandments in general are part of the moral law which was confirmed and made even stricter by our Lord (St. Matthew 5:17-48). The moral principle of the Fourth Commandment is that there should be one holy day of rest out of seven. But the observance of this rule on the seventh day of the week was part of the ceremonial law (St. Mark 2:27). In the apostolic age Jews who had become Christians continued to keep the Sabbath with the rest of the Jewish ceremonial law (Acts 16:13, 21:20), but Christians who had never been Jews were excused. All Christians, however, observed the Lord's Day in remembrance of Jesus Christ's resurrection on that day. That was the day, the first day of the week, on which the Christians assembled to "break bread" (for the Holy Communion) (Acts 20:7; cf. Heb. 10:25 and Rev. 1:10). This Lord's Day was first a day of worship; and when the Roman Empire became Christian, it was made a legal holiday, in order that Christians might have an opportunity to fulfill their obligation of Eucharistic worship.

The notion, widespread in English-speaking countries, that the Lord's Day is the Jewish Sabbath, is a mistake made by the Puritans of the sixteenth century. In Latin the first day of the week is *Dies Dominica* (French "dimanche"), the Lord's Day; the seventh day is *Dies Sabbati* (French "samedi"). We are to keep the Lord's Day, first, by being present at the Holy Eucharist (Holy Communion), then, as far as possible, by avoiding unnecessary work, or causing others to do it; always excepting works of necessity ( such as milking cows) and works of mercy (such as tending the sick).

**56. What is the basic difference between the Roman Vulgate and the King James Bible?**

The Vulgate is the translation of the Bible from the original Hebrew and Greek into Latin, made by St. Jerome (Hieronymus) in 382-404. The King James Bible is the translation from the original Hebrew and Greek into English made by a committee of divines under the direction of King James I (VI of Scotland) in 1611, and is generally known as the "Authorized Version" of the Bible. The chief difference is that the books called Apocrypha are collected together in one place between Malachi and St. Matthew in the King James Bible, but in the Vulgate they are scattered through the Old Testament, and some of them are parts of other books: II Chronicles, Daniel, and Esther. Another difference is that the books of the Old Testament are in a somewhat different order in the Vulgate from that in the King James Bible.

The King James Bible is generally agreed to be the supreme masterpiece of English literature. The Vulgate, considered as literature, though it has many beauties, is on the whole poor Latin. Both translations contain mistakes. The Vulgate regularly reads "do penance," which does not fairly represent the Greek word; the English Bible reads "repent." What the Greek really means is a change of heart. In Isaiah 9:3 the King James Bible reads "not increased the joy." The word "not" is a mistake for "to it," due to the confusion of two similar Hebrew words. The Psalms in the Vulgate Bible are translated not from the original Hebrew but from a Greek translation of the Hebrew. This makes the Vulgate Psalms very obscure and inaccurate. Coverdale's version, which we have in the English Prayer Book, was made from this Latin version. Coverdale did not know any Hebrew.

**57. What are the criteria for saying that some parts of the Bible are fact and others legend or symbolism?**

The ordinary criteria of literary and historical criticism. (To answer the question fully would require a large book.)

The Book of Genesis is based on traditions passed on by word of mouth for centuries. The earlier chapters are almost entirely symbolical, but not the less important for that. The books of Samuel and Kings are historical on the whole, but some parts of them, especially the story of David's reign, are better history than others; still others, especially the stories about Elisha, are partly legend. The Books of Chronicles present history as the Jews of the third century B.C. thought it must have happened. Some of the books are poetry. Daniel, the Revelation of St. John, and parts of some other books are highly symbolical. The Gospels and Acts are on the whole good contemporary history. The Epistles of

St. Paul, except perhaps the Epistles to Timothy and Titus (and Hebrews, which is certainly not by St. Paul), were written or dictated by him. In Galatians 5 there is a passage added by his own hand.

**58. Is the image of God (Gen. 1:26) obliterated or blurred? Are "image" and "likeness" different?**

The image of God is not obliterated by the Fall. The doctrine that it was obliterated is one of the errors of Calvin. Man is "very far gone from original righteousness" (Article 1), that is, he is very different from what God intended him to be; but man is nevertheless capable of being restored by Divine grace. But the image of God is blurred. Theologians from St. Irenaeus in the second century onward have distinguished between the "image" and the "likeness" of God, but in Hebrew (of which language most of the ancient theologians were ignorant) there is no difference at all. Any distinction must therefore be rejected; image and likeness are the same thing.

**59. Are stories such as that of Adam and Eve stories of actual events?**

No (see Question 38). The story of Adam and Eve is based on an origin-myth such as is found in all primitive races. It was changed by Divine inspiration into an allegory teaching the Fall of man, a teaching which is of the utmost importance and a necessary part of the Christian Faith.

The story of Cain and Abel seems to be based on the opposition between pastoral nomads (like Abel, who sacrificed a sheep) and settled farmers (like Cain, who offered the produce of his fields) which runs through much of the Old Testament. As we have the story, it is a warning against envy and murder. The story of the Flood is based on a historical event, a flood which covered all of Mesopotamia and of which traces have been found by archaeologists. As we have it, the story is a warning of what happens to men when they neglect God, and it contains several other lessons as well (St. Luke 17:26; Heb. 11:7; I Peter 3:20; II Peter 2:5).

**60. How do men come to be of different races and colors if they are all descended from Adam and Eve?**

The story of Adam and Eve is not historical. The origin of different races is a question for the anthropologists which we cannot yet answer. We know that man has been on the earth for at least a hundred thousand years, probably much longer. The black skins of some races are certainly caused by the heat of the tropical sun. It is generally agreed that the American Indians came from Asia over the Bering Strait, which may at one time have been closed by a land bridge. The Australian aborigines seem to have come from India at a much more remote period.

**61. Whom did Cain and Abel marry?**

Cain and Abel were not historical persons, but types of different stages of human progress, both of them quite late (see Question 59). Cain is the typical settled farmer who grows crops; Abel is the typical wandering shepherd. Both types are later than the food-gathering type (like the Australian aborigines) and the hunting type (like the Eskimos).

**62. "And there shall be, like people, like priest" (Hos. 4:9). What does this mean? How far is the communicant responsible to and for his priest?**

The prophet is denouncing the priests of Samaria and saying that they are no better than their people, to whom they ought to be examples and teachers of the law of God. Instead these priests are idolaters, whoremongers, and drunkards, and it is their fault that their people commit all these sins. These priests were the priests who worshiped the golden calves (I Kings 12:28–31; II Chron. 13:9), but the prophet Jeremiah found the priests at Jerusalem a century later not much better (Jer. 6:13, 23:11). The Christian priest is not the same kind of priest as the Hebrew priests, true or false, under the Old Covenant, but, like them, he is responsible to God for teaching the people God's Will and setting them a good example.

The communicant is responsible to his priest for listening to and obeying his preaching and teaching, supporting his work with gifts and personal service, and defending him against any slander, injury, or malicious story. He is responsible for paying the stipend of the priest, if required (I Cor. 9), although this may be done through diocesan rather than through parochial channels. The communicant is also responsible for his priest, whose work depends upon the prayers of his people. These should be offered daily. When you wish to criticize bishops, pray for them instead.

**63. What is the full meaning of "Be still, and know that I am God"? (Psalm 46:10)**

We cannot expect to know the *full* meaning of any text of Scripture. The most we can know is what God means us in particular to learn from it. It may have other meanings for other people and other ages. The literal meaning, as intended by the writer of this verse, appears to be that God speaks to the enemies of His people, who are attacking Jerusalem, and says to them: "Stop! let it alone; it is under my protection, and I am God Almighty."

St. Augustine, the great African bishop (died 430), says: "Be still; like Mary at the Lord's feet, go with the Hebrews three days' journey into the solitude, in the contemplation of the Blessed Trinity; like the Apostles, refuse to serve the tables of fleshly appetites, that thou mayest give thyself wholly to the ministry (Sermon on Martha and Mary, see J. M. Neale, *Commentary on the Psalms*, Vol. 1, p. 110). St. Ambrose says that our Lord is exalted among the heathen, by the preaching of the Cross, and in the earth, that is, the new heaven and the new earth, by His ascension to the right hand of the Father.

**64. Was our Lord crucified on Friday? Did He rise again on Sunday? Was that Sabbath a high day? (Our Lord gives it as a proof of His Divinity in St. Matthew 12:40.)**

Yes; the day of the Last Supper was Thursday, and the first day of the Passover (St. Mark 14:12). According to St. John (13:1), it was before the Passover. Our Lord was crucified on Friday; the following day was the Sabbath (St. Mark 15:42; St. Luke 23:56; St. John 19:31). He rose from the dead on the first day of the week, which is called the Lord's Day, and is observed by Christians for that very reason. The sign promised by our Lord in St. Matthew 12:39 is not a sign of His Godhead, but of His resurrection after three days in the grave; that is, part of Friday, all of Saturday, and part of Sunday.

**65. Did the miracles, such as the Feeding of the Five Thousand, really happen, or are they mere stories?**

The miracles of our Lord really happened; all attempts to strip the miraculous element away from the Gospels have failed. The Feeding of the Five Thousand is related in all the four Gospels. It is true, of course, that some of the miracles related in the Old Testament, especially those of Elijah and Elisha, are probably based on legend.

**66. Are persons afflicted by mental disease possessed by devils? If so, why cannot disciples of Christ cast them out? Is there a service for exorcising devils?**

There are many kinds of mental disease. It is by no means true that all persons so afflicted are possessed by devils; perhaps some of the persons mentioned in the Bible as possessed by devils were only believed to be so by their neighbors. But possession by devils does sometimes take place. Such possession is rare in Christian countries but common in Africa, India, China, and Melanesia. The disciples of Christ can and do cast out devils. It requires a great deal of faith and prayer to do this, a naturally strong will, and careful training; otherwise it is extremely dangerous (see Acts 19:13). The Reverend Charles Harris, Vicar of South Leigh near Oxford (the parish where John Wesley preached his first sermon), was a well-known theologian and a specialist in casting out devils. He once told me how he had freed from devil-possession, and completely cured, a young man whom the doctors had given up as a hopeless lunatic. (See also Maynard Smith's *Frank [Weston]*, *Bishop of Zanzibar*, Chap. 6.) No one should attempt to cast out devils without special training (St. Mark 9:29). I believe there is a service of exorcising in the Roman Ritual but no one is allowed to use it except priests who have received special permission to do so.

**67. What is meant by "until the times of the Gentiles be fulfilled"? (St. Luke 21:24)**

The meaning of this passage is uncertain. The two best explanations are: (1) that "the times of the Gentiles" are the seasons when the Gentiles will be allowed to execute the judgments of God; (2) that these times are the opportunities which the Gentiles will have for possessing the privileges which had been forfeited by the Jews. It is suggested that these opportunities will not last for ever.

**68. Was there any special ritual of the scribes at washing hands before meals?**

The Jewish scribes had special prayers and thanksgivings provided for almost every act of daily life.

**69. Who was St. Paul, anyway?**

St. Paul was a wealthy Jew of Tarsus, brought up to speak Aramaic (Phil. 3:5; Acts 21:40) and possessing the rare privilege

of Roman citizenship by birth (Acts 22:25–29). He was trained
at Jerusalem to be a rabbi, or teacher of the Law; he was a
Pharisee and he belonged to the Sanhedrin, or Great Council
of the Jews (Acts 26:10). He was active in persecuting Christians
and while on his way to Damascus for this purpose was wonder-
fully converted by a vision of our Lord (Acts 9, 22, 26). He was
the "chosen vessel" (Acts 9:15) especially selected by God to
preach the Gospel to the Gentiles. It was St. Paul, more than anyone else, who turned the Christian Church from a Jewish sect
into a universal religion.

The story of his three missionary journeys is told in Acts 13–21.
His great theological task was to work out the doctrine that
men are not saved as a reward for doing the commands of the
Jewish Law but by the free gift of Divine grace which is given
in answer to faith. Through St. Paul's work members of all nations were allowed to become Christians without submitting to
the requirements of the Jewish Law. It seems likely that he must
at one time have been married, for otherwise he could not have
been a member of the Sanhedrin.

After many sufferings, of which he gives a list in II Corinthians 11:23–27, he was arrested on a charge of bringing Gentiles
into the Temple at Jerusalem. Knowing that he had no chance
for obtaining justice from the Jews, he appealed to the Roman
Emperor. As a Roman citizen he had a right to do this. Conse-
quently, he was sent to Rome as a prisoner, and was shipwrecked
at Malta on the way (Acts 27). After two years of imprisonment
at Rome, he is believed to have been acquitted of the charge
made against him. Some time later he was arrested and then be-
headed at Rome. He was, perhaps, the greatest of all Christian
teachers and missionaries. Of the twenty-seven books of the New
Testament ten are letters written by him and three others (the
Epistles to Timothy and Titus) are attributed to him, although
scholars are not agreed that he actually wrote them himself.

**70. Was St. Paul's "thorn in the flesh" physical? (II Cor. 12:7)**

The "thorn in the flesh," perhaps better translated "stake in
the flesh," was some intermittent disease from which St. Paul
suffered. Sir W. M. Ramsay's explanation is to me completely
convincing: the stake in the flesh was malaria, and the severe head-
ache which malaria brings. St. Paul was first attacked by this at

Perga (Acts 13:13), a district heavily infected with malaria. He was compelled to go up into the mountains. At this time John Mark went away just when he was most needed, which made St. Paul very angry (Acts 15:38). He was suffering from malaria when he was at Pisidian Antioch and at Iconium and was first preaching to the Galatians (Gal. 4:13). Later St. Luke went with him on his travels so that he might have a physician always at hand (Acts 20:6; Col. 4:14), and passed himself off as St. Paul's slave so that he might accompany him to Rome (Acts 27:1), since wealthy prisoners who were Roman citizens were allowed to have two slaves with them (see W. M. Ramsay, *St. Paul the Traveller and Roman Citizen*).

**71. If God's Will for us is health, why should we pray, "If it be Thy will"?**

In general, God's Will for us is health, but it is not always His will for each one of us. Some people are sick through their own fault or the fault of others. Some people are brought to God through sickness, people who would never have known Him if they had always been well. St. Ignatius Loyola, the founder of the Jesuits, was converted through a long sickness caused by a wound received in battle; and there are many similar cases.

*Chapter Five*

# ORIGINAL SIN

**72. What is the doctrine of Original Sin?**

"Original sin" is the name given by St. Augustine and other ancient Latin writers to the tendency to do evil rather than good, a tendency found in every human being (except our Lord Jesus Christ) and in every corporate society of men. It is not "actual sin," which is a deliberate act of the human will in disobedience against God; but unless it is stopped, original sin will certainly result in actual sin. St. Paul does not use the phrase "original sin" but he does teach the doctrine in Romans 5:12: "Wherefore, as by one man sin entered into the world, and death by sin; and so death passed upon all men, for that all have sinned . . . therefore as by the offence of one judgment came upon all men to condemnation; even so by the righteousness of one the free gift came upon all men unto justification of life."

St. Paul and St. Augustine assumed that the story of the Fall, as told in Genesis 3, was historical fact. We cannot now believe this (see Question 60) but the doctrine of the Fall and of Original Sin does not depend upon the belief that Adam was a historical person. The universal tendency of human beings to do evil rather than good is a matter of experience as well as of revelation. Since it is universal, it must be the result of some event in the distant past, an event of which we do not and cannot know anything. The denial of this truth by Rousseau and many others in the past two hundred years has led to the greatest disasters. It has encouraged the delusion that a good time coming may be expected if only we can free mankind from ignorance and prejudice and change its environment. As we might have learned from the Gospel (St. Mark 7:15), the chief troubles of men come not from ignorance nor from defects in their environment, but from the corruption of their own hearts, and that corruption cannot be permanently removed as long as the world lasts. Therefore all hopes of any utopia or millennium in this world, a good time coming, are bound to fail; for if the utopia of the reformers were to come about, it would soon cease to be a utopia, because men will always be subject to original sin. The chief problem of government, as Dr. Niebuhr has shown us, is that men cannot be governed without power, and yet no man, or class, or community, is fit to be trusted with power. Belief in necessary progress and belief that men can be permanently helped by education and science alone, all religious and political optimism, are contrary to the doctrine of Original Sin; and they have been thoroughly refuted by the experience of the past forty years. "The day in whose clear shining light all wrongs shall stand revealed, when justice shall be throned in might and every hurt be healed" is not to be expected in this world, but only in that new heaven and new earth which God is preparing for us when this world shall have ceased to exist (Heb. 11:16; Rev. 21:1).

The only remedy for original sin is the grace of God. Without grace, knowledge and power, education and science, excellent gifts of God in themselves, are much worse than useless. You can be more wicked in a comfortable house with all modern conveniences than if you lived in a cave. You can hurt your neighbors much more effectively with atomic bombs than with a bow and arrows. But the grace of God can overcome everything, if we are willing, at whatever cost to ourselves, to let it have free course.

**73. What does the Episcopal Church say about Original Sin?**

"Original sin standeth not in [that is, does not consist of] the following of Adam, (as the Pelagians do vainly talk;) but it is the fault and corruption of the Nature of every man . . . whereby man is very far gone from original righteousness, and is of his own nature inclined to evil" (Article 9). This statement is strongly influenced by the teaching of St. Augustine, which is supported by the experience of us all. It is not Calvinistic. "Very far gone from original righteousness" was not sufficient for the Calvinists, whose Westminster Assembly in 1643 rejected this phrase; they preferred "we are utterly indisposed, disabled, and made opposite to all good, and wholly inclined to all evil" (Westminster Confession, Article 6).

St. Paul tells us (I Cor. 11:7) that man is the image and glory of God and St. James (3:9) says that man is made after the likeness of God; in spite of the Fall, that image is not entirely destroyed, as Calvin taught. But at the present time the errors of Pelagius are far more dangerous than the opposite errors of Calvin. Pelagius (died about A.D. 418) held that there is no such thing as original sin and no necessity for Divine grace; he taught that without grace a man may, if he chooses, avoid all actual sin. This is the besetting heresy of the English (and, I suspect, of the Americans), which leads them to think that they can live a good life by their own strength; a delusion only too clearly held by many of those who submitted questions for this book. The Episcopal or Anglican tradition is to reject the teaching of both Calvin and Pelagius, as the Bible requires us to do.

**74. Explain the concepts of the Old and the New Adam. Explain Genesis 3.**

See Questions 59 and 60. Adam and Eve represent the race of men. They were created good by God. He gave them the power to obey Him or to disobey Him, the power of a limited free will. In the story told in Genesis, this truth is represented by the power to obey or disobey God's command not to eat the fruit of the tree of knowledge of good and evil. Adam and Eve misuse their power of free will; they eat the fruit; this gives them the knowledge of what it is to be separated from God. They are no longer innocent; they become conscious of sex and are ashamed of being naked. In normal human life man tills the ground and woman bears the children. The Hebrews regarded these labors as the punishment inflicted on man and woman for their disobedience to God. The serpent in Genesis is not the devil (this is a later conception) but simply the first snake, the creature which crawls on the ground and bites the heel of the passer-by. The snake was believed to have been punished in this way for tempting Adam and Eve. The whole story is a legend intended to explain to primitive man the origin of human occupations, of sex, and of the nature of the snake. But the passage "He shall bruise thy head, and thou shalt bruise his heel," which originally referred to the normal relations between men and snakes, has always been taken by Christians as a prophecy that the devil would bring our Saviour to His death, but that He would, by His resurrection, finally crush the devil's power.

St. Paul means by the Old Adam the fallen corrupt nature of man apart from grace, and by the New Adam the risen life of our Saviour which is imparted to us at baptism and which gradually overcomes and replaces the old corrupt nature in each of us (Rom. 6:6; I Cor. 15:47). Adam is the Hebrew word for man; it is not a proper name. Hebrew (or Aramaic) was St. Paul's mother tongue (Phil. 3:5) though he wrote in Greek.

**75. What is the soul? Is it the same as the spirit? Is there something Divine in us, as some think?**

The word "soul" in the Bible often means simply "life." When our Lord said, "What shall it profit a man, if he gain the whole world, and lose his own soul? Or what shall he give in exchange for his soul?" He was not referring to the eternal destiny of man, but to his life here on earth (St. Mark 8:36, 37; St. Matthew 16:26). In St. Paul's epistles "soul" is contrasted with "spirit." "It is sown a natural body; it is raised a spiritual body" (I Cor. 15:44); the word "natural" should be "soulish" if we had such a word; it means connected with earthly life.

But the word "soul" is often used also with the meaning of "spirit," that part of a man which is not material and which does not die when the body dies. It is this "soul" of the believer to which our Lord promised eternal life (St. John 3:16, 10:28). The Bible does not tell us that the soul or spirit is immortal, as Plato and other Greek philosophers taught; it promises that those who believe in Jesus Christ and are incorporated into Him by Baptism shall have eternal life, not only in the next world but here and now; and that the soul shall receive a new body, a spiritual body, at the final judgment.

Man is made in the image of God, but the opinion that he has in him a spark of the Divine is not Christian and there is no reason for believing it. We are to be made partakers of the Divine nature (II Peter 1:4), but only by union with Christ and His Church.

**76. When does a human being receive a soul?**

We do not know.

**77. Do animals have souls?**

We do not know. The Christian tradition teaches that they do not. It is pleasant to think that your pet dog has a soul which will survive death; but are you ready to think that every wolf, every shark, every mosquito has one? If not, there seems to be no place where we can draw a line, and no reason for drawing a line, between one animal and another.

## Chapter Six

# GRACE AND SALVATION

**78. Give a simple definition of grace. Explain "grace of God," "state of grace."**

Grace is the favor or kindness of God and this is always its meaning in the New Testament. Later it came to mean also the spiritual power which the favor of God gives us. We cannot do anything good without it and God alone can give it to us. It may also be defined as God the Holy Spirit in action. It is not a substance and there are not different kinds of grace, but grace is given in different ways and for different purposes.

A baptized Christian is said to be in a state of grace when he is trying with all his heart to love and serve and obey God and is not guilty of any unrepented sin. The state of grace normally begins with Baptism. The Prayer Book says that children who die after Baptism, before they have committed any sin, are undoubtedly saved.

**79. How does grace work? What is meant by "salvation by grace" and "by grace ye are saved"?**

We do not know how grace works (St. John 3:8). But God has given us the means of grace; prayer, the sacraments, reading the Bible, the preaching of His word, etc. If we use these means faithfully we may expect God's favor and power, although He can and does give us grace apart from them. St. Paul says, "by grace are ye saved through faith; and that not of yourselves: it is the gift of God: not of works, lest any man should boast" (Eph. 2:8, 9).

We are saved, that is, reconciled to God, not by anything that we are or have or do, but entirely by God's free gift. St. Paul is claiming that we cannot get salvation for ourselves by keeping the law, as the Jews believed; we must not boast of our good deeds, because it is God Who has given us the wish and the power to do them. English and American people, who are always inclined, as these questions show, to think that they can earn salvation by leading a conventionally "good" life (which is for them what the Law had become for many of the Jews), need to be constantly reminded of St. Paul's teaching. It was the great work of Martin Luther to bring it once again to men's minds; but it is held by all orthodox Christians.

**80. Is a blessing a means of grace in any way?**

To bless God is to praise Him: "O all ye Works of the Lord, bless ye the Lord; praise him, and magnify him for ever." To bless human beings is to pray that God will give them His favor and help. Priests have to bless their people, especially those who are being married. Parents ought often to bless their children. To bless things (including living animals) is to set them apart for the service of God and to pray that He will use them for His glory. The answer, therefore, is Yes.

**81. What is salvation? How is it achieved? Is Christianity the only gate to salvation? What about good pagans, such as Gandhi?**

Salvation means to be reconciled to, accepted by, and finally united with God; but "united" does not mean absorbed; we are to remain forever separate persons, to praise God freely, which is the purpose for which we were created.

Those who want salvation must first repent, and this includes sorrow for sin (contrition), confession, and amendment. Secondly, they must believe in Jesus Christ, which means committing themselves, and all that they are and have, entirely to Him. Thirdly, they must be baptized with water in the Name of the Father, the Son, and the Holy Ghost. This makes them members of Christ's Church, outside of which, as far as we know, there is no salvation. Finally, they must persevere until death, as faithful members of Christ's Body. Repentance, faith, Baptism, and perseverance are all His gifts.

There are two stages in salvation: present and final. Those who are living the life of the Church, obeying its rules and using its means of grace, and who are not guilty of any unrepented sin, are said to be in a state of salvation (Church Catechism). This is what the Quicunque Vult means by "Whosoever wishes to be saved," that is, to be in a state of salvation. We must always be on the watch lest we should fall away from this state. Even St. Paul thought this possible for himself (I Cor. 9:27). Final salvation will be reached when, having lived and died in a state of grace, we shall be acquitted at the Particular Judgment; after which we shall not be subject to temptation (St. Luke 16:19–31). The difference may be illustrated by this allegory: A ship was wrecked and was sinking rapidly. A lifeboat was sent to rescue the crew. Many of them got into the boat, but some remained in the ship and some preferred to swim. Those who were in the boat and some of those who swam reached land safely. The ship with its crew is the race of men. The wreck is the Fall of man. The boat is the Church; those who are in it and remain in it have present salvation but they may fall out of it. Those who have reached the land have final salvation. The allegory is defective because it does not refer to our Lord, to Whose death and resurrection our salvation is entirely due.

Good pagans who have never had a chance to hear the gospel

(such as Socrates, Vergil, and the Buddha) will be judged by their use of the opportunities which they have had (St. Matthew 25:31–46). Gandhi was in a different position; he knew the gospel, and rejected it, but we do not know how much blame for his rejection lies at the door of the Christians with whom he was in contact. In any case, he is under God's judgment, not ours. All who are saved, whatever their history may have been, will have been saved by Christ alone (Acts 4:12).

**82. How does the Church interpret personal redemption? How do we know whether we are redeemed? Is individual effort required?**

Each one of us, who has repentance and faith and has been baptized, is personally redeemed or "bought back" by the death and resurrection of Christ. We know that God wills all men to be saved (I Tim. 2:4), and if we have obeyed the conditions which He has laid down we trust Him to fulfill His promises. We must do all we can to serve Him; "faith without works is dead" (James 2:26).

**83. How does the Episcopal Church differ from and compare with other churches in their teachings of salvation?**

I suppose that most of the sects think of salvation as offered to us as separate individuals and do not recognize the necessity for Church membership and for the sacraments. The Roman Communion holds that submission to the Pope is necessary to salvation (Bull of Pope Boniface VIII).

**84. If faith without works is dead, what about works without faith? Will salvation come for the very works sake?**

Nobody can obtain salvation through works, with or without faith. "By grace are ye saved through faith; and that not of yourselves: it is the gift of God: not of works, lest any man should boast" (Eph. 2:8, 9).

"For the very works sake" is here quoted out of its proper context. Our Lord asked His disciples to believe in Him, if only because of His miracles which they had seen. The verse has nothing to do with the question.

I rather think that there are no good works without some faith. A deed which appears to be good must be done either for a good or for a bad motive. If the motive is good, there must be some faith in the doer: faith in goodness, even if not faith in God.

That faith, however imperfect, is the gift of the Holy Spirit. If the motive is bad, the deed is not a good deed. Perhaps this is a possible explanation of the difficult Article 13 with its technical terms taken from medieval theologians.

**85. Does it make any difference what you believe, as long as you live a good life?**

This question expresses the ancient and widespread error whose classical form is in Pope's couplet:

> For forms and creeds let fools and bigots fight.
> He can't be wrong whose life is in the right.

There are two fallacies here. The first is that we are all agreed about the kind of life that is "good." But in fact men differ as much about morals as they do about doctrine. Every religion has a different moral system, and every version of the Christian religion has different opinions about morals. Romanists think divorce wicked but gambling permissible. Methodists think gambling wicked but divorce permissible. The Archbishop of Canterbury, rightly in my opinion, thinks neither divorce nor gambling permissible. One might add to such instances indefinitely.

The second, and more profound, fallacy is that we can lead a "good" life by our own strength. The truth is that we can do nothing that is good without grace; we shall not be given grace unless we pray for it, and use the sacraments and other means of grace, and we cannot pray or use the means of grace without faith.

This question implies far too low a standard. Probably the "good life" means a life conventionally decent. The conventions of our neighbors are for many of us what the Law was for the Pharisees—sufficient, if we observe them, to establish a claim upon God. Our Lord requires of us not conventional decency but perfection (St. Matthew 5:48). He said, "Except your righteousness shall exceed the righteousness of the scribes and Pharisees, ye shall in no case enter into the kingdom of heaven" (St. Matthew 5:20).

What we do depends to a large extent on what we believe. If your belief is false your behavior will be bad. If you believe in Hitler's God you will behave like Hitler. If you do not believe that there is any life hereafter your conduct will be very different from what it will be if you believe that your conduct here and now will take you to Heaven or to Hell.

## Chapter Seven

## FREE WILL AND PREDESTINATION

**86. Why did God give us free will? If He made everything and made it good, how could any evil course present itself?**

This is the mystery of the Origin of Evil, which no one has ever been able to solve. All we can say is this: God wished to be served freely; He wished to have love, courage, and all the virtues in His creatures. These virtues could not have existed if there had been no power of choice. Without free will there could be nothing good or holy. Human beings would be things, not persons. But it was God's Will to have *persons* as objects of His love.

**87. What is predestination? What is the Anglican view of it, as opposed to the Calvinistic view?**

The Church teaches that God predestines some men to privileges which are not given to all. The Hebrews were the chosen people; they were united to God by a covenant as the Greeks and Romans, the Indians and the Chinese, were not. This privilege was given to them for the sake of others. God said to Abraham, "In thy seed shall all the nations of the earth be blessed" (Gen. 22:18; Acts 3:25). Some people have the opportunity of hearing the gospel while others do not. We who have had that opportunity, and have accepted it, are responsible for preaching it to others.

The "elect" are the baptized. "All the elect people of God" means those who have by Baptism been made members of Christ's Church. "Many are called, but few are chosen." Only few are chosen because only a few have accepted the call. This is the constant teaching of both the Bible and the Prayer Book. "God will have all men to be saved, and to come to the knowledge of the truth" (I Tim. 2:4). "God so loved the world, that he gave his only begotten Son, that whosoever believeth in him should not perish, but have everlasting life" (St. John 3:16).

The Calvinistic doctrine is that "by the decree of God, for the manifestation of His glory, some men and angels are predestinated unto everlasting life, and others foreordained to everlasting death. Neither are any redeemed by Christ, but the elect only" (Westminster Confession, 1643, Article 3).

**88. Discuss clearly and fully election, predestination, and conversion. Has God predestined our actions, thought, and destiny? Does He know what we shall decide tomorrow, whether we shall go to Heaven or Hell?**

See Question 87. Conversion is the conscious turning of the will to God. All men are offered salvation, while some men are predestined to privilege for the sake of others. All men are called to conversion, while some men are given the privilege of a special conversion, like St. Paul (Acts 9) and St. Augustine. Conversion requires the cooperation of the will. It must not be confused with regeneration or the New Birth which is given through Baptism, even to unconscious infants.

God has a plan for each of us but He does not compel us to carry it out, for He has given us free will. He wishes all of us to be saved but He does not save us against our will. Our thoughts and actions are not decided entirely by ourselves. "God knows whatever is to happen, but what He knows is determined by what will happen, and not vice versa" (Francis J. Hall, *Dogmatic Theology*, Vol. 3, p. 285).

**89. Is grace irresistible?**

No. This was one of the errors of Calvin. If grace were irresistible, God would break our free will, which He never does.

**90. Define free will. How does God's foreknowledge enter into our faith?**

Free will is the power to choose between good and evil, between obeying God and disobeying Him. It is limited in many ways. Most attacks on human free will assume that it is supposed to be unlimited. If there were no free will there would be no right or wrong. I do not understand the last sentence. God's foreknowledge does not alter our faith or our conduct.

**91. Christ said, Many are called, but few chosen. Why should I try hard to be good? I may be one of those whom He does not choose.**

You are to try to be good, not for your own sake but for His, and you are to seek His help, without which you can do nothing good. If you are not chosen, it is only because you have not accepted His call; the man who would not put on the wedding garment provided for him (St. Matthew 22:11, 12) was called, but it was his own fault that he was not chosen.

**92. Explain what the problem of evil is. How does the Church provide an answer that the man in the street can understand?**

The problem of evil is the mystery of how there came to be sin in the world which God created good (see Question 86). The Church cannot give an answer to this mystery, for no answer has been revealed.

**93. Are there degrees of sin? Is one sin more serious than another in the sight of God?**

Yes. Our Lord said to Pilate, "He that delivered me unto thee hath the greater sin" (St. John 19:11). In I John 5:16 a distinction is drawn between the sin unto death and the sin not unto death. This is the source of the distinction between mortal and venial sin (roughly, between sins of deliberation and sins of weakness). All sins, however "venial," are sufficiently serious for us to make every possible effort to avoid them.

**94. What is the difference between the Catholic and the Protestant interpretation of Justification by Faith?**

In place of "Catholic and Protestant" read "Roman and Lutheran." The placing in opposition of "Catholic" and "Protestant" should always be avoided. The opposite of Catholic is not Protestant but heretical; the opposite of Protestant is not Catholic but Romanist. The Episcopal Church is Catholic. It is also Protestant in the historical use of that term, and, in this sense only, that means non-Roman.

Justification by faith is the teaching of St. Paul (Rom. 5:1, etc.). The Greek word means "accounted righteous," as Luther held, or, perhaps, "vindicated." But St. Augustine, who knew little Greek and no Hebrew (the root idea here is Hebrew) thought it meant "made righteous," and Rome has followed this false translation. "Faith" did not have the same meaning for Luther that it had for his opponents. Neither side understood the other. For Luther, as for St. Paul, the experience that he was justified by faith and did not need to rely on his own good deeds was an overwhelming religious experience. But Luther (and still more his followers) was tempted to think that nothing else was of much importance. He added two further doctrines which are not found in Scripture: the doctrine that Christ's merits are imputed to us and our sins imputed to Him, and the doctrine that we are accepted by God when we feel "assurance" of it. The Anglican Communion does not accept these doctrines, which the Church has never taught.

The truth for which Luther stood (and we with him) is that salvation is the free gift of God and cannot be earned or "merited." The truth for which Rome stands is that the act of acceptance by Christ is not the end but the beginning of a long process. Rome includes sanctification in justification, whereas we, with Luther, regard them as separate, but both necessary. The difference is very difficult to explain simply or briefly. There is much more in common between the two sides than either was ready to admit in the age of the Reformation.

**95. Why should you complicate the beautiful and simple ethical teachings of Jesus with all the dogma about blood sacrifice and sacraments and ceremonies?**

You appear to think that you are wiser than God and know what men need better than He does. The Son of God did not come to give us "beautiful ethical teachings," which many prophets and sages have done; He came to save us from our sins, which no one else has ever done or even claimed to do. He could do it only by being nailed to a cross. Ethical teaching is useless unless it is put into practice. Even St. Paul found that he could not keep the Law, however hard he tried; still less could he or anyone else live up to the far higher standard of the Sermon on the Mount, which is by no means "simple," as anyone will discover who seriously tries to obey it. We cannot do anything good without grace; if we think we can "we deceive ourselves, and the truth is not in us" (I John 1:8).

We can obtain grace only by means of our Saviour's death. That is the only "bloody sacrifice" in the Christian religion. Sacraments are the chief means by which we receive grace, and they are "a pledge to assure us thereof" (Church Catechism), that is, we know we have received grace when we have been baptized, or been confirmed, or received the Holy Communion.

The Christian religion is not a philosophy but a way of life. Therefore it requires ceremonies. The vast majority of mankind would rather take part in a ceremony than sit listening to "ethical teaching." You may have a Puritan background, and prefer sermons to ceremonies; if so, that is your misfortune (like being color-blind or having no sense of humor); and the Church, which provides for everyone, also provides dull services and long sermons for those who like them and are benefited by them.

*Chapter Eight*

## THE BLESSED VIRGIN MARY

**96. What is the Anglican doctrine about our Lord's Mother? Is she in glory? Do we pray to her or have pictures and statues of her in the Episcopal Church?**

Two doctrines about our Lord's Mother are proved from Scripture and are binding on all Christians. The first is that when her Son was born she was a virgin, which is an article of the Creed (see Question 40). The second is that she is rightly called *Theotòkos* (God-bearer), which in the First Prayer Book of 1549 is translated "Mother of our Lord and God Jesus Christ." This was decided by the General Council of Ephesus (A.D. 431) which was accepted by all the ancient churches and by the chief Reformers. (Even the Church of the East, Assyrian, which did not recognize the decrees of the Council of Ephesus, accepted the Council of Chalcedon, which ratified them.) This means that our Saviour was God from the first moment of His existence as Man.

The ancient Christian writers, from the second century onward, called our Lord's Mother the "Second Eve." As in the old story the temptation of Eve led to the fall of Adam, so the acceptance by the Blessed Virgin, the Second Eve, of her call to be the mother of the Second Adam ("Be it unto me according to

thy word"—St. Luke 1:38) led to the conquest by the Second
Adam of sin and death. As Bishop Ken (d. 1711) wrote:

> As Eve, when she her fontal sin reviewed,
> Wept for herself, and all she should include,
> Blest Mary, with man's Saviour in embrace,
> Joyed for herself and all the human race.

It has also been held by most Christians from early times that
she was a virgin not only when her Son was born but also till her
death. This cannot be proved either way: there is not, and perhaps
could not be, any evidence. (St. Matthew 1:25 does not, in the
original Greek, throw any light upon this matter.)

Our Lord's Mother foretold that all generations would call her
blessed (St. Luke 1:48). She was nearer to her Son than anyone
else, and she probably lived under the same roof with Him for
thirty years (St. Luke 3:23), ten times as long as most of His disciples. She has always been regarded as the first and holiest of
saints.

In the Church of England since the Reformation many writers,
in both prose and verse, have maintained a tradition of devotion
toward the Blessed Virgin; such as Bishop Joseph Hall (d. 1656),
George Herbert (d. 1633), Bishop Ken (d. 1711), Bishop Mant
(d. 1848), John Keble (d. 1866), Stuckey Coles (d. 1929). There
are five festivals of the Blessed Virgin in the English Prayer Book
Calendar and more than two thousand churches, old and new,
are dedicated to her. Statues and pictures of her in churches are
very common; perhaps the most famous is the statue which Archbishop Laud placed over the porch of the University Church at
Oxford, and which is still there.

However, the Anglican Communion is unwilling to go beyond
its knowledge in honoring our Lord's Mother. We know nothing
about her except what is told us in Holy Scripture or may be
proved from the Bible. There are many legends about her but
they have no historical value; even the oldest of these come from
the Apocryphal Gospels, which are certainly fictitious. That
she is "in glory" is more than we know. No doubt she is in the
highest condition of honor possible for any human being who
is not also Divine. Without claiming to be certain about things
so far beyond our knowledge, we think that human beings will

be given new bodies at the Last Judgment and that they will not
be in glory until they are clothed with the resurrection body.
Since there is no evidence for the legend of the Assumption of the
Blessed Virgin, we have no reason to suppose that she differs in
this respect from all other human beings. We have no doubt that
she prays for us, but we do not know whether she can hear our
requests to her to do so and we have no right to ask her for anything but her prayers. For this reason there are no direct addresses
to the Blessed Virgin, or to any other saint, in Anglican public
services. Those who do not feel certain that she can hear what
we say ought to be free not to address her directly. Those who
think she can hear our prayers may freely address her in private,
but they have no right to compel others to do so.

**97. Did Jesus have brothers and sisters? As the Bible clearly
says that He did, why is there belief in the perpetual virginity
of His Mother? Who were the brothers mentioned in the Gospel?
Would bearing other children have made her less holy?**

The question as to who were the Lord's "brothers and sisters"
is not so simple as some people think. It has been disputed ever
since the fourth century and even today is frequently argued. In
the fourth century there were three rival theories: St. Epiphanius,
Archbishop of Cyprus, held that the "brethren" were sons of
St. Joseph by a former marriage and were therefore our Lord's
older stepbrothers. Helvidius taught that they were the sons of St.
Joseph and St. Mary. St. Jerome (Hieronymus) believed that
their mother was the Blessed Virgin Mary's sister.

The opinion of St. Jerome is rejected by all modern scholars,
though it is commonly held in the Roman Communion. The
opinion of Helvidius was rejected by almost all Christians during
his lifetime and by Catholic tradition ever since. But the Reformers took up this theory out of a prejudice against celibacy,
and it has been widely taken for granted in Evangelical circles.
There are, however, indications in the Gospels that it is mistaken.

St. Joseph took his wife and our Lord to Jerusalem when He
was twelve years old. On the theory of Helvidius there were at
least six younger children who must have been left alone at
Nazareth. The attitude of His brethren toward Him (St. John
7:3-5) sounds more like that of older stepbrothers than of
younger half brothers. Again, our Lord entrusted His Mother
to the beloved disciple (St. John 19:26, 27). According to a highly

probable tradition, the "beloved disciple" was St. John, and he was her nephew for St. John's mother, Salome, was her sister (St. Mark 15:40, St. Matthew 27:56, St. John 19:25). If St. Mary had had sons of her own, it would have been their duty to support her. If our Lord had entrusted her to another man, they would have been jealous. This argument seems to me, if we accept St. John's Gospel as accurate, quite conclusive.

There remains the theory of St. Epiphanius, that the "brethren" were the sons of St. Joseph by a former wife. If St. Joseph was an old man at the time of our Lord's birth (he seems to have died before our Lord was thirty), it is probable that he had been married before, since Jewish boys were encouraged to marry at eighteen. Joseph, being the heir of David, needed sons to carry on the royal line from which the Messiah was expected to be born. This theory also explains why St. James, the eldest son, had such a great reputation among the Jews; it was not due to his character alone but to the fact that he was the heir of David. I think the theory of Epiphanius is practically certain.

**98. Why are there such different teachings from the clergy about the Blessed Virgin?**

Because they have been trained in different traditions and because some people delight in expressing opinions on subjects about which nothing is known.

**99. What is the Immaculate Conception?**

The Immaculate Conception is the opinion that our Lord's Mother, from the first moment of her existence, was miraculously preserved from all stain of original sin, and from actual sin also. It was proclaimed as a dogma binding on all Romanists by Pope Pius IX in 1854.

There is no evidence for this opinion. The texts of Scripture given as authorities, Genesis 3:15 and St. Luke 1:28, have nothing to do with the case. It is contrary to Romans 3:23, which declares that all men have sinned (except, of course, our Lord—St. John 8:46). It was quite unknown to the early writers, some of whom, such as St. John Chrysostom (d. 407), accuse the Blessed Virgin of actual sin. It seems to have appeared about the eleventh century. The Eastern and Old Catholic Churches reject it as heretical.

**100. What is the authority for believing in the Perpetual Virginity of the Blessed Virgin, and in her Assumption?**

Belief in her perpetual virginity was almost universal from the

third century. Most Christians have been unable to believe that
she who was the mother of the Word of God could have had
other children. But there is no evidence for this and, in the very
nature of the case, probably could not be any (see Question 97).

If the Blessed Virgin had had other children it would not have
made her any less holy, but there is no evidence that she did
have any.

The legend of the Assumption was unknown in the early centuries of the Church and there is no historical evidence that it is
true. It came to be generally accepted in all parts of the Church
during the early Middle Ages and was proclaimed as a dogma
necessary to salvation by Pope Pius XII in 1954. For several reasons most Anglican Churchmen find it quite incredible.


*Chapter Nine*

# THE CHURCH


**101. I don't need the Church. I can be just as good staying at
home, reading my Bible, and not being annoyed with others.**

Your religion seems to be entirely selfish. The important thing
is not what you think you need but what God requires of you.
The purpose of religion is not to make you "good," but to carry
out the Will of God. You say you read the Bible. How often
do you read it? Certainly you don't understand it. The Bible
could teach you many things of which you evidently know nothing; it shows, for example, that no one can serve God rightly
except by being united with Him by a Covenant. To be under
the Old Covenant men had to be Israelites. To be under the
New Covenant we must be members of the Church, the New
Israel (Acts 2:38; Rom. 6:3; Phil. 3:3). You cannot do anything
good, not even "not being annoyed with others" (which is a
negative kind of goodness), without the help of Divine grace.
You cannot, normally, have Divine grace except through the
sacraments and other means of grace given only to members
of the Church. In St. John 6:53 our Lord said, "Except ye eat the

flesh of the Son of man, and drink his blood, ye have no life in you." You cannot do this except as a member of the Church. You would not even have a Bible if the Church had not written it and preserved it for you. You cannot understand the Bible (and evidently you don't!) unless you study it with the help of scholars of the Church who explain it for you. You cannot serve your fellow men unless you join with others in the life of the Church. You must think again.

**102. Let me alone. Why must you constantly interfere with my personal life? Why must I pledge? Why must I worship God? Isn't living a good clean life enough?**

God made you and keeps you alive. You are not your own but His. Your first duty is to worship Him, because it is the purpose for which you exist. You cannot lead a "good clean life" without God's grace, which you receive even without knowing it: for of yourself, apart from that grace, you can do nothing good (Rom. 7:18). The Pharisees thought that they were living a "good clean life," but even Christ Himself could do nothing for them because they were satisfied with themselves. "Except your righteousness shall exceed the righteousness of the scribes and Pharisees, ye shall in no case enter into the kingdom of heaven" says our Lord (St. Matthew 5:20). You ought to be grateful to those who are trying to rescue you from your present dangerous condition of self-satisfaction, a condition that will certainly lead you to destruction if you do not acknowledge that you are a sinner in need of pardon.

**103. How can the Church, as a human institution, claim any authority over me? How can the Church, or a clergyman, be so arrogant and audacious as to tell me that I must believe or do this or that? Is not this to interfere with my freedom of religion?**

*If* the Church were an entirely human institution and you were a member of it, it would have a right to authority over you. The United States is a purely human institution, yet, as an American citizen, you are bound to obey its laws, because you benefit by the services it performs for you (too many to mention) and because you are required by God to render unto Caesar the things that are Caesar's (St. Mark 12:17).

But the Church is not an entirely human institution. It is the Body of Christ (I Cor. 12:27), the New Israel (Gal. 3:29), the representative of God on earth (Acts 1:8). You are not forced to be a member of the Church, but if you refuse to be a member you must assume full responsibility for the consequences to yourself, both in this world and in the next (St. Mark 16:16). If you have chosen to be a member of the Church you are bound to believe its doctrines and to obey its laws, both those which have been revealed by God (the Ten Commandments, etc.) and those which are made by men with authority given to them by God (St. Matthew 18:18). The clergy, as officers of the Church, are bound to teach you, as a member, what you are to believe and to do (Mal. 2:7; I Thess. 5:12, 13). They are doing their duty, and you ought to be grateful instead of resentful toward them.

Freedom of religion is freedom under the civil law. You are not forbidden to worship Jupiter or Baal, or any other false god, if you wish to. But if you neglect to worship the true God, or put any other god in His place, you will suffer the fate which befalls those who misuse their freedom. If you have deliberately chosen to be a member of the Church you have put limits to your freedom, as everybody does who joins any society. If you belong to a club you must pay your subscription; if you are an American citizen you must pay your taxes; if you are a member of the Church you must pay your share toward the stipends of the clergy and the other Church expenses.

**104. Our prayer group decided that Christians today were less Christian than those before the beginning of the organized Church. Are we losing ground?**

There was no time when the Church was not organized and there were no Christians before there was an organized Church. The Church was organized from the beginning, as you can see from reading the New Testament. Your prayer group has no means of judging who is more and who is less Christian. In any case, "judge not, that ye be not judged (St. Matthew 7:1).

**105. Why should people belong to the Church and go to church?**

Man is a social being: none of us liveth to himself (Rom. 14:7). We cannot serve either God or our neighbors in solitude. The Church is the family of God, into which we were adopted when we were baptized. It is God's chief instrument for bringing mankind back to Himself. It is only through the Church that we can receive the sacraments and other grace. It is only in the Church that we can be most fully ourselves, because only in the Church can we carry out to the utmost of our power the worship and service of God for which we were made. The highest kind of worship, that commanded by our Lord Himself, is the Holy in that act of worship every Sunday, whenever possible. That Eucharist. It is the duty of every member of the Church to join is what Sunday is for; not a day of rest but a day of worship. We are told not to forsake the assembling of ourselves together (for the Eucharist), for it was the only assembly practiced by early Christians (Heb. 10:25).

**106. What do you mean by "the Church is the Body of Christ"?**

It is the teaching of St. Paul that the Church is the Body of Christ (I Cor. 12:12–27; Rom. 7:4; Col. 1:18). The Church is an organism with one life imparted to it by Christ its Head. No one can understand the doctrine of the Church if he is under the delusion that men are entirely separate individuals. Neither a family nor a nation is simply the sum of its members; rather it is like an arch instead of a heap of stones, or a tree instead of a wood. Much more is this true of the Church of Christ. As our body is the means by which we express ourselves, so the Church is the means by which our Lord expresses Himself in this world. We are the members, the living parts, of that Body. The life of Christ, that is, His living power, which indeed is God the Holy Spirit, is given to us by the sacraments and other means of grace. If we do not use it we become like withered limbs on a tree, fit only to be destroyed. As each member has its own function in the human body, so each of us has his or her own function or vocation in the Church, some great, some small, but all necessary to its fullness. In the same way every race and every nation has its function in the Body of Christ. The Jews had their function, but they refused it, and the Church still suffers from the loss of them. The Greeks and the Latins, the Germans and the Russians, the British and the Americans, all have had their work to do in the filling up of the Body of Christ, and many other nations with them. Hereafter, with God's help, the Indians and the Africans, the Chinese and the Japanese, will take their places beside them. Every race, however small, every individual, however obscure, has a function foreordained by God.

**107. What is the analogy of the Church as the Bride of Christ?**

The prophets sometimes spoke of God as the Husband of Israel (Jer. 3:20, 31:32; Ezek. 16; Hos. 2:16–20). Israel's worship of false gods is compared with adultery. Psalm 45 was regarded by the Jews as a prophecy of the position given to Israel as the Bride of the Messiah. "Hearken, O daughter, and consider, incline thine ear; so shall the king have pleasure in thy beauty." In the Gospels our Lord is sometimes compared to a bridegroom (St. Mark 2:19; St. Matthew 22:2). St. Paul compares man and wife to Christ and the Church (Eph. 5:22–33; cf. II Cor. 11:2). In the final vision of Revelation we read of the marriage of the Lamb (Rev. 19:7–9), and the seer is shown "the bride, the Lamb's wife," which is the heavenly Jerusalem (Rev. 21:9).[1]

**108. Is not the Golden Rule the sum and substance of the teaching of Jesus?**

The Golden Rule (St. Matthew 7:12) is "Whatsoever ye would that men should do to you, do ye even so to them." It is part of our Lord's teaching but it does not cover all that He taught about our duty toward our neighbors and it does not even touch His teaching about our duty to God and to ourselves.

Our Lord said that the most important commandment was: Thou shalt love the Lord thy God with all thy heart, and mind and soul and strength (St. Mark 12:30). He quoted as a commandment: "Thou shalt worship the Lord thy God, and Him only shalt thou serve" (St. Matthew 4:10); He proclaimed, "Ye cannot serve God and mammon" (St. Matthew 6:24); He said, "Be ye perfect, as your Father in heaven is perfect" (St. Matthew 5:48), "Blessed are the pure in heart, for they shall see God" (St. Matthew 5:8), and "Whosoever doth not bear his cross, and come after me, cannot be my disciple" (St. Luke 14:27). These sayings, and many others, have nothing to do with the Golden Rule, even though they are all concerned with conduct. Besides these, however, Christ also taught doctrine, which is even more important because what you do depends upon what you believe. Here are some of His teachings about doctrine: "These shall go away into everlasting punishment: but the righteous into life eternal" (St. Matthew 25:46); "Except ye eat the flesh of the

[1]See Claude Chavasse, *The Bride of Christ* (London: Faber and Faber, 1939).

Son of man, and drink his blood, ye have no life in you" (St. John 6:53), and more fundamental still, "Before Abraham was, I am" (St. John 8:58).

**109. Are not the precepts of Christianity really contained in the words "Live and let live"?**

There is nothing specially Christian in these words; they are observed by all human beings who value their own interests, and even by other kinds of animals. The first duty of a Christian is to believe in, to worship, and to love God.

**110. Isn't Christianity really trying to follow the teachings of Jesus?**

That is certainly necessary, but by itself it will not carry us far, because we cannot do this without grace, however hard we try. To be Christians we must first repent of our sins (realizing, of course, that we are sinners), then believe (that is, commit our-selves and all we have and are to Jesus Christ), be baptized into His Church (St. Matthew 28:19; St. John 3:5), be confirmed (St. John 14:26; Acts 8:17), receive the Holy Communion regularly (I Cor. 11:25; St. John 6:56), and live as faithful members of His Church.

**111. I believe in God and try to follow the teachings of Jesus, but why is the Church necessary?**

See the preceding question. You might believe in God and yet not believe that He is Three in One and therefore love, or that Christ died and rose again for you, if the Church had not taught you. You might try to follow the teachings of Christ, but you would not be a Christian unless you had entered His Church by baptism. Our Lord did not need to teach His hearers to worship God; they were all practicing Jews and were worshiping God already. Our first duty is to worship God, for that is the purpose for which we were made. And we must do this corporately, in union with others. It is for this purpose that we must go to church, and it is for this purpose that the Lord's Day is observed. The Church is the principal means by which the work of God in this world is carried on. You, like every other human being, have your appointed place and function in that work. If you do not take that place, God's work is to that extent incomplete; you are letting Him down, though He has done everything for you.

**112. A man, who is a better Christian than anyone else I have ever met, never goes to Church; how will he fare at the Day of Judgment?**

You do not know that he is a better Christian than anyone else you have ever met. You cannot know what he or anyone else is in the sight of God, and you have no right to offer an opinion on such a subject. We must all stand at the judgment seat of Christ (Rom. 14:10): it is our own eternal fate, not that of others, that should be our concern (St. John 21:22).

**113. Why missions? There is plenty to do here; and, after all, other people have their own religions.**

Indeed there is plenty to do here; how much of it do you do? Our Lord commanded us to make disciples of all nations. A black man in Central Africa is just as dear to Him as you and I are. There is no respect of persons with Him.

You evidently know very little about other religions. In many parts of the world the local religion is the fear of malicious spirits and the tyranny of the witch doctors. The gospel of Christ comes as a great deliverance. Some forms of Hinduism are simply devil worship. Temple prostitution is practiced on a large scale.

I heard the former Bishop of Melanesia tell this story: During Hitler's war, American airmen were warned by the authorities that if they landed on a certain island in the Pacific they would be killed and eaten. Those authorities were two generations behind the times. An American aircraft did crash on that island. The native lay reader and his congregation were gathering for Evening Prayer at the time. They rushed to the scene of the crash and, under the guidance of a doctor, who had been on board and was himself hurt, gave first aid to the injured. Then these same natives carried their patients on stretchers to the nearest American post, a task that took most of the night. The lay reader refused to accept a reward or even to give his name for a decoration. "We are Christians," he said, "it is only our duty to help those in need." That was the result of missions.

In many parts of the world there is a race between Christian missions and Islam (the religion of polygamy, fanaticism, and contempt for non-Moslems) or communism (the religion of atheism and class hatred). The Christian religion is the religion of love; Jesus Christ alone is the Saviour of all men.

**114. Why should people give money to the Church?**

If they are members of the Church they are bound to pay for Church expenses and for the stipends and training of the clergy because they benefit by them. If they are servants of Jesus Christ they must help to carry out His will for the sick, the orphans, the missions, and many other works. He said, "Inasmuch as ye have done it unto one of the least of these my brethren, ye have done it unto me" (St. Matthew 25:40).

**115. What is the basis of the idea that the world exists to support the Church?**

Since the Church is God's chief instrument for carrying out His purpose, we may say that the world exists to support it. It would be better, however, to say that the Church exists for the glory of God, a purpose which is to be fulfilled by serving the world, that is, the human race. God may have other purposes for the world besides those which He has revealed to us.

**116. How can we more effectively present the Catholic truth that one cannot be a practicing Christian without sharing in the life of the visible Church?**

By sharing in it ourselves with all our power and trying to make it as attractive as possible to those who do not yet share it.

**117. Why cannot I have the music I want at weddings and funerals? Why cannot my child be baptized when and where I want?**

The music at weddings and funerals, as at all other services of the Church, is entirely under the control of the rector of the parish. It must be so, since various interests are involved. A reasonable priest will consult the bride (and possibly the bridegroom) at a wedding and the next of kin to the dead person at a funeral, but he is not bound to give them what they ask for if he thinks it unsuitable. His decision is final; there is no appeal from it.

Baptism is a public service of the Church, which desires that as many as possible should be present to welcome the new member into the family of God. The rule is that whenever possible baptism should take place at or after one of the public services on a Sunday or Holy Day, and in the parish church. Baptism in private houses is allowed only in cases of extreme sickness. (In England this rule is strictly enforced.) It is a common but deplorable custom for wealthy people to attempt to have their children baptized at a semiprivate service in church, at which no one is expected but the family and friends of the candidate. The more enlightened priests are trying to break down this custom by administering baptism only at a fixed hour on a fixed day. It is contrary to the Christian spirit to give a privilege to the wealthy which would not be given to the poor (James 2:2–5).

**118. Why must I be active in the Church if I am to be a Christian?**

Because our Saviour died for you and therefore you ought to do all you can for Him. Because He has given you some piece of work to do, and if you do not do it, it will not be done. Because, if you do not make use of whatever gift God has given you, you will lose the power to use it, and you will be of no service to God, to man, or to yourself (St. Matthew 13:40 ff.).

But being active in the Church does not necessarily mean that your vocation is to do what is commonly called "Church work." It may be your vocation only to do your ordinary work as well as you can, as a service to God, and to set an example of Christian living to your neighbors.

**119. What is the minimum requirement for a Christian? Is the average Churchman considered a "saint"?**

There is no minimum requirement for a Christian. What is required of us all is perfection (St. Matthew 5:48). However, the Archbishops of Canterbury and York have declared that the following are duties binding on every member of the Church:

(1) To follow Christ's example in home and daily life, and bear personal witness to Him.
(2) To be regular in private prayer every day.
(3) To read the Bible carefully and regularly.
(4) To receive the Holy Communion faithfully and regularly.
(5) To give personal service to the Church, neighbors, and community.
(6) To give money for parish and diocese, and for the work of the Church at home and overseas.
(7) To uphold the standard of marriage entrusted by Christ to His Church.
(8) To take care that children are brought up to love and serve the Lord.

**120. In what tangible provable ways is the world a better place to live in through the life and death of Jesus Christ, compared with the world before His time?**

Read Mr. Stewart Perowne's recent life of Herod the Great for a picture of what even the Jews, the chosen people, who were far more moral than the Greeks or Romans, had come to by the time of our Lord.

Here are a few of the reforms due to the Christian religion: The gladiatorial shows (as popular as football and racing are today), in which men killed each other for the entertainment of the audience, were stopped by Christian emperors, because of the martyrdom of St. Telemachus, who protested and was lynched by the spectators. The murder of unwanted infants, an everyday practice among the Romans, was stopped. The foul practices in heathen religions were forbidden. Slavery was at last abolished, largely through the work of Christians such as Clarkson, Wilberforce, Fowell Buxton, David Livingstone, and many Americans. The Mexican religion, the chief feature of which was human sacrifice on a large scale, was abolished by Cortes.

**121. Should not the Church steer clear of politics? Should a priest lead a political group?**

In my personal opinion the Church as such should steer clear of *party* politics. There are good men as well as bad men in all parties. The Church will have much more power to defend what is right if it is able to say to any party, "Do that, and we all, whatever our party, will vote against you." But the Church should use any such power only for a clearly moral cause and must not identify in its own material or even spiritual interests with the Will of God. Only seldom is one side in politics so certainly right and the other wrong that all members of the Church are morally bound to vote one way.

The clergy should never attach themselves to any political party for several reasons: (1) The priest in charge of souls must be the same to all his people, whatever their politics; but he will not be this if he is known to belong to a political party. (2) He will find it impossible to make people distinguish between his personal opinions and the beliefs he is required to teach as an officer of the Church; either they will think that his opinions are those of the Church or they will think that the doctrines of the Church have no more authority than do his personal opinions. (3) Politics is always an affair of compromise; but the priest's theological training should have accustomed him to think of truth as absolute truth and of right conduct as absolutely right; therefore, as history shows, clerical politicians are usually bad politicians or else bad priests (Laud was the former, Wolsey the latter). (4) Priests are required to give their whole time to their proper work; they ought to have no time for political activity.

But the Christian laity ought to take their full share in politics. If good men avoid political action, it will be misused by bad men for selfish purposes.

**122. Why do not the Church and its parishes oppose more actively communism and socialism, as the Roman Communion does?**

Socialism is to be sharply distinguished from communism. Every member of the Communist party must be a militant atheist and try to destroy every kind of religion, according to the teaching of Marx. Socialism, on the continent of Europe, is said to be opposed to religion, but in Britain many Socialists are practicing Christians. Such leading Socialists as George Lansbury and Sir Stafford Cripps have been ardent members of the Church. Other Socialists are members of the Roman Communion, and the Pope, who does not allow Romanists to be Socialists on the Continent, permits them to join the (Socialist) British Labour party.

The best way for the Church to oppose communism is to preach and practice the Christian religion, especially in its social aspects, and to show those to whom communism appeals that it is not true that "religion . . . is the opium of the people" or that the Church is allied with the wealthy against the poor. The Roman Communion is not in quite the same position as we are. Many of its members, especially the Irish, are accustomed to look to their priests for guidance in politics. That is not our tradition; we think that the priest is no more competent than any educated layman to give guidance in politics and that in some ways he is less competent because he is trained to study truth and conduct absolutely rather than relatively.

**123. What is the proper role of the Church in the social order?**

To answer this question a treatise would be required. I assume that the "Church" here means the laity as well as the clergy. The duty of the Church and its members to the social order is based on the doctrine and moral teaching of the New Testament, as understood by the Universal Church. The application of Christian principles to the complex problems of modern social life requires long and careful study. No one's opinion on any subject is worth listening to unless he has studied that subject and has the intelligence to use his knowledge. I have neither the knowledge nor the experience (never having had to earn my living as a layman) and therefore I cannot answer this question except to say that the Church and its members, in judging such a matter, ought to lay aside all selfish interests, both their own and those of their class or race or country or even Church, and, as far as possible, consider only what seems to be according to the revealed Will of God.

**124. Is excommunication still practiced by the Church? If so, on what grounds may one be excommunicated?**

Excommunication is the severest punishment which the Church has the right or power to inflict. The excommunicated person is excluded from all the rights of membership, including Communion and burial with the Church service (see Article 33, American numbering, which declares that the excommunicated person is to be boycotted, a practice now obsolete). In the Roman and Orthodox Communions excommunication is not uncommon.

In the Anglican Communion it is chiefly found in the mission field, especially Africa, and is imposed for idolatry, witchcraft, and sexual offenses. In English-speaking countries it is rarely used, for several reasons. The purpose of excommunication is to bring the offender to repentance and restoration and to warn the faithful against his errors. In modern England a sentence of excommunication, and the trial in the Church court which must precede such a sentence, would bring the offender much undesirable publicity. He can always join one of the many sects which give communion to everyone who asks for it, and the sort of person who would be likely to be excommunicated in English-speaking countries would not hesitate to do this, especially as public sympathy would probably be on his side. Two centuries of individualism in religion have made the sin of schism almost meaningless. In England, where the Church courts are controlled by the State, the legal difficulties and the expense of a prosecution make excommunication almost impossible.

Excommunication may be imposed only by the bishop of the diocese, and is inflicted for grave offenses against faith or morals. A modern American case is that of William Montgomery Brown,[1] who was deprived of his bishopric and excommunicated because he declared that he believed in God only "in a symbolic sense." J. W. Colenso, Bishop of Natal, was excommunicated in 1863 by the Church of South Africa for rejecting the doctrine of the Atonement and for other heresies, as well as for refusing to recognize the authority of the Provincial Synod. The excommunication led to a small schism, which still exists.

**125. What happens to the nonbeliever?**

We do not know. We cannot judge how far his lack of belief is his own fault. He is under both the justice and the mercy of God.

*Chapter Ten*

# THE ANGLICAN COMMUNION

*Introductory Note.* Since the standpoint from which the next chapters are written will be strange to many readers, I must explain it as briefly as I can.

There is, and can be, only One Church, which is the Body of Christ (I Cor. 12:12; Eph. 1:22, 23). This is an article of the Creed: I believe one Holy Catholic Apostolic Church. The Church is partly in this world and partly in Paradise; it is the New Israel, the chosen people of God. In this world, like the Old Israel, it is visible; that is, we know who belongs to it and who does not. Those who have been baptized, and only those, are members of it. Some of these are good and some are bad. A bad man may be a member of the Church (Acts 5:1, 8:21); an unbaptized man, however holy, cannot be a member of the Church in this world.

---

[1] He was consecrated Bishop Coadjutor of Arkansas in 1898 and the next year became diocesan; he resigned his jurisdiction in 1912 and was deposed in 1929. He died in 1937.

When the New Testament speaks of churches, it means local communities of Christians; the Church of Corinth or of Ephesus means the Christian community in that city, organized under apostolic authority and including all baptized persons; for the New Testament knows nothing of an unbaptized Christian.

Over against the Church we find the sects. A sect is a society of Christians, large or small, organized for a particular purpose, such as to promote some special doctrine or method, in opposition to, or as a supplement to, the official apostolic Church. I wish to show no disrespect toward the sects (commonly called "churches"). Many of them have plainly received the Divine blessing, for they have done immense work for Christ, sometimes work which the Church could not or did not do. Members of these sects, if baptized, are members of the Church, though in most cases not full members because they have not been confirmed and do not recognize apostolic authority. But the sects themselves, properly speaking, are not churches; they do not, in most cases, accept the whole faith of the Apostles, and they do not possess authority derived from the Apostles nor are they historically connected with the Apostles. Hence a member of one of the sects, if baptized, is a member of the Church, not because he belongs to the sect but because he has been baptized; although he is not a full member of the Church because he has not been confirmed.

The Catholic Church ought to be a single united society. Through quarrels in past centuries about secondary matters, it is now divided into different sections, which we call "Communions." It is like a nation divided by a civil war or like Israel from the time of Jeroboam to the Captivity, which was divided into two kingdoms, yet both belonged to the chosen people. All these Communions possess the same Creed, sacraments, and ministry; the same religious life is found in them all; they are all governed by the apostolic authority of their bishops. They are not completely separated, but are rather like members of one family who have quarreled, as Israel and Judah had quarreled.

In England, we claim that the Provinces of Canterbury and York are the Catholic Church in England. They possess the apostolic faith and authority and they have been here since the gospel was first preached to the English. The majority of the English people have always belonged to these provinces and, nominally, still do. We make the same claim for the Welsh and Scottish Churches in communion with Canterbury, although the majority of the Welsh and Scots do not recognize the authority of their bishops. It is a claim that has nothing to do with "establishment." We say that every baptized person in England is a member of the Catholic Church and therefore of the Church of England, for there is no other. (Resident foreigners, belonging to the churches of their own countries, are the only exceptions.) They may not be full members of the Church, but by their baptism they have a measure of membership.

In the United States the position is not so simple. The Church of England was brought to Virginia by the first settlers in 1607. It remained an outlying part of the Diocese of London until the American Revolution. Then it was organized as an independent national Church, in full communion with the Church of England. Every member of the Church of England, if he lands in America, becomes automatically a member of the Episcopal Church, and vice versa. Meanwhile different groups of settlers had brought various sects with them, and other sects were founded in America. The French, Italians, Poles, etc., brought the Roman Communion. The Greeks, Russians, Serbs, etc., brought the Orthodox Eastern Communion. The Armenians and Assyrians brought their own national Churches.

The Episcopal Church, therefore, cannot claim to be exclusively the Catholic Church in the United States, as the Church of England claims to be in England. What it can claim is this: an American who wishes to live the Catholic life as a full member of the Catholic Church, cannot belong to the Roman Communion unless he is willing to submit to the papal claims and dogmas, which all who are not Romanists believe to be false and unscriptural. If he belongs to one of the Eastern Churches, he will be a member of a church attached to some foreign nation, whose history, traditions, and usually language are foreign. There is as yet no one American Orthodox Church. To be Orthodox you have to belong to the Greek, or Russian, or some other foreign Church. But an American may belong to the Episcopal Church, which is thoroughly American, keeps to American traditions, and is subject to no authority outside the United States. It does not claim exclusive jurisdiction, as the English Church does in England. (The Romanists and the Eastern Churches have their own jurisdictions in America, which the Episcopal Church recognizes.) But the Episcopal Church has the right to claim allegiance from Americans, as the one Communion which is Catholic, free from papal additions to the faith, and entirely American. How far it makes that claim, or lives up to it, is for the reader to judge, but I cannot see any other ground on which the Episcopal Church can claim the allegiance of its members or even the right to exist.

**126. "The Episcopal Church has the historic Catholic Faith." What does this mean?**

Catholic means universal. The teaching of the Episcopal Church and of the other Anglican Churches is the same as that of the Church of the early centuries and is based entirely on the Holy Scriptures, as they were understood in the ancient Church and as modern scientific discovery and criticism have thrown new light upon them. The Episcopal Church also maintains the ancient Church order and government based on the Catholic doctrine of the ministry. It accepts, as a summary of the faith and order of the ancient Church, the Lambeth Quadrilateral drawn up at Chicago in 1886 by the General Convention of the Episcopal Church and accepted by the Lambeth Conference of all the Anglican bishops in 1888. This statement is not a binding doctrinal formulary and does not include the whole Catholic faith; it was put forward as a preliminary basis for negotiations with other Communions. It consists of four points, the Bible, the Apostles' and Nicene Creeds, the two great sacraments, and the three orders of the historic ministry, bishops, priests, and deacons.

**127. What is the real meaning of "Catholic" as used in the Episcopal Church?**

Remember, "Catholic" means universal. Strictly speaking, only those doctrines and practices are Catholic which have always been believed and used in all parts of the Church. More loosely, the word is applied to practices and traditions (such as the observance of Christmas Day or the use of special dress by the clergy) which have a long continuous history and are universally accepted, even though they do not go back to apostolic times. The word also implies "orthodoxy," holding the right faith and worshiping God in the right manner as required by the Church.

Every member of the Church, who is baptized, in communion

with the bishops, and not excommunicated, is a Catholic. The opposite of Catholic is heretic, a person who, being a member of the Church, rejects any part of its defined faith; or schismatic, a person who is separated through his own fault from the fellowship of the bishops or encourages those who are separated to remain separated.

**128. Is the Episcopal Church a denomination within the Holy Catholic Apostolic Church?**

The word "denomination" means a religious society of any kind, in relation to the State and to society in general. It has no theological significance.

According to the standpoint from which this book is written, the Episcopal Church is the Catholic Church in the United States, without prejudice to the jurisdiction over their own people of the Roman and Eastern Communions (Orthodox, Assyrian, and Armenian) and the National Polish Church.

**129. How do we know that the Anglican Communion is part of the Body of Christ?**

The Anglican Communion, which is represented in the United States by the Episcopal Church, holds the faith or doctrine based on Holy Scripture which the ancient Catholic Church held to be necessary to salvation; it has neither added anything to that faith nor left anything out. It has maintained continuity both in the faith and in the orderly succession of the bishops from the earliest times. In the British Isles the Anglican Communion has continued the ancient hierarchy of the bishops holding the ancient faith, and therefore it has exclusive jurisdiction there. In the United States the Episcopal Church may claim to have been the first part of the Church to be planted in the country and to be the only part of it not necessarily connected with any foreign nation or under the jurisdiction of any foreign bishop.

The Anglican Communion cannot be justly accused of any act of heresy or schism, except by those who believe that the papal claims and dogmas are necessary to the Christian religion. The abundant life which this Communion displays, its extension throughout the world, and the growth within it of all the normal features of Catholic devotion, such as the retreat movement, the honor given to the saints, the practice of daily Communion, the life of men and women under vows of poverty, celibacy, and obedience, and the heroism of its missionaries and martyrs, show that it belongs to Catholic Christendom and has received the blessing of God on its work.

### 130. What is our relationship with the Polish National Catholic Church?

The Polish National Catholic Church, which is the American part of the group of Churches called the Union of Utrecht, or Old Catholic, is in full communion with the American Episcopal Church. The basis of the full communion is the agreement drawn up at Bonn (of which I was one of the signatories) between the representatives of the Church of England and the Old Catholic Churches of Europe. It was accepted by the Polish National Catholic Church in 1936. (For the text of the agreement, see *Lambeth Report,* 1948.)

Full communion means that any member of either Church has all the rights of a member in the other Church; just as the members of the Church of England and of the Episcopal Church have in one another's Churches. What is unique about the Polish National Catholic Church is that it is the only Old Catholic Church in the same country as an Anglican Church. This is technically irregular, because normally there can be only one Church in one country, and the Anglican Churches are careful to respect the jurisdiction of other Communions which they recognize as Catholic. But in this case it is necessary because the Polish National Catholic Church consists entirely of Poles and Lithuanians, whose language and religious habits and traditions are different from those of the Episcopal Church. The other Old Catholic Churches are those of Holland, Germany, Switzerland, and Austria, and two or three smaller groups in Europe. They are grouped round the ancient archbishopric of Utrecht, which was founded in 696.

### 131. Discuss our Faith and Reunion (Ministry).

Reunion of the Church requires, as a first condition, agreement on what is meant by the Church and by Reunion. On this there are at least three different doctrines:

(1) The Church is visible, and cannot be divided (Roman). In this case reunion means submission to the Pope.

(2) The Church is visible, and reunion requires agreement in fundamental doctrine but not submission (Anglican and Eastern).

The Anglican Churches hold that the Church is divided by schism; the Orthodox Churches hold that it cannot be divided, and that the Orthodox Eastern Communion is the only true Church.

(3) The Church is invisible, consists of all who are converted, and is found wherever the Word of God is preached and the (two) sacraments are administered. Those who believe, as the Easterns, Romanists, Anglicans, and some Lutherans do, that the Church is visible and is composed of the baptized must hold that it ought to have one government, which can only be that of the apostolic ministry of bishops, priests, and deacons.

Those who believe that the Church is invisible and manifests itself in a number of independent sects do not think that it matters what sort of ministry they choose to have. They do not believe that historic continuity or apostolic authority is necessary.

**132. Give a list, and explanation, of the legitimate traditions of Catholic, Orthodox, and Protestant Communions.**

This is too big a question to be answered here. The term "Protestant Communion" should be avoided, for, strictly speaking, there is no such thing. The Anglican Communion, which is neither Eastern, Roman, nor, in the usual modern sense, Protestant, is not mentioned.

**133. Why don't we admit we are Catholic without papist addition or Puritan subtraction? Why should we double-talk about being both Catholic and Protestant?**

The first sentence of this question is a fair description of the Anglican position: it comes from the will of Thomas Ken, Bishop of Bath and Wells. The Anglican Communion declares that it is Catholic, for it recites the Catholic creeds and in the Prayer Book refers to the Catholic Church. As long as the Episcopal Church uses the word "Protestant" in its title, it cannot deny that it is in some way Protestant; in the eighteenth century the word meant only non-Roman or Anglican; but it has now changed its meaning and ought to be dropped.

**134. A Catholic friend once told me that the Episcopal Church is merely a branch of the Catholic Church. What is the reply?**

The word "Catholic" as used in this question appears to mean Romanist. This is a meaning of the word which no member of the Anglican Communion should ever allow to be used in his presence, still less use it himself. In the case where the Episcopal Church is referred to, as in this question, the reply is, "Of course it is, and I am glad you admit it; but I don't see how, on your [Roman] principles, you can." For no Romanist can consistently admit that we, who reject the papal claims and the dogmas of the Councils of Trent and the Vatican, can be a part of the Catholic Church.

On the other hand, we are not a part of the Roman ecclesiastical empire, sometimes, but incorrectly, called "the Western Church." The Anglican Churches are Catholic, but neither Roman nor Latin.

**135. What is the authority of the Church in pronouncements on faith and morals? How is it promulgated? How far are such pronouncements binding on the laity?**

We must distinguish between the two meanings of "authority." It may mean moral and intellectual weight, as when one says, "F. J. Hall is a great authority, or has great authority, in dogmatic theology." Or it may mean the right to be obeyed; the policeman exercises this kind of authority when he tells us to stop. The Church has both kinds of authority but the second appears to be meant here.

The Church Universal (except the Roman Communion) is normally governed by national or provincial synods or councils, consisting of bishops, in whom the final authority rests, with representatives of the clergy and laity. The General Councils, of which we recognize six, were summoned as extraordinary assemblies to deal with particular cases. Their decrees on faith and morals, as far as they may be proved from Scripture and have been accepted by all the local churches, are binding on all members of the Church. The best known of these decrees is that in which the Council of Chalcedon (451) promulgated the Nicene Creed (except the clause "and the Son"). There is no council for the whole Anglican Communion. The resolutions of the Lambeth Conference (to which all Anglican diocesan bishops are invited) have no binding force, unless and until they have been ratified by the national or provincial synods. The synod of the American Episcopal Church is called the General Convention.

Such a synod may issue decisions on faith and morals, if they can be proved to be in agreement with Holy Scripture and the decisions of the General Councils and if they do not alter the universally accepted conditions for the validity of a sacrament. For instance, it is universally agreed that the wine used for the Holy Communion must be fermented grape juice and that no woman is admissible to Holy Orders. No local or national synod can disregard these rules, which are certainly in accordance with Scripture; for if it did, other local churches would not recognize its sacraments (including the ministry). The Anglican principle is: "The Church hath power to decree rites or ceremonies, and authority in controversies of faith; and yet it is not lawful for the Church to ordain anything that is contrary to God's Word written, neither may it so expound one place of Scripture, that it be contrary to another" (Article 20). See also Article 6, which lays it down that no man is required to believe, as necessary to salvation, what cannot be proved from Scripture. Within these limits, the decisions of provincial synods on faith and morals are binding on both the clergy and the laity. But Anglican synods rarely issue such decisions.

**136. What is the difference between Catholic and Protestant?**

Both terms require careful definition. Catholic means that which belongs to the whole Church and to the true faith. The opposite to it is "heretical." Protestant, in the old sense, meant antipapal. The opposite to it is Romanist or papalist. But in the present age the word "Protestant" is loosely used to cover all persons, in some sense Christian, who not only reject the papal claims but also deny that the Church on earth is a single, organized, visible society to which all Christians ought to belong; that there is any need for historic continuity from the Apostles' time; and that there is any ministerial priesthood in the Church on earth, distinct from the corporate "priesthood of all believers." In practice, Protestant now means "belonging to the sects."

**137. Is the Episcopal Church Catholic or Protestant?**

Both; it is Catholic positively and Protestant negatively. It is Catholic in its essential nature because it maintains the Catholic and apostolic faith and order. It is Protestant, in the old sense, negatively because it rejects the papal claims to supremacy, infallibility, and universal jurisdiction, and the decrees of the Councils of Trent and the Vatican. It is not Protestant in attaching any authority to the teaching of the Reformers as such or in rejecting the doctrines of the universal visible Church, baptismal regeneration, apostolic authority or ministerial priesthood. It is not one of the "Protestant Churches" and has not necessarily anything in common with the sects that are thus described.

**138. Why don't we omit "Protestant" from the name of our Church, since its meaning has changed?**

The word is highly misleading and ought to have been omitted long ago.

**139. What does Protestant mean in the Church's title?**

In the eighteenth century the word "Anglican" had not come into use. "Protestant" was the word commonly used to distinguish the Church of England from the Roman Communion and sometimes also from the Puritan sects. Even in this century I once heard the following dialogue in a play by Lennox Robinson (in Ireland): "Are you a Protestant? Certainly not, I am a Presbyterian." In Germany "Protestant" means Lutheran but not Calvinistic. "Protestant" in the title of the Episcopal Church means Anglican, or American, Catholic.

**140. What constitutes an act of schism?**

Formal breach of the unity of the Church or any act which tends toward it. Schism may be within the Church, such as the many historical quarrels between the Greeks and the Latins or the breach between Rome and Canterbury in 1570, or it may be from the Church, such as the setting up of new sects as rivals to it. To say or do anything that is likely to encourage the belief that it does not matter to what church or sect you belong is an act of schism. It is usually held that members of the Church are guilty of an act of schism if they take part in the worship, and still more in the sacraments, of sects which do not recognize the authority of the Church unless for some special reason and with due permission.

**141. Why are we not in full communion with the Church of South India? Why not make concessions for the sake of unity?**

Concessions can never be rightly made in matters of truth, even for the sake of unity. For instance, most of us are agreed that we cannot accept the papal claims, even for the sake of unity, because we do not believe them to be true. The union of the Church must be a greatest common measure rather than a lowest common multiple: it is a fatal mistake to give up what you believe to be valuable, even if not absolutely necessary, because someone else has a prejudice against it.

There appear to be two main obstacles in the way of full communion with the Church of South India. One is that many of its ministers have not been ordained by a bishop, which implies the principle that episcopal ordination is not necessary. If we were in full communion with the C.S.I., some of these men, who are not priests, would be permitted to celebrate the Holy Communion in Anglican churches. This would almost certainly lead to a widespread schism. The time may come when all the ministers of the C.S.I. will have been ordained by bishops, for there have been no ordinations by anyone else since 1945. When that time comes no one will be committed to the principle that episcopal ordination is not necessary. But that principle must be explicitly rejected before full communion can be accepted.

A much greater obstacle is that the C.S.I. is in full communion with the Presbyterians, Methodists, and Congregationalists in other countries. This implies either that these sects are Churches in the Catholic sense (which they themselves do not claim) or that the C.S.I. does not think the differences between a Church and a sect are important. It is hard to see how this obstacle can be overcome.

There are various minor difficulties. The C.S.I. gives some authority to that intolerable formulary, the Westminster Confession. It is also said to use some substance which is not wine in its Communion service, and its rules of marriage are said to be lax.

*Chapter Eleven*

# THE EASTERN CHURCHES

### 142. What are the essential differences between the Anglican and Orthodox Communions?

Strictly speaking, there are no essential differences. The chief formal difference is that the Orthodox Churches regard the decrees of the Seven General Councils as their doctrinal basis, but the Anglican Churches recognize only six. There is no real reason why the Anglican Churches should not accept the Seventh Council, which forbade both irreverence and superstition toward sacred pictures.[1]

The two chief practical differences are that the Orthodox Churches do not officially regard churches which are outside their communion as belonging to the true Church and that the great variety of belief and practice among Anglicans is not acceptable to the Orthodox, who are accustomed to a closer conformity of belief and practice everywhere. The psychological difference caused by differences of history, tradition, and language also is very great.

Some Orthodox bishops think that the clause "and the Son" in the Nicene Creed, which was added in the West without the consent of the Eastern Church, has been explained satisfactorily by the Anglican bishops. But others are not so sure of it. There is also misunderstanding about some of the Articles of Religion in the Anglican Prayer Books. At the present time by far the larger part of the Orthodox Communion is under Communist rule; it is doubtful whether the Orthodox Churches are free enough to take any decisive common action.

**143. Why is not a more visible pathway of unity with the Orthodox Church set up?**

**144. Why is not the Episcopal Church a pioneer of closer relations with the Orthodox Churches, as it has been with the Protestants?**

The majority of our lay people (and many priests) know nothing about the Orthodox Churches. Some are even prejudiced against them. If the Episcopal Church would drop the misleading word "Protestant" from its title it would remove from Orthodox minds and hearts one great obstacle to closer relations with us. We might also formally accept the Seventh General Council and omit the "and the Son" clause from the Nicene Creed, for it has not, like the rest of the Creed, the authority of the whole Church.

**145. Do the Orthodox Churches accept us as part of the historic Church?**

[1] See my book, *The Church of England and the Seventh Council.* New York: Morehouse-Gorham, 1957.

Officially they do not. I do not see how they could. The ignorance and false belief which are so constantly found among our laity, and even among our clergy (as these questions show), make it hard for our Orthodox friends to treat all Anglicans as being of the same religion as themselves.

**146. What is the relationship between the Anglican and Orthodox Communions?**

It has been very close and friendly for many years. Active proselytism is discouraged on both sides. The Archbishop of Canterbury regularly exchanges letters of greeting with the heads of Orthodox Churches, at the great festivals and on their enthronements. Anglican students spend periods in Orthodox colleges and Orthodox students in Anglican colleges. The bishops attend one another's consecrations as guests, but do not take part in them.

The Greek and Rumanian, but not the Slavonic, Churches, up to now, have recognized Anglican ordinations as equivalent to Roman ordinations. (Strictly speaking, the Orthodox Churches do not fully recognize any ordinations which are not Orthodox.) In many ways, at the higher levels, the two Communions support one another. But most of the clergy and laity on each side know very little about those on the other side.

**147. How can intercommunion with certain Orthodox groups be hastened?**

The word "intercommunion" has no meaning for the Orthodox Churches. A Church or a person is either Orthodox, and therefore in full communion with other Orthodox, or not Orthodox, and therefore not in communion. The whole Orthodox group of Churches acts together; we could not be in communion with some and not with others.

The best way to promote reunion with the Orthodox Churches is to pray regularly for them, to make friends with their members, to study their history and their point of view, and to take part in *their worship* (which, in this case, is not an act of schism). They are the masters of us all in the art of liturgical worship, and to accustom ourselves to their liturgy is the best way to understand them. For orthodoxy is not only "right belief" but also "right worship." Their liturgy has behind it a richer tradition than any in the West can claim.

*Chapter Twelve*

# THE ROMAN COMMUNION

**148. Is it not plain from the Bible that Peter was selected to be the head of the Church?**

Nowhere in the New Testament is St. Peter ever called the head of the Church. St. Paul calls our Lord the head of the Church (Eph. 1:23, 4:15). In I Corinthians 12:27 he says, "ye are the body of Christ," and refers (v. 28) to different members, placing Apostles first. In II Corinthians 11:5 and 12:11 he claims to be "in nothing behind the very chiefest apostles."

St. Peter was the leader and spokesman of the Apostles. He had the position of first among equals; their eldest brother, not their father. He was sent on a mission by the "apostolic college," the Apostles corporately (Acts 8:14) and was sometimes called upon to account for his actions (Acts 11:2; Gal. 2:14). Our Lord said to him, "Thou art Peter, and upon this rock I will build my church" (St. Matthew 16:18). This verse is explained in different ways, but if St. Peter is the rock, he is compared to the foundation stone of a building because he was the first to declare openly that our Lord was "the Christ, the Son of the living God." But a foundation stone can, as foundation stone, have no successors. All members of the Church are the stones laid afterward (I Peter 2:5; though here our Lord, not St. Peter, is called the foundation stone) but there can be only one foundation. The power to bind and loose, of which the keys were a symbol, was not given to St. Peter alone, but to all the Apostles (St. Matthew 18:18).

The popes are not the successors of St. Peter, for there is no evidence at all that he was ever Bishop of Rome. According to the earliest evidence, that of St. Irenaeus a century later, St. Peter and St. Paul consecrated Linus to be the first Bishop of Rome. The two Apostles were like our missionary bishops, founding Christian communities in different places (I Peter 1:1; II Cor. 11:28) but seem to have had no fixed sees. However, it appears likely that St. Peter did not continue to be the leader and spokesman of the Apostles all his life. Dr. Cullmann, in his recent book on St. Peter, argues convincingly that St. Peter took charge of the mission to the Jews, as St. Paul did of the mission to the Gentiles (Gal. 2:7), leaving St. James, the Lord's brother, in charge of the home Church at Jerusalem. Thus St. James takes the chair at the Council of Jerusalem (Acts 15:13) and sums up the discussion. In Acts 21:18 he is the head, in later terminology the bishop, of the Church in Jerusalem. In St. John 14:26 the Holy Ghost is promised as the Teacher of all Christians. In the letter which the Pope sent to Kubla Khan, the Mongol Emperor of China, giving him a summary of Christian doctrine, he said much about the teaching authority of Rome but hardly mentioned the Holy Ghost, Who is the true Vicar or Representative of Christ on earth. As the papal claims increased, the Holy Ghost was half forgotten.

**149. Was Peter the rock on which the Church was built?**

That is one explanation, but in any case it does not apply to his successors, if he had any. Many early writers explain the rock as Christ Himself, for in the Old Testament God is the Rock of Israel (II Sam. 22:2, etc.) and in I Peter 2:4–8 Christ Himself is the foundation. But even if St. Peter is the rock, he is not unique, for all the Apostles are foundations of the wall of the New Jerusalem (Rev. 21:14).

**150. Was St. Peter the first Pope?**

No; he was not even Bishop of Rome; the first Bishop of Rome was Linus (see Question 148). There were no popes, in the later sense of the word, for centuries after St. Peter. Monsignor Duchesne, the great Romanist historian, writing of the fourth century, says: "The Papacy, as the West was to know it later, was still to be born" (*Early History of the Church*, Vol. 2, p. 522). All bishops were called pope (father) until the sixth century. It was Gregory VII in the eleventh century who forbade other bishops to be called pope. The claim to universal authority first appeared about the fifth century.

**151. Define our differences from Rome for those who say that "is just like the Catholic Church."**

We claim that the Episcopal or Anglican Church is Catholic and has as much right to the Catholic heritage as the Romanists have. In all that is really Catholic in faith, such as the creeds, sacraments, and priesthood; in order, such as episcopal government, and diocesan organization; and in worship, such as the Church Calendar, and the use of such ornaments as chasubles, etc., for priests, miters for bishops, crucifixes and sacred pictures, candles and incense, we resemble the Romanists, although our tradition is independent and sometimes different in detail.

Where we differ from them in faith we do so because we believe that our doctrine is true, scriptural, and Catholic, and theirs is not. Where we differ from them in order and worship we do so because we claim that we are not bound by any rules which are only Latin or "Western" and that we are as independent of Rome as we are of the Eastern Churches.

The differences between the Anglican and Roman systems can be given here only very briefly. We have no wish to dwell on what unhappily divides us from our brethren in Christ.

(1) We deny that the Pope is the successor of St. Peter or the Vicar of Christ, that St. Peter was ever Bishop of Rome, that the Bishop of Rome has by Divine right any superiority over other bishops, that it is necessary to salvation to obey the Pope or to be in communion with him, that he is infallible, and that he has universal jurisdiction, or any patriarchal jurisdiction beyond Italy and the adjacent islands (for this was all that was given him by consent of the General Councils). We believe that the highest authority in the Church belongs to the bishops as successors of the Apostles (St. Luke 22:29; Acts 5:13; I Cor. 12:28; Eph. 4:11) and that the Romanist interpretation of the "Petrine texts" is quite unhistorical and was unknown for several centuries.

(2) We do not believe in autocratic and irresponsible government. Our bishops are not dictators; they may act only with the consent of the other bishops and of the priests and laity of their dioceses. Our church government is corporate and synodical, as it was in the ancient Church and as it is still in all the Eastern Churches. We think that the Church in each nation ought to be free to govern itself, within the limits set by Scripture, the definitions of the General Councils, and the conditions of the validity of the sacraments which are universally recognized.

(3) We reject the authority of the Council of Trent (1545–1563) and the Vatican (1870), and all other Latin Councils; also the authority of all papal bulls and briefs. Therefore we repudiate

the new dogmas of the Immaculate Conception (1894) and Assumption (1954) of the Blessed Virgin Mary, and the dogmas of Purgatory, Indulgences, Transubstantiation, etc., which were made binding by the Council of Trent.

(4) We assert that every dogma necessary to membership of the Church, that is, to present salvation (for the conditions of future salvation are not known to us), must be found in, or proved by, Holy Scripture. We accept the definitions of the General Councils, not because the Pope has ratified them, but because they can be proved from Scripture and have been accepted by the whole Church for many centuries. We reject the doctrine of Trent, that tradition is equal to Scripture as a source of dogma, because it has enabled the Pope to proclaim as necessary dogmas opinions which cannot be proved from Scripture and were unknown to the ancient Church.

(5) We claim freedom for the clergy to marry at their discretion and for the laity to receive Holy Communion in both kinds, according to our Lord's command (St. Matthew 26:27). We value confession to a priest as a means of grace, but we enforce it on no one. We claim that it is the right and the duty of all Christians to read the Bible in their own language (but not to insist on their own interpretation of it, for "no prophecy of the scripture is of any private interpretation"—II Peter 1:20); and to have the liturgy and other services of the Church in a language which they can understand.

(6) We claim for ourselves political, intellectual, and liturgical freedom; we are not in any way bound to the political interests of the Vatican; we are free from the censorship and the index of prohibited books, from the decrees of the Biblical Commission and other Vatican pronouncements, and from the traditions and superstitions which have survived in the Roman Communion from medieval, and even pagan, times; we have our own Prayer Book, which we are free to change when our synods wish, instead of the rites and ceremonies of the Missal and Breviary, which have no authority for us.

(7) Finally, our tradition was separated from that of the Latin Churches in the sixteenth century, and we distinguish between customs which we have inherited from the Middle Ages, such as the use of vestments and incense, and customs which sprang up in

Southern Europe after the Reformation, which are not part of our tradition, however harmless they may be in themselves, such as the use of the Italian cotta, biretta, and zucchetto, or the feasts of the Sacred Heart and Our Lady of Victories. We ought to do nothing in our Church life which implies or suggests that we are pretending to be Romanists or that we recognize any authority or anything peculiarly Catholic in the Roman Court or in the Latin language and culture.

**152. What is the answer to Where was your Church before the Reformation?**

The traditional answer is, Where was your face before it was washed? A more polite way of putting it would be, Where was Virginia before George Washington? Where it is now. Virginia, Massachusetts, etc., before the American Revolution were subject to the British crown. Then they ceased to be so, but they were not new states. The provinces of Canterbury and York, Armagh and Dublin, were subject to the Pope before the Reformation. Then they ceased to be subject to him, but they were the same Churches that they had been before.

**153. Why does "Catholic" usually mean "Roman"?**

Because Romanists claim it for themselves and deny the title to all other Christians. But no Anglican should ever use "Catholic" in the sense of "Romanist" or allow anyone else to do so in his presence without protest. If the Roman Communion is Roman, it is not universal. It claims to be the whole Church, whereas the Anglican Communion claims to be only part of the Church.

**154. On what ground were Anglican (Episcopal) Ordinations declared invalid by the Pope?**

On the ground that the Church of England did not intend that its ministers should be "sacrificing priests" and that the words "for the office and work of a bishop" were not used in the Anglican consecration service before 1661.

These objections were fully answered by the Reply of Archbishops Frederick Temple and Maclagan, as well as by Dr. Gregory Dix and others. I cannot go into details here but two things ought to be said: (1) The Bull Apostolicae Curae of Leo XIII assumed that Rome was right and that so far as the Anglicans differed from it they were wrong. The only question was whether they were so far wrong that Rome could not recognize their ordinations. The Pope's answer was that they were, and therefore their ordinations could not be recognized. We do not admit that Rome was right. We say that Rome had altered the proportion of the various functions of the ministry: that while the priest had indeed to lead his people in sharing the self-offering of Christ in Heaven, that is not his only function; therefore we changed the rite, which as a self-governing Church we were entitled to do, to correct this proportion. It does not matter to us whether the Pope recognizes our ordinations or not; it makes no difference to anyone but his own subjects, for we do not recognize his authority. (2) The Pope was bound, on his own principles, to take such action as would lead the greatest number of persons to become Romanists; for he believed that salvation could be found only in obedience to himself. He was advised that, if he rejected Anglican ordinations, many Anglicans would become Romanists, but if he recognized their ordinations, they would stay where they were. He could be expected to act only according to the advice given to him, but it turned out to be entirely mistaken.

**155. Are there any discussions for reunion or intercommunion with Rome going on now?**

Not as far as I know. Reunion with Rome is impossible for this reason: The Roman Communion is held together by belief in the supremacy and infallibility of the Pope. If the Pope were to admit that he was wrong by giving up these doctrines he would shake the faith of millions and break up his Communion, for the people have been taught to base all their belief on the Pope's authority. But we could never, even for the sake of reunion, submit to these Romanist beliefs, for reasons which have been given above, nor surrender our religious and political freedom.

**156. How did the Church get divided into Anglican and Roman in Henry VIII's reign?**

**157. Was Henry VIII the founder of the Church of England?**

No. But to answer these questions fully would require a history of the English Reformation. Briefly, what happened was this: The great revolt against the religious, political, and economic system of medieval Europe had begun in Germany and was already finding adherents in England when Henry VIII, who had no sympathy with it, determined to get rid of his wife, Katharine of Aragon, because she had not borne him the male heir needed for the security of the kingdom and because he wished to marry Anne Boleyn, with whom he had become infatuated. The Pope would not grant a decree of nullity for Henry's marriage with Katharine, because he was afraid of the Emperor Charles V, who was Katharine's nephew. Henry therefore threw off obedience to the Pope, made himself master of the clergy, dissolved the monasteries, and confiscated their property. He had a translation of the Bible set up in every parish church, and this greatly promoted the Reformation because men found that much that they had been taught by the Church had no foundation in the Bible. During Henry's life no great change was made in doctrine, worship, or organization, but under his son, Edward VI (1547-1553), the first English Prayer Book was issued, and used everywhere, and other changes were made through the influence of the foreign Reformers. When Edward VI died, Mary, the daughter of Henry VIII and Katharine of Aragon, brought the Church and nation back to the obedience of Rome and tried to undo all that her father had done. On Mary's death in 1558 Elizabeth I, the daughter of Henry and Anne Boleyn, succeeded her. Elizabeth, under pressure from her people, among whom the Reformation had now made great progress, restored most of what had been done under Edward VI. In the meantime the Council of Trent (1545-1563) had tightened up the Roman system of faith and order, made tradition equal to Scripture as a source of dogma, and issued the Creed of Pope Pius IV, by which many medieval beliefs against which the Reformers had revolted were declared for the first time to be necessary dogmas. Elizabeth and her people had to choose between the Reformation and the new system of Trent; they had no hesitation in choosing the Reformation. But during the whole period the old faith and order continued: the succession of bishops was maintained, the vast majority of the clergy and laity accepted the Reformation settlement. Those who wished to destroy the old order, and set up a new sect on the model of Geneva, struggled to do so for a hundred years. They were finally defeated in 1660, when many of them seceded and formed the Presbyterian, Congregationalist, and Baptist sects.

It is absurd to call Henry VIII the founder of the Church of England. Even the final break with Rome did not take place till

1570, when Pope Pius V excommunicated Elizabeth I and all who adhered to her. This was inevitable, since they had refused to submit to the Council of Trent.

**158. Do the difficulties between us and Rome really matter?**

There is only one Church. It is of the utmost importance to be a full member of that Church, outside of which no one can live the full Christian and Catholic life. We believe that the Episcopal or Anglican Church is for us the true Church, that God has placed us in it, and that we have no right to leave it. No one can belong to the Roman Communion without accepting the papal claims and dogmas (see Question 151). If we believed them to be true, it would be our duty to become Romanists. Since we are convinced that they are not true, that they are contrary to Scripture, history, and reason, and that they refuse the freedom to which every Christian has a right, we could never say that they are true; even if the Anglican Communion did not exist, we could never be Romanists.

**159. Am I right in thinking myself as Catholic as the Romanists?**

Yes; in some respects more Catholic, because you are not required to submit to uncatholic dogmas. But if you wish to be regarded as Catholic you must be as faithful to the fundamental faith and practice of the Catholic religion as the Romanists are.

**160. What are the best talking points in defense of the Catholicity of Anglicanism and the validity of its priesthood against Roman propaganda?**

Never enter into controversy with Romanists if you can help it; it serves no useful purpose, and needless controversy is bad for the soul. We have no wish to convert to our religion Romanists who are content where they are; therefore we have nothing to gain by controversy. But if you are forced to enter into controversy, always take the offensive. Whether we are right or wrong, it is certain that Rome is wrong; our Lord never gave to St. Peter any such position as the Pope now claims, nor did the Apostles or anyone else for centuries recognize that He had, nor was St. Peter ever Bishop of Rome, nor are the popes his successors. The validity of Anglican ordinations is a side issue, about which it is futile to argue. If the Pope were what he claims to be, his word would be final and the question would be settled. We deny that he is what he claims to be or that he has any authority to judge in such a matter (especially as he is an interested party). No one else denies the validity of the Anglican priesthood. If the Pope's claims are false (as we can prove them to be), the question of Anglican ordinations is not worth discussing.

**161. Was there a break in the Anglican episcopal succession, and if so, when?**

No; the succession was carefully preserved. The Romanists say that Matthew Parker, the first Archbishop of Canterbury consecrated with the English rite, was not properly consecrated. We have a full contemporary record of this consecration. Matthew Parker was consecrated in Lambeth Palace Chapel on December 17, 1559, by four bishops, Barlow of Bath and Wells, Scory of Chichester, Coverdale of Exeter, and Hodgkins of Bedford. There is a second line of succession through Hugh Curwen, Archbishop of Dublin, 1555–1567; and a third through Marcantonio de Dominis, Archbishop of Split in Dalmatia, who joined the Church of England in 1616 and became Dean of Windsor. All present Anglican bishops have a succession through all these three.

*Chapter Thirteen*

# THE CHURCH AND THE SECTS

**162. Should we consider merger with another church when we have two different schools of thought in our own church?**

There are at least six schools of thought in the Anglican Churches, but they shade into one another with various cross-currents. There are no clear-cut divisions. Similar schools of thought, in one form or another, are found in all the great Christian Communions, but it is only among us that they show themselves in worship. This is a feature of the Anglican Communion with which all workers for reunion must reckon, but the differences may be modified by mutual understanding, as we see happening in England. We cannot amalgamate (or form a merger) with any other part of the Church; reunion must be based on agreement in necessary dogma, but even then we live in different countries, or at least serve different nations with different languages and traditions (as in the case of the Polish National Catholic Church—see Question 130). Amalgamation with any sect is impossible except on condition that it shall accept the whole faith and order of the Church and give up the notion that a Christian may believe and do what he pleases.

**163. Why cannot I do my bounden duty in the Methodist Church as well as I can in my own?**

You are a Churchman and not a Methodist, and your duty is to the society of which you are a member. But besides this, the Methodists are not a Church, but a society founded by John Wesley. He knew this or he would not have written in the last year of his life (I have seen the letter in his own handwriting, in the British Museum): "If the Methodists leave the Church, God will leave them." You have the privilege of being a full member of the true Catholic Church. Your duty is to join in the worship which it alone has Divine authority to offer. No doubt God accepts the worship of the Methodists, but He will not accept yours if you neglect your duty to His Church.

**164. When I have time I shall read the Bible right through. Then I shall really know which church is the right one and shall not have to take my priest's word for it.**

To read the Bible straight through is not an intelligent way to read it. The Bible consists of over sixty separate books, and you must give separate attention to each of them. You will need the help of priests and other scholars or you will not understand what you read (Acts 8:31). Even so, to read the Bible through will not teach you which is the true Church, for all Churches and sects accept the authority of the Bible; they disagree only about its interpretation. There are in practice only three beliefs among which you have to choose:

(1) the Church is visible, and the papal claims are true.
(2) the Church is visible, and the papal claims are false.
(3) the Church is invisible, and all sects are equal.

The first belief is Roman, the second Anglican (and Orthodox), the third is that of the sects. You would have to read not only the Bible but a great deal of Church history in order to choose between them, for each of them is believed by its adherents to be based on the Bible. If you have not time nor capacity to undertake the necessary study, you had much better stay in the denomination in which you were brought up, follow its teaching and practice faithfully, and leave controversy alone.

**165. Are not all churches much the same? What does it matter to which one I belong?**

There is only one Church, the Catholic Church, which was refounded by our Lord as the New Israel, and which derives its authority from Him. It matters very much that we should say only what we believe to be true. I am an Anglican priest, and I believe that the Anglican Churches are part of the Catholic Church, the part in which God has placed me; whereas I am entirely convinced that the papal claims are false and contrary to Scripture; if possible, I am even more entirely convinced that the sects' doctrine of the Church is false, unscriptural, and disastrous. People who take the trouble to find out which belief is true will tell you that all churches are not the same, and that it does matter which one you belong to.

**166. If we are made members of the Church by Baptism, what right have we to withhold the Lord's Supper from any baptized Christian in good standing? Did not our Lord say, "All of you drink of this"?**

Our Lord said so indeed, but only to the Apostles when no one else was there (St. Matthew 26:20, 37). Baptism alone does not make us full members of the Church; it requires to be completed by Confirmation. The Church is a society; the bishops are its officers, and the Holy Communion is the highest privilege of membership. No one may be admitted to that privilege who does not recognize the authority of the officers of the society. The clergy are stewards of the mysteries (I Cor. 4:1; I Peter 4:10). It is their duty to see that no one is admitted to the Lord's Table who is not entitled to be there. Only those may receive Communion who are confirmed (or ready and willing to be confirmed) and under the care of the bishop of the diocese or some other bishop who is in full communion with him (that is, each acknowledges the other). In our case that means Anglican and Old Catholic bishops.

**167. Why can't anyone receive Communion who loves God and his neighbor?**

We cannot know that anyone loves God and his neighbor. We should have to take his word for it. The Christian religion requires us to be members of the Church. We do not receive Communion just as ourselves, but as members of the Church which is Christ's Body. We cannot be full members unless we are baptized, confirmed, and subject to the bishops who are the successors of the Apostles. If we are to join in the breaking of bread and the prayers we must accept the Apostles' doctrine and fellowship (Acts 2:42).

168. Where does the Church stand on open and closed Communion? Why?

169. How do priests who not only permit but encourage open Communion justify this action?

170. Is it permissible to bring a baptized member of another religious body, such as a Methodist minister, to Communion?

171. Who speaks for the Episcopal Church in offering Communion to members of other Protestant faiths? What is the practice of other Anglican Churches?

172. How are we to interpret the Confirmation rubric charitably when communicants of other churches wish to come to our altars?

173. How can those of other faiths be allowed to communicate when they do not believe or have not been confirmed?

174. Why do some priests invite everyone to receive Communion?

175. Why do some churches [i.e., parishes] have open Communion and others restrict Communion to confirmed members?

176. Does the Church have "closed" Communion?

177. Does the Episcopal Church invite members of other Christian Churches to Communion?

178. How can the Confirmation rubric be applied to non-Anglicans? Is it not unchristian to exclude from Communion anyone who wants it?

179. Why do we not welcome all the baptized to Communion, as children of God?

These twelve questions all relate to the same problem and will therefore be answered together.

The rule of the Church is quite clear: "There shall none be admitted to the Holy Communion, until such time as he be confirmed or ready and desirous to be confirmed" ("The Order of Confirmation," last rubric). This rule is not merely Anglican. The whole Catholic Church has always required four conditions for communicants: (1) Baptism; (2) Confirmation, or at least willingness to be confirmed; (3) submission to the bishops; (4) they must not have been excommunicated. The reason for this is that the Church is a society and the highest privilege of its members is to receive the Holy Communion. The unbaptized are not members at all and are incapable of receiving the Body and Blood of Christ. Those who are not confirmed are not full members. Confirmation is, or should be, preceded by careful instruction; we cannot be responsible for admitting to the most solemn mysteries of our religion those whom the Church has not tested. The bishops are the chief officers of the Church; those who do not accept their authority have no right to privileges which the bishops alone have authority to bestow. Communion is the chief of these. No one may administer it unless he has been ordained by a bishop, and also been licensed or given permission to administer it in that diocese.

The notion that charity requires us to give Communion to anyone who asks for it shows failure to understand what charity is. The Good Samaritan was given by our Lord as an example of charity, of the man who loved his neighbor as himself, even though he belonged to a different religion (St. Luke 10:30–37). He risked his life to help him, he gave personal service and money, but one thing he did not do: he did not invite him to take part in the sacrifices on Mount Gerizim. That would have been contrary to the religion of them both. We can perform no more charitable action toward our separated brethren than to bring them to accept with us the whole faith and full membership of the Church (which does not mean that we should proselytize them against their will). But if, mistaking sentimentalism for charity, we invite them, or even permit them, to receive Communion without accepting the faith or submitting to the rules of the Church we shall only be encouraging their errors and their separation from the Church.

The false belief which appears to lie behind the desire, or craze, for "open Communion" appears to be that the Covenant of God is made not with us as members of the chosen people (as the

Bible clearly teaches) but with us as individuals. It is mistakenly supposed that everyone who has accepted Christ's offer of salvation is a member of the Church, that he does not have to be baptized or belong to any particular society. The Church is believed to be manifested in a multitude of sects, none of which has any superiority over the others. Some of them do not administer baptism, many of them think it quite unimportant, most of them administer it carelessly. The Communion service appears to be regarded by many of them as only a symbol of love, a memorial of our Lord's death and nothing more. Therefore to refuse to welcome anyone to share in it is regarded as a refusal of love: like a refusal to shake hands with someone or to dine with him.

The Catholic sacrament of Holy Communion is all this, but it is much more. It is the means by which those who have been made members of Christ's Body by Baptism, and have received the Holy Spirit in Confirmation, are permitted to share in the sacrifice of Himself which our Saviour continually offers in Heaven. No one is admitted to this tremendous mystery unless he believes the doctrine and obeys the rules which our Saviour gave. Those who are confirmed openly declare their belief, and the Church does its best to assure that all communicants have repentance and faith, as well as charity.

But the Church has no control over the sects. They have their own rules, but some of them appear to exercise no discipline over their members at all. Question 171 speaks of "other Protestant faiths." There is only one faith, faith in Christ; those who have it are required to accept His teaching and to obey His commands: these include the Creed and Commandments in which candidates for Confirmation are instructed and which they promise to obey; and if they break their promise in a notorious manner they can be, in theory, excommunicated. The Episcopal Church, as has already been shown, is "Protestant" only in the sense of non-Roman. It has nothing in common with the sects, except as far as they share, as most of them do, the fundamental beliefs common to all Christians (including the Roman Communion). We welcome all baptized Christians to be present at our services, including the Holy Communion, but if they wish to receive Communion they must be confirmed and be in fellowship with the bishops.

I am not an American citizen; if I were staying in the United

States during a presidential election, no one would invite me, nor should I wish, to vote. If I wished to vote I should have to apply to be naturalized. It is the same with the Church. You must be a full member if you are to have the rights of membership.

In all special and doubtful cases the bishop of the diocese alone can decide who may receive Communion, subject to any conditions laid down by the synods. In England we have foreign, chiefly Lutheran, students, whose beliefs do not differ greatly from ours, and who are far from their own Church. They cannot join the Church of England (though some of them would like to) because there is no Anglican (or Old Catholic) Church in their own country within reach. In such cases the bishop may give them permission to receive Communion, but no priest has authority to do so. In England, Scotland, and Ireland the Confirmation rubric is observed fairly strictly. There are some sentimentalists and some rebels among the clergy. But most people see clearly that it would be difficult to get young people to attend a long series of Confirmation classes, in order to become full members of the Church, if they saw members of the sects admitted to the privilege of full Church membership without any such requirement. There was in the ancient Church a practice called the love feast, or *agapē*, which survives in the "antidoron" ("instead of the Gift") in the Orthodox Churches. A piece of unconsecrated bread is given to all who are present at the Liturgy, whether Orthodox or not (I have often received it). Those who wish for a symbol of Christian love, which would not necessarily imply agreement in doctrine or Church order, might well consider reviving the love feast, which has been successfuly tried in England by Anglicans and Methodists. But care must be taken that it shall not resemble, or be mistaken for, or be confused with, the Holy Communion.

So far I have referred only to the sects. There is no reason why we should not admit to Communion members of other parts of the Church, except for the rules to which they are subject. The Lambeth Conference has authorized Communion to be given to members of the Eastern Churches, with the permission of their own bishops. This permission has sometimes been given, when their is no Orthodox priest within reach. But the Roman Communion would not give such permission in any case, and forbids its members even to be present at our services. We ought not to encourage anyone to disobey his own Church, which, on its own principles, is quite right to give such directions.

**180. Are those outside the historic Church members of the Church?**

All baptized persons, if rightly baptized with water in the Name of the Trinity, are members of the Church, and cannot be baptized again. But they are not full members of the Church until they have been confirmed, and they are not full members of the Church if they belong to any sect which does not recognize the authority of the bishops of the Church.

*Chapter Fourteen*

# THE APOSTOLIC SUCCESSION

**181. What do you mean by the Apostolic Succession?**

**182. Why is the Apostolic Succession (admitting it to be historical) important?**

**183. What is the importance, historical and theological, of the Apostolic Succession?**

The Church on earth is a society. It must therefore have a government and officers who are everywhere recognized. (Those who deny that it is a society see no reason why it should have a universally recognized government.) In modern democracies the government derives its authority from the people, but there is no trace of such a democracy in the New Testament. The Church is not, and never has been, democratic; it is theocratic.

Our Lord appointed His twelve Apostles, whom He had carefully trained for the purpose, to be both witnesses to His resurrection and rulers of His Church (St. Matthew 19:28; St. Luke 22:30). As witnesses they could have no successors; as rulers they had to have successors. In the Acts, and throughout the New Testament, the Apostles are shown as ruling the Church, consulting the other members as constitutional rulers always do. There is no authority in the Church aside from theirs, and they are guided by the Holy Spirit. St. Clement of Rome, the first Christian writer after the New Testament (about A.D. 96), says: "The apostles appointed the first fruits of their labors when they had proved them by the Spirit, as overseers and ministers of those who should believe: and afterwards issued a direction that when these fell asleep, other approved men should succeed to their ministry." Less than twenty years later St. Ignatius knew of no local Church which had not bishops, priests, and deacons, and these three orders have continued ever since in all parts of the Church.

The Apostolic Succession is important because it is the means, all down the centuries and in all parts of the world, by which the authority given by our Lord to the Apostles has come down to the modern Church. This authority has two functions: to govern the Church and to administer sacraments. All spiritual authority in the Church is derived from the bishops, because they are the successors of the Apostles; there is no other source of authority in the Church. Every priest receives at his ordination the power to celebrate the Holy Communion, to absolve sinners, and to bless in the name of the Church, and the authority to use these powers in a fixed area. The former is given by the bishop's sacramental authority; the latter by his governing authority. The governing authority can sometimes be delegated; the sacramental authority cannot.

### 184. What do Episcopalians believe about the Apostolic Succession and the Protestant ministry?

I assume that "Protestant ministry" here means the ministry of the sects, not that of the "Protestant Episcopal Church." The ministry of the sects is a different kind of ministry from the three orders of bishops, priests, and deacons. The duty of the bishop is to govern the Church and to administer the sacraments; the duty of the priests and deacons is to assist him, with authority derived from him. The function of preaching is not confined to the clergy; laymen are sometimes licensed to preach and priests and deacons (though usually licensed to preach) do not necessarily preach as part of their duty. But the Reformed ministry is a ministry of preachers: its authority, in the Calvinist tradition, is derived from the people, who elect the minister whom they believe to have been called directly by God; in the Methodist tradition, from Conference, which was originally founded by John Wesley and derives its authority from him. Now, the sacramental ministry, as distinct from the preaching ministry, is entirely dependent upon authority. The Communion or the Absolution, which is administered by a man who is not authorized and is known not to be authorized, is of no value at all. On the other hand, the preacher who preaches without authority may still edify his hearers. Authority is absolutely necessary to the priest; it is important, but not absolutely necessary, to the preacher. The priest must have been ordained by a bishop who has received authority through succession from the Apostles, for otherwise no one will recognize him as a priest. The preacher in the Church ought to have a license from the bishop, but he does not need to be ordained. Since the sects do not believe that the Church is a single universal visible society, they do not believe it needs a universally recognized ministry; and they deny that the minister is any more a priest than the layman. They feel no need for, and so do not believe in, the Apostolic Succession.

The ministry of the sects, then—Presbyterian, Congregationalist, Baptist, and Methodist—is not in our eyes invalid or defective; it is a different kind of ministry from the ministry of bishops, priests, and deacons; it has different functions and a different kind of authority; and it is irregular, because its authority is not apostolic. The reason why many people do not recognize this is that they have been taught that the Anglican Churches are "Protestant" and that their ministry is the same as that of the sects; they do not realize that the Anglican ministry of bishops, priests, and deacons is the same ministry, with the same origin, authority, and functions, as the ministry of the Roman and Eastern Communions, and therefore different from the ministry of the sects. Two facts show quite clearly that this is true: The preface of our Ordinal (American Prayer Book) says: "It is evident unto all men, diligently reading Holy Scripture and ancient Authors, that from the Apostles' time there have been these Orders of Ministers in Christ's Church—Bishops, Priests, and Deacons. . . . And therefore . . . that these Orders may be continued . . . no man shall be accounted or taken to be a lawful Bishop, Priest, or Deacon, in this Church, or suffered to execute any of the said Functions, except he be called, tried, examined, and admitted thereunto, according to the Form hereafter following, or hath had Episcopal Consecration or Ordination." The other fact is that ministers of the sects have to be ordained by a bishop if they are to be Anglican deacons or priests, whereas Romanist deacons or priests who come to us (and many more do than is commonly realized) are accepted by us as they are. If ministers and members of the sects (and many full members of the Church who ought to know better) understood this, they would not expect us to give them privileges which they would never expect (and certainly would not receive) from the Roman or Eastern Communions.

**185. Discuss the development of the orders of the ministry and the Apostolic Succession.**

**186. Which came first, bishops or priests?**

The Apostles came first: all forms of the regular ministry, which did not include prophets, were derived from the Apostles. In Acts 6:6 we find the Apostles laying hands on the seven (traditionally known as deacons, though they are not called so). In Acts 14:23 St. Paul and St. Barnabas appoint "elders" (priests) in each city, as the regular resident ministry. In Acts 13:5 St. Mark ("John") is "minister" (deacon) to the two Apostles. In Acts 20:17 St. Paul addresses the elders of Ephesus, and in verse 28 he calls them "overseers" (bishops). These three words, "episkepos" (overseer), "presbyteros" (elder), and "diakenos" (minister), had not yet acquired their later technical sense of bishops, priests, and deacons. This fact has misled many, from St. Jerome in the fourth century onward, into thinking that in the New Testament bishops and priests are the same officers. The evidence shows that in the apostolic age the Apostles were the first order of the ministry (I Cor. 12:28); they, like pioneer missionary bishops now, had no fixed sees, but went about founding Christian communities in different places. In each city the community or local church was governed by a group of "elders," also called "overseers," assisted by "deacons." So St. Paul addresses the overseers (bishops) and deacons in Phil. 1:1, and in I Tim. 3:1 and Titus 1:7 the "bishop" evidently belongs to the second order, for Timothy and Titus are in control, like Apostles. These are just the sort of letters that might be sent from the Archbishop of Canterbury or the Presiding Bishop to a young missionary bishop. In St. Ignatius' letters, at most fifty years later, the Apostles are all dead, the pioneer period is over, there is one bishop with his priests and deacons in each city. St. Ignatius knows of no other form of church government; "without these," he says, "there is not even the name of a Church" (Letter to the Trallians). (I use the word "priest," which is derived from presbyter, because the word presbyter is misleading, as it is used by Calvinists in a different sense.) There is no reason to suppose that St. Ignatius' "presbyters" preached or governed; and they celebrated only in the bishop's absence.

We do not know precisely how authority was transferred from the Apostles to the bishops; there is no evidence except what St. Clement tells us (see Question 153), but there is no doubt that it was transferred without any controversy. In the New Testament the Apostles are the only source of authority (II Cor. 11:28, etc.): fifty years later, the bishops. There is no other source from which the authority of the bishops can have come; and this agrees with the Jewish precedent, for the rabbis claimed succession from Moses by laying on of hands. From the time of St. Ignatius bishops, priests, and deacons have continued to the present day. In the sixteenth century the Reformers, misinterpreting the New Testament, and knowing nothing of the letters of St. Clement and St. Ignatius, failed to recognize the bishops of their time (who were, in Germany and elsewhere, great feudal princes) as the successors of the Apostles; and they set up a new ministry different from the historic one.

**187. Is there any real doubt that the Apostles transferred their authority to others, or that our Lord intended this?**

Our Lord seems to have left the organization of the Church to the Apostles, guided by the Holy Spirit. The method of succession was arranged by them. When you see a train entering a tunnel at one end and a train like it coming out at the other end a few minutes later, you do not doubt that it is the same train. In the New Testament the Apostles governed. In St. Ignatius, and ever afterward, the bishops governed. It has always been held that the authority of the bishops comes from the Apostles. There is no reason for doubting it.

**188. How do Lutheranism and Calvinism differ from the Churches with Apostolic Succession?**

Lutherans consider Justification by Faith alone as the most important of all dogmas. They are inclined to think that questions of church organization are of no great importance. However, in Sweden and Finland the Apostolic Succession was maintained, and more importance is now attached to it than formerly. In Denmark, Norway, and Iceland the first Lutheran bishops were consecrated by John Bugenhagen, who was only a priest, but since then the succession has been carefuly preserved. Most other Lutherans do not maintain or claim a succession.

Calvinists believe that the Church is the invisible company of the elect, and they reject the principle of institutional succession. The only kind of succession which they recognize is continuity of belief, which indeed is necessary but not enough. Some Scots claim a "presbyteral succession," but this claim does not seem to have arisen until long after the Reformation (about 1650), in opposition to Anglican claims, and to have no historical basis because the Presbyterian meaning of "presbyter" is not and has never been intended to be what the Church means, and because the Scots abolished, for a time, the laying on of hands. I cannot here deal with the other beliefs of Lutherans and Calvinists. They differ sharply from one another, and both are divided among themselves.

**189. What is the difference between the professional ministry and the priesthood of all believers?**

The word "priest" represents two Greek words, "presbyteros" and "hiereus." In the Catholic Church, and therefore in the Anglican provinces of it, they both refer to the same office. Hitherto I have used the word "priest" in the first sense, as a member of the second order of the ministry. But a bishop or a priest is also "hiereus," a man who offers sacrifices (though the word is not applied to the Christian ministry in the New Testament, because its first readers, accustomed to Jewish and heathen sacrifice of animals, would have been misled). The only sacrifice in the Christian religion is the offering of Jesus Christ (Heb. 3:1, 4:14, 5:5, etc.).

> Offered was He for greatest and for least,
> Himself the Victim, and Himself the Priest.
> (Ancient Irish Hymn, 7th century)

He was slain on the Cross, presented His life to the Father at the Ascension, and, since everything in Heaven is eternal, continues to do so forever, as it is written of Him: "Thou art a priest for ever after the order of Melchisedec" (Heb. 5:6).

The Christian Church is the Body of which He is the head, and therefore its members are permitted to take part in the offering of Himself, and to offer with it themselves and all they are and

have. The only passage which refers to the corporate priesthood
of the Church is I Peter 2:9 (with the highly symbolical texts
of Rev. 1:6 and 5:10) and it is a quotation from Exodus 19:6.
The priesthood of the New Israel, as of the Old Israel, is a corporate priesthood. The ordinary Israelite was not, as an individual,
a priest, as the stories of Korah (Num. 16) and Uzziah (II Chron.
26:18) show; and the Christian layman, by himself, is not a priest,
any more than he is a king: he is a member of a society which
shares the royal and priestly functions of Jesus Christ its Head.

This priestly function is chiefly exercised in the Holy Eucharist.
The Christian priest (hiereus) is the organ by which the Church
joins in the one sacrifice of our Saviour in Heaven. He alone is
authorized to lead the local church in the offering of this sacrifice; it cannot be offered without him, as a man without eyes cannot see or without ears cannot hear. But the priest cannot offer
the sacrifice by himself; no priest may celebrate the Eucharist by
himself, without a congregation; nor may he do so (except in
emergency) without the authority, direct or indirect, of the
bishop, who represents the whole "college" or body of bishops
throughout the world, the modern representatives of the Apostles. It would be more correct to speak of the "ministerial" rather
than the "professional" priest. The clergy have a right to be paid
for their services (I Cor. 9:1–11), but in the ancient Church, and
in some countries today, especially under Communist governments, priests have another profession, such as physician or
engineer, and are paid for that and not for their work as priests.
It is, however, generally considered that the priest's work should
normally occupy all his time, and therefore the priesthood is
thought of as a profession.

## Chapter Fifteen

# THE SACRAMENTS IN GENERAL

**190. Are the sacraments absolutely necessary or just a better
means to salvation?**

They are absolutely necessary to membership in the Church,

and to present salvation (Question 81). "Except a man be born of water and of the Spirit, he cannot enter the kingdom of God" (St. John 3:5). "As many of us as were baptized into Jesus Christ were baptized into his death" (Rom. 6:3). "Except ye eat the flesh of the Son of man, and drink his blood, ye have no life in you. Whoso eateth my flesh, and drinketh my blood, hath eternal life" (St. John 6:53, 54).

**191. What is meant by "generally necessary to salvation"?**

"Generally" means for all persons, as "General Thanksgiving" means giving thanks for all things. Everybody need not be married or ordained, but everybody must be baptized and a communicant, if he is to take part in the life of the Church. Salvation here means present salvation (see Question 81).

**192. Does the Episcopal Church teach that there are two sacraments or seven?**

There are two sacraments, Baptism and Holy Communion, which were instituted by Christ Himself; He commanded the use of water in one, bread and wine in the other. These sacraments are universally necessary to salvation (see Questions 190, 191). The Church Catechism and Article 25 state the Church's teaching. There are also five other rites which are commonly called sacraments: Confirmation, Penance, Holy Orders, Matrimony, and Unction of the Sick. They have no visible sign commanded by Christ, nor are they (except Confirmation, without which Baptism is not complete) necessary for everybody, but they certainly convey grace. The word "sacrament" does not occur in the New Testament. The sacraments have been usually reckoned as seven since the twelfth century, but to believe that there are exactly seven sacraments is not necessary to salvation; it is a widespread and highly probable opinion.

**193. Why is there such a difference in the sacraments of our Church? How are they comparable to those of other churches?**

This question is not clear. The sacraments of the Church are the same everywhere. They are differently administered, but the necessary conditions are: Form (the words said), Matter (the substance used), Minister (one authorized to administer them), Subject (one capable of receiving the sacrament, e.g., a baptized person), and Intention. Most of the sects recognize two sacraments only, and they differ widely in their doctrine, from the Church and from one another. Many of them either do not use sacraments at all or do not think them necessary to membership. (The Lutherans recognize three sacraments, Baptism, the Sacrament of the Altar, and Penance. Their teaching about these differs little from that of the Church.)


*Chapter Sixteen*

## BAPTISM AND CONFIRMATION

**194. What happens to those who do not believe in the doctrine of Baptism as taught in St. John 3:5?**

We do not know. They are under the justice and mercy of God.

**195. Can one who has not been baptized be a Christian?**

He cannot be a member of the Christian Church. But some people who have not been baptized, such as members of the Society of Friends, believe in our Lord Jesus Christ as God and Man, and serve Him so well that we cannot refuse to group them with Christians.

**196. When should baptisms be scheduled, and why?**

Perhaps this means, when should baptisms be entered or recorded in the Church register? The Baptism should be registered immediately; if it is a private Baptism (which is allowed only in cases of emergency) as soon as possible afterward. The registration of baptisms is most important. Nobody ought to be confirmed or ordained without trustworthy evidence of Baptism. If it is not forthcoming, the candidate must be baptized conditionally. The Confirmation or Ordination of an unbaptized person is null and void and must be repeated after Baptism. No unbaptized person may be married or buried with the service of the Church.

Perhaps this question means, When should baptisms be administered? The Prayer Book directs that baptisms shall be administered on Sundays or other Holy Days and in connection with the public services of the Church. The reason for this is that Baptism, by its very nature as the means of admission into the

membership of the Church, is the concern of all members of the
Church, who should be present to welcome and to pray for the
new member, to witness the vows of the candidate or, if an
infant, the vows of the Godparents.

**197. I have already been baptized. Why should I be con-
firmed?**

**198. Is a baptized person committed to confirmation? If so,
why?**

Confirmation is the second part of Baptism, which is not complete without it (Acts 19:1-8). Confirmation is the means by
which we receive the gifts of the Holy Spirit, wisdom, understanding, counsel, knowledge, spiritual strength, godliness, and
holy fear (Isa. 11:2). It makes all the difference to the life of the
Christian, as I know by my own experience. Confirmation makes
us full members of the Church, entitled to receive the Holy
Communion, without which we have no life in us (St. John 6:53).
Confirmation classes are in most cases the only opportunity for
being instructed in the whole Christian system of faith and morals.
If you have been baptized, you have promised, personally or by
your sponsors, to be Christ's faithful soldier and servant. He bids
you, through His Church, to be confirmed; you are not keeping
your promise if you refuse.

**199. What is the difference between the gift of the Spirit at
Baptism and at Confirmation?**

The gift of the Spirit at Baptism is the new birth (St. John 3:5).
His gift at Confirmation is sevenfold (Isa. 11:2; see Question 198).
The precise relation between them is much disputed, but as both
are necessary, the dispute is not important. You cannot be confirmed without having been baptized. If you have been confirmed,
and there is any doubt whether you have been baptized, you
must be baptized conditionally, and confirmed again (conditionally).

**200. Explain in detail Baptism and Confirmation, and Church
laws about them.**

Baptism conveys the New Birth, forgiveness of sins, both
original and actual, and membership in the Church. If, being an
adult, you had been baptized without repentance or faith, which
are the conditions required for Baptism, you would still have
become a member of the Church (otherwise we should not know

who is and who is not a member), but you would not have had forgiveness of sins; and the New Birth would only have made your responsibility and your condemnation greater. For sin is much more serious in the baptized than in the unbaptized. Baptism makes us children of God by adoption, and brings us within His Covenant.

Baptism is administered by pouring (not sprinkling) water on the head of the candidate or dipping him beneath the water (which should be done three times, but this is not absolutely necessary), and saying, "I baptize thee In the Name of the Father, and of the Son, and of the Holy Ghost. Amen." That is all that is necessary. It should be performed by a priest, or in his absence by a deacon, but in case of necessity it may be performed by anyone, male or female. No one can be baptized again: to rebaptize anyone already baptized is both profane and impertinent, unless there is some doubt about the first Baptism, in which case it should be performed with the words: "If thou art not already baptized, I baptize thee . . ." Any living human being may be baptized unless he has been baptized before (see also Question 196).

Confirmation is the bestowal of the sevenfold gift of the Holy Spirit by the laying on of hands (or by anointing with chrism, a consecrated oil), but in the Anglican Churches the laying on of hands is sufficient, accompanied by prayer for the gifts. The scriptural authority is Acts 8:17, 19:1–6; Heb. 6:2. In Anglican Churches only bishops are authorized to administer Confirmation. Those who are confirmed are required first to renew their baptismal promises. Confirmation, which is not a peculiarly Anglican rite, but is regarded as a sacrament in every part of the Church, admits us to full membership in the Church. No one may receive the Holy Communion until he has been confirmed, or is ready and willing to be confirmed. In the ancient Church, as in the Eastern Churches still, infants were confirmed immediately after Baptism. The Anglican rule is that Confirmation is not to be administered until "years of discretion," that is, when the child knows right from wrong, traditionally at seven years of age (the age at which, for instance, John Wesley was confirmed). In practice it is usually administered at about twelve. No one, of course, can be too old to be confirmed.

**201. Do we join the Church at Confirmation?**

No. "Joining the Church" is a phrase used by the sects. We do not join the Church; God admits us into it at Baptism. Every baptized infant is a member of the Church because he is baptized, and for no other reason.

**202. Discuss the bearing of infant Baptism on its relation to Church membership and Confirmation.**

Baptism, if rightly performed, makes us members of the Church and cannot be repeated. It has the same effect, no matter who administered the Baptism, but it ought, if possible, to be administered by a priest or deacon.

Confirmation makes us full members, and it is often used to bring those who have been baptized in some other body into the full membership of the Church. They should be received into the Church first, as is done after a private Baptism, so that they may have godparents. (Those who have been confirmed in the Roman Communion must be received as confirmed persons.)

**203. Why infant Baptism? Would it not be more important later?**

**204. Since God's service must be freely chosen, is not Baptism of infants an infringement of free will? Does not God wish us to be aware of alternatives?**

Freedom of will is not the right to do what we like, but the power to do what we ought. From our birth our free will is perverted, so that we always find it easier to do wrong than to do right. Baptism is given at the earliest possible age (see Question 72) so that we may have every opportunity of resisting by God's grace this tendency to sin. We do not infringe the free will of children by offering them food, clothes, education, and other necessities; and Baptism is necessary for the spiritual life, like food for the life of the body. God's Will for us is life; Baptism is the beginning of the way to it. We remain free to reject God's offer of life, as we are continually tempted to do, but at least we are given the grace of Baptism, and the instruction which should follow it, to help us to resist temptation. The Church baptizes infants only on condition that they shall be instructed in the Christian faith and brought forward for Confirmation; if this condition is not likely to be fulfilled, Baptism should be postponed.

Perhaps the inquirer imagines that Baptism is one of several possible alternatives. There are in fact only two alternatives: God's service and the devil's: Baptism is the normal way of entering God's service.

**205. Does not infant Baptism ignore the human part in God's Covenant with man?**

God did not offer Abraham the choice between accepting and refusing His Covenant; He said, "Thou shalt keep my Covenant" (Gen. 17:10). The Covenant between God and man is not a bargain between equals, and it is not made with you or me, but with the Church. It is an offer made by God to us which He bids us accept. We can refuse, and if we do, so much the worse for us. The offer is made to infants, that they may have every opportunity of accepting it, and be admitted to the Church. Freedom is not the right to do what you like, but the power to do what you ought. If you were a father, and someone offered your infant son a large sum of money, to be paid at once, on condition, let us say, that he was not convicted of a felony, would you refuse it on the ground that when he grew up he might wish to be a burglar?

**206. Why infant Baptism? It is so difficult to explain to outsiders.**

According to some sects, Baptism is not a means of grace, still less the necessary means of the New Birth. It is a public assertion that the candidate has been converted, that is, has accepted Christ's offer of salvation. This is what "the Baptism of John" was (St. Mark 1:5; St. John 1:33). It was not Christian Baptism (Acts 19:4,5), and those who received it had to be baptized again if they were to be Christians.

If you think that Baptism is only a public proof of conversion, you will not believe in baptizing infants too young to be converted. But if you believe that Baptism is God's gift of the New Birth, and that as we are not asked whether we wish to be born, so we need not be asked whether we wish to be baptized, you must accept the universal belief of the Church that children should be baptized as early as possible. St. Paul says, "Children, obey your parents in the Lord" (Eph. 6:1). He would not have bidden them obey their parents if they had not been young: he would not have said "in the Lord" if they had not been baptized, for they would not have been members of Christ's Body.

**207. Why do we have lay Baptism in case of emergency?**

The Church has always desired that no one who wished to be baptized should die unbaptized. Therefore, if anyone is in danger of death and there is no ordained man within reach, as may easily happen, any man or woman is allowed to baptize. Every member of the Church ought to know how to baptize and be ready to do so in case of emergency: such as a sick child or a soldier on the battlefield.

**208. Why does not the Episcopal Church baptize by immersion, as that is scriptural?**

Immersion is allowed by our rubrics, if anyone wishes to be baptized or to have his children baptized in that way. It is often practiced in hot countries. But the Church in the West, from early times, laid down that pouring (not sprinkling) water on the head was sufficient. The Church has authority to interpret Scripture; our doctrine must be scriptural, not necessarily our ceremonial details. For instance, the Apostles lay on couches at the Lord's Supper, but that is no reason why we should. Baptism by immersion was easier when people wore only a single garment. This principle that Scripture does not bind the Church in such details was proved by Richard Hooker, perhaps the greatest of Anglican theologians.

**209. "One baptism for the remission of sins." Is the emphasis on "one" or on "remission"?**

I should say on both.

**210. Is it irregular for a priest to baptize his own children?**

Certainly not. What a strange idea! It may be his duty as well as his privilege. I was baptized by my grandfather; my brother, by my father.

**211. Why do newly confirmed members attend church only on special occasions?**

Judging by English experience, I should say that either they have not been sufficiently instructed, or their parents do not encourage them to come, or the clergy do not take enough trouble to keep them together and give them something really attractive to do for our Lord, whereas the world, the flesh, and the devil always give them plenty to do.

**212. Is instruction in preparation for Confirmation often too haphazard?**

Only too likely. I used to require four months' regular attendance both at church and at classes. I think now that it was not nearly enough. My experience is that the decisive factor is nearly always the parents' influence.

**213. At what age should one be confirmed?**

It depends on the person and the conditions. Some people are as mature at eleven as others are at sixteen. The worst possible age is usually fourteen to seventeen for physical reasons. If the home is entirely satisfactory, it matters little how young the candidate is. If the parents are uninterested or hostile, it may be better to wait until the candidate is able to stand on his own feet. There is no general rule; and I know nothing of conditions in America.

**214. Some people think it uncharitable, or High Church, to require Confirmation before Communion. Please explain.**

It is useless to argue with people's prejudices. Probably what they mean by "High Church" is something to which they are not accustomed and which therefore they dislike; by "uncharitable," something that imposes discipline upon those who regard religion as entirely a matter of personal choice, and not as membership in a society. They cannot mean that it is Romanist, for the modern Roman practice often is to put one's First Communion some years before one's Confirmation. This is quite contrary to the practice of the Church in ancient and medieval times, and is partly due to a defective doctrine of Confirmation dating from the ninth century, and widely prevalent in the Roman Communion.

If Confirmation is not to be before Communion, when is it to be? It appears that it is to Confirmation, as such, that they object. The answer is that it is clearly required by the Bible and by the Prayer Book. The references in the Bible are Acts 8:17, 19:1–6; Heb. 6:2. The rubric in the Prayer Book is quite explicit. The suggestion that to insist on Confirmation is "uncharitable" is to fail to understand what is meant by "charitable" and what is meant by membership. Anyone may receive Holy Communion if he fulfills the conditions of membership: he must be baptized, be confirmed, and obey the bishops (see Questions 168–79).

**215. Why is Confirmation required? Why is it done by a bishop?**

For the answer to the first question see Questions 168–79, and 214. In the Anglican Churches only the bishops are authorized to give Confirmation. This is the apostolic practice. Philip, who was only one of the Seven, could not do it; it required St. Peter and St. John as Apostles. By Confirmation every member of the Church is once in his life brought into direct personal contact with the bishop, the successor of the Apostles and the chief authority in the local Church.

**216. What should the newly confirmed do as soon as possible?**

Begin the lifelong habit of regular Communion, at least once a month, and at Easter, Christmas, and Whitsuntide.

**217. Why does Confirmation take place at the chancel steps?**

If there is a chancel, it is the most suitable place, where the whole congregation can see and hear it. Besides, the chancel gate, on the way to the altar, symbolizes confirmation as the way to Communion.

**218. What significance has the rubric requiring Confirmation before Communion in our day of widespread denominationalism?**

It is of the very greatest importance, because it safeguards the membership of the Church, and it is our only means of doing so. To have been baptized as a baby may mean very little, but to have been confirmed means, or should mean, that one has been taught the doctrine of the Church and has voluntarily promised to believe and practice it. The rule also prevents members of the sects, many of which exercise no discipline at all over their members, from claiming privileges to which they have no right.

*Chapter Seventeen*

# THE HOLY COMMUNION

**219. Is it correct to say that the Holy Spirit is with us always, but God the Son is found not only, but especially, in the consecrated elements, at the Holy Communion?**

Yes, but you must not draw the distinction too sharply. Our Saviour said, "Lo, I am with you alway, even to the end of the world" (St. Matthew 28:20), and "Where two or three are gathered together in my name, there am I in the midst of them" (St. Matthew 18:20). God the Holy Spirit is the Agent of Holy Communion (see St. John 16:14). We must not claim to understand fully the mystery of the Trinity or ignore the fact that God is One.

**220. Does the Church believe that the bread and wine in the Holy Eucharist become the flesh and blood of Christ, or just that Christ is present?**

They become the Body and Blood of Christ, but not in a local or material sense. "When the Sacrament is moved, the Body of Christ does not move" (John Henry Newman). It is a mystery which we cannot expect to understand. The bread and wine continue to have all the properties of bread and wine; but they are also much greater than bread and wine, as we know by experience.

**221. Is Christ really present in the consecrated elements?**

**222. What is meant by the Real Presence?**

Christ is really present in the consecrated elements, but the words "real" and "presence" may mean several different things. He is present to feed us with His life and to enable us to share in His offering of that life to the Father. In my opinion it is wiser to think in terms of power than of presence. The bread and wine are changed by the Holy Spirit: they have Divine power which before consecration they did not have.

**223. In professing to believe in the Real Presence of Christ in the Eucharist, do we mean the Son as opposed to the Holy Spirit?**

Yes; for the Holy Spirit has not taken to Himself a body or blood (but see Question 219).

**224. Why should I believe in the Real Presence in the Holy Communion?**

Because our Lord taught us to believe it. He said, "Take, eat: this is my body, which is broken for you: this do in remembrance of me" (I Cor. 11:24; see also St. Mark 14:22; St. Luke 22:19; St. John 6:51–54). Every part of the Church in every age has believed it. Even Luther held it strongly, and Charles Wesley ended one of his eucharistic hymns with these words:

> We need not now go up to heaven
> To bring the long-sought Saviour down.

Thou art to all who seek Thee given:
  Thou dost e'en here Thy banquet crown.
To every faithful soul appear,
And show Thy real presence here.

The rubric in the English Prayer Book says: "If any of the bread and wine remain unconsecrated, the Curate shall have it to his own use; but if any remain of that which was consecrated, it shall not be carried out of the church, but the priest . . . shall immediately after the blessing, reverently eat and drink the same" (part of this is omitted in the American Prayer Book). This distinction between the consecrated and the unconsecrated elements shows that Anglican teaching agrees with that of the rest of the Church.

**225. Is the Real Presence the same as Transubstantiation?**

**226. Do we believe in Transubstantiation?**

Transubstantiation is a theory devised in the twelfth century to explain the Real Presence in terms of the philosophy then universally current. It was made compulsory for Romanists by the Lateran Council of 1215 and the Council of Trent (1563). We are not bound by these Councils. Our Article 28 condemns Transubstantiation, but whether the official doctrine or a popular corruption of it is uncertain. Transubstantiation cannot be proved from Scripture, and there are serious technical objections to it (see Charles Gore, *The Body of Christ*). There seems to most of us to be no need for any explanation or definition of the mystery of the Eucharist.

**227. What exactly happens at the consecration? Do the bread and wine turn to the actual Body and Blood of Christ, as Roman Catholics believe?**

They do not become the *material* Body and Blood of Christ, as you appear to mean. That is certainly not the official Roman doctrine (even if some Romanists think it is). Romanists do not believe that they are cannibals. The best Anglican divines teach that the bread and wine become the Body and Blood of Christ after a heavenly and spiritual manner. What happens at the consecration is that in answer to the prayer of the congregation led by the priest, who is ordained and authorized to lead it, the Holy Spirit changes the bread and wine, so that while remaining bread and wine they also become the spiritual Body and Blood of Christ. It is a mystery which we cannot define further.

**228. What is the official teaching on the Holy Communion, since the Articles are vague?**

See the Second Office of Instruction in the American Prayer Book (in the English Prayer Book, the Church Catechism). The mystery of the Holy Communion cannot be fully understood and there have, and still are, different opinions about it. The Church is wise to avoid sharp definitions. The Holy Communion was given to us to be received reverently, regularly, and thankfully, not to be a subject for disputes.

**229. Why is the Holy Communion the most important service of the Church?**

It is the one service which our Lord expressly commanded, when He said, "Do this in remembrance of me." From the earliest days of the Church, all its members gathered on the Lord's Day for the "Breaking of Bread" (Acts 2:42, 46, 20:7). Hebrews 10:25 commands regular attendance. The whole Church in all ages has regarded the Holy Communion, or Liturgy, as the chief service round which all others are grouped. The Lord's Day, or Sunday (which is not a continuation of the Sabbath of the Jews), was made a public holiday in order that Christians might be free to worship at the Eucharist. The Church of England directs sermons to be preached and notices issued at this service, and at no others, and the Episcopal Church follows its example.

**230. Why has Morning Prayer superseded the Holy Communion as the main service on Sunday morning?**

This custom, which is peculiar to the Anglican Churches, and is now rapidly breaking down, has a long history. The intention of the Prayer Book was that the Sunday morning service should be Morning Prayer, Litany, and Holy Communion with sermon. In the sixteenth century people had long been accustomed to communicate only once a year. The Reformers wished to abolish "solitary Masses," at which only the priest communicated, and to restore frequent Communion by the laity. They laid down that if no one had given notice that he wished to communicate the service should proceed only to the Prayer for the Church Militant. This was the usual order of service until about a hundred years ago. The belief had long become general that no one ought to be present at the Holy Communion who did not at the time intend to communicate. (There is no trace of this in the Prayer Book, nor is it known in any other part of Christendom. It is supposed to be due to the Elizabethan Puritans.) So when there was a Eucharist, the greater part of the congregation, as they were not communicating, trooped out.

The followers of the Tractarians, in order to induce people to prepare for Communion more carefully, especially by receiving it fasting, introduced the early Communion service, which is now almost universal in the Church of England. When choral services became common, Morning Prayer and Ante-Communion became choral, and the choir and most of the people, when there was to be Communion, departed after the Prayer for the Church Militant. Then came the demand for shorter services; the Ante-Communion was dropped, and the sermon was preached at Matins. Other parishes introduced a Choral Eucharist at which people were not supposed, or even allowed, to communicate, for fear they might not be fasting. So arose the contrast of parishes with Sung Morning Prayer and parishes with Sung Eucharist. The distinction is now being broken down by the Parish Communion at nine or ten o'clock, sometimes followed by a parish breakfast; this service combines general Communion with music, but Morning Prayer disappears. (For its advantages and disadvantages, see the Archbishop of York [Michael Ramsey], *Durham Essays*.)

**231. Where there is but one priest, ought he to celebrate three times on Sunday? Might one of the services be replaced by the Mass of the Presanctified?**

I cannot say without knowing the conditions. A priest ought not to celebrate more than once a day without necessity, but for many reasons it often is necessary. If there is a parish or family Communion, as the inquirer says, I see no reason for a late one as well. The laity might fairly put themselves to some inconvenience rather than expect their priest to celebrate three times in one day.

The Mass of the Presanctified would not solve the difficulty. This is an ancient service, based on Communion from the Reserved Sacrament, and held on days when the ordinary Liturgy was not thought suitable: among the Greeks, on all Wednesdays and Fridays in Lent; among the Romanists, on Good Friday and Easter Eve only. It has no Anglican authority and would not satisfy anyone's needs on a Sunday; there is no consecration, so that the congregation is not joining in the Sacrifice, for which

Communion from the Reserved Sacrament is not a sufficient substitute.

**232. If the Holy Communion is the chief service, why is it at eight o'clock rather than at a decent hour when most people are present?**

It is at an early hour in order that the communicants may be fasting, according to the universal custom of the Church. The first hour of the day is the best time to give to the worship of God.

**233. If Holy Communion is the chief service, why do many parishes have Morning Prayer?**

See Question 230. We ought to attend both, and it is quite possible, by not having too many hymns or too long a sermon, to get both into an hour, or a little more. This seems the more urgently required if there is no Evensong, which in many English parishes is the best-attended Sunday service.

**234. Why is Morning Prayer frowned on unless it is accompanied by the Holy Communion?**

There is nothing whatever against Morning Prayer, which every member of the Church ought to know and love, but it should never be a substitute for the offering of the Holy Eucharist; if you have not attended the latter you have not done your Sunday duty and are breaking the Fourth Commandment.

**235. How can the importance of the Mass, not only on Sundays but on weekdays, be better emphasized?**

If you are one of the fortunate few who have the time and opportunity to go to the Holy Communion (Eucharist, Mass, or Lord's Supper) every day you ought to live up to that great privilege by showing yourself specially kind, patient, and self-sacrificing toward your less fortunate neighbors: "to whom much is given, of them much will be required" (St. Luke 12:48).

**236. Does the Church believe that the sacraments (Holy Communion) are God, or only symbolic of Him?**

Neither. The sacraments are means by which God's grace and power are conveyed to us; they are not bare symbols (such as, for instance, the sign of the cross in baptism), but "effectual signs" (Article 25). They are not God: God is almighty and eternal; the Holy Eucharist is not almighty or eternal.

**237. How should I receive the Holy Communion?**

Go to church early: be in your place at least five minutes before the service begins; fasting (unless you are sick or aged), that is, having eaten or drunk nothing that day. Make sure that your hands and nails are perfectly clean. If you are a woman, put on no lipstick, for obvious reasons. When the time comes, proceed quietly to the altar, take off your gloves, and kneel at the rail. When the priest comes to you with the Bread, be ready, with the palm of your right hand held out and your left hand cupped underneath it (as St. Cyril of Jerusalem in the fourth century directed), making your left hand a throne for your right. The priest will place the Bread in your palm; raise it to your mouth but don't touch it with your fingers, and be careful that no crumb or fragment is lost. When the priest comes to you with the Cup, he will have a firm hold of it. Grasp the base of the Chalice with your right hand, and tilt it carefully to your lips. Drink only the least quantity that you can swallow. If you are a woman, don't wear a hat with a broad brim, which would prevent the priest from seeing your face; that is how accidents easily happen. Kneel straight upright throughout, and don't bow your head. Wait until the next person has communicated, then rise and return to your place; in some churches it is the custom to return by a different way, so as to avoid confusion between those coming and those going. Unless it is absolutely necessary, never leave the church until the priest has returned to the sacristy; to leave before he does is very bad manners. Never leave the church without offering a thanksgiving. Be careful what you say immediately after Communion, for the reaction on returning to the world is the devil's opportunity: if you can do so without hurting anyone's feelings, it is best to go home silently.

**238. Being an Anglican member of the Catholic Church, may I communicate in the Roman Church?**

Certainly not. If the Roman priest knew who you were he would not communicate you. To communicate without telling him would be a lie, and a very grave one; to communicate in unrepented sin is to be guilty of the Body and Blood of the Lord, and to bring judgment on yourself (I Cor. 11:27). To receive Communion in any Church is to commit yourself to its beliefs; in this case to the papal supremacy, etc. The Orthodox Church will sometimes, in exceptional cases such as that of the former Queen of Rumania, give Anglicans Communion when there is no Anglican priest at hand; and there is no Orthodox doctrine which we are bound as Anglicans to reject. But this is perhaps unlikely in the United States. No Anglican should do so without special permission from the Orthodox bishop.

**239. May intinction be used, and in what way consistently with Catholic usage and Anglican tradition?**

**240. Why do some priests and some dioceses object to intinction? Has it been sanctioned by the Lambeth Conference or the American bishops?**

Intinction is Communion with the Bread dipped in the Chalice or touched with the Wine. It has been the regular practice of the Eastern Churches since the thirteenth century, and recently of the Dutch Old Catholics (who formerly communicated in one kind only). There is no Anglican tradition or authority behind it, as far as I know. Intinction is permissible, with the leave of the bishop, in special cases, such as for alcoholics or persons with diseased lips. However, it does not really fulfill our Lord's command (St. Matthew 26:27): "Drink ye all of it." The notion current in some quarters that the common cup (which has great symbolic value) is dangerous to health is nonsense. The person most likely to suffer, if there were any truth in this silly idea, would be the priest: and statistics show that priests live longer than anyone else.

**241. How often should I receive the Holy Communion?**

Provided you come in repentance, faith, and charity, and make proper preparation and thanksgiving, you should aim at once a week at least. An old writer says: "If he asks how often he should receive, tell him as often as he can, that the old Serpent, seeing the Blood of Christ on his lips, may tremble to approach." No one, except a priest who has to celebrate more than once, is allowed to communicate twice in one day.

**242. Does a priest have to consecrate specially to take Communion to a sick person?**

No. He may bring the Body and Blood of Christ from the altar or he may keep the sacrament permanently in the church, so that a sick person, or anyone who cannot get to the church, may be communicated at any time. But those who are permanently house-bound should be given a private celebration from time to time, if conditions permit. The priest who celebrates will always himself receive.

**243. How much wine may a priest consecrate at one time?**

As much as is needed, but not more than enough.

**244. Why is not the Host reserved in all Episcopal churches, as there seems to be always a tabernacle built in?**

I suppose some priests do not know how to reserve and do not feel the need for it. The standing tabernacle is not a good place because it distracts attention from the altar, which is more holy than the tabernacle. It is more usual to reserve in an ambry (small cupboard) at the side.

**245. Need one make a formal preparation before every Communion if one communicates often?**

I do not think so, if one is careful to make frequent self-examination, to be sure one is in charity with all men, and to beware of letting Communion become formal. You should have a spiritual adviser and consult him.

**246. How can Communion in one kind be justified, in view of the words of institution?**

It cannot be justified: and it is forbidden in the Anglican Communion as it is in all the Eastern Churches (see Article 30). Even Communion from the Reserved Sacrament, if not in both kinds separately (which may be impossible), should be by intinction (see Question 239).

**247. How about the use of one cup for Communion?**

The Church requires the use of the common cup, out of which all are to drink. This has high symbolic value. Fear of infection is an idea which should be ignored. The Chalice must be cleansed by the lips of the celebrant, and not by a purificator. If the consecrated wine touches any fabric, that fabric must be carefully washed, and the water drunk by the celebrant. See Question 240.

**248. Does the Invocation in the Canon imply a Receptionist theory?**

The Invocation is: "We most humbly beseech thee, O merciful Father, to hear us; and, of thy almighty goodness, vouchsafe to bless and sanctify, with thy Word and Holy Spirit, these thy gifts and creatures of bread and wine; that we, receiving them according to thy Son our Saviour Jesus Christ's holy institution, in remembrance of his death and passion, may be partakers of his most blessed Body and Blood." There is nothing here that implies Receptionism, but, like all Anglican consecration prayers, it does not exclude Receptionism; which is not a heresy, for it has never been condemned by the Church, though it is contrary to the usual teaching of the Church. The elements are here called "bread and wine" after the recital of the words of our Lord, "This is my body, This is my blood." At the same place in the Roman Canon the following words occur: "the holy bread of eternal life, and the cup of perpetual salvation" (in *Unde et memores*). The theory that the use by the celebrating priest of the words of our Lord (which were His words of administering, not of consecrating) effects the consecration is a medieval belief which has given rise to many superstitions. The Canon of the Roman Mass is much older than this theory. The belief shown by all the ancient liturgies is that the consecration is effected by God the Holy Spirit in answer to the prayer of the Church, which has already offered thanks over the bread and wine. Every ancient liturgy known to us, with the doubtful exception of the very obscure Roman Mass, contains an Invocation of the Word or the Holy Spirit. The American Church (with the Scottish and other Anglican Churches) has, by restoring this invocation, returned to the practice of the ancient Church.

**249. Who may be admitted to the Holy Communion, and why?**

See Questions 168–79. Those who have been baptized and confirmed (and have not been excommunicated), and are under the bishop of the diocese or some bishop in full communion with him (that is, are Anglican or Old Catholic communicants) are entitled to receive the Holy Communion as full members of the Episcopal Church, which is the Catholic Church in the United States (see Questions 127, 128). Communicants of the Orthodox, Armenian, and Assyrian Churches may be communicated at our altars, with the permission of their own bishops. This permission must be obtained in every case and on every occasion; and they must on no account be admitted to Communion without it (except at the point of death). Our authority is the resolutions of the Lambeth Conference, subject to the consent of the American bishops.

The Church of England has formally permitted communicants of the Churches of Sweden and Finland, and some other national Churches of the Lutheran tradition, to communicate at our altars. They believe as we do about the creeds and the two great sacraments; they never seceded from the Church of England, whose authority they recognize; and they could not become Anglicans even if they wished to, as there is no Anglican Church in their native countries.

**250. Is it not superstitious to think the condition of the stomach before Communion more important than the condition of heart and mind?**

The condition of heart and mind is indeed the most important thing: to communicate without repentance, faith, and charity is profane. The reason for the rule of fasting Communion is that we may honor our Lord's Body and Blood by making it the first food of the day. This has been a custom of all parts of the Church from early times. It is also the experience of most people that they are not in a fit condition for religious exercises after a meal, for this there is plenty of biblical authority (Ex. 34:28; I Kings 19:8; Dan. 10:3; St. Matthew 4:2; Acts 10:10). The best time to communicate is early in the morning, before the cares and distractions of the day have begun.

**251. Has the Episcopal Church an official or majority doctrine of the Real Presence?**

See Questions 220–24. The Episcopal Church has no doctrine on this or any other subject that cannot be proved from Scripture or has not been defined by the Universal Church. There is no definition of the Universal Church on this subject. We must not be explicit where Scripture is not explicit. In any case doctrine is not decided by majorities, which have no spiritual authority. The Holy Eucharist is a mystery, and the less we try to explain it the better.

**252. Why is the Eucharist a sacrifice?**

See Question 189. The only sacrifice in the Christian religion is the sacrifice of our Lord Jesus Christ, made on the Cross and offered in heaven (see the Epistle to the Hebrews). The Eucharist is the principal means by which we are permitted to take part in that sacrifice and to offer all that we are and have, that we may be united with our Saviour's perfect sacrifice. When we take part in the Eucharist, even without receiving Communion, we are carried into heaven and share the worship of the angels and archangels; when we receive Communion we take part more fully, for then we feast on the Sacrifice.

**253. What is "Benediction"? How can it be reconciled with Articles 25 and 28?**

"Benediction" is the practice of using the consecrated Bread for blessing people: either in a glass vessel called a "monstrance" or in a closed vessel called a "ciborium." It is a modern Romanist ceremony, unknown in ancient times or in the Eastern Churches. It was not in use even among English Romanists before the nineteenth century. The Articles quoted only say that Christ did not command the sacraments to be carried about, or gazed at, and this cannot be denied by anyone.

Benediction is forbidden or strongly discouraged in most Anglican dioceses. Such learned and holy men as Pusey, Scott Holland, Richard Benson (founder of the Cowley Fathers), and Bishop Gore (who forbade it in his diocese) were strongly opposed to it. Benediction encourages simple people to believe that our Lord is *locally* present in the tabernacle and to offer adoration to the outward visible signs of His presence; but we must not offer adoration, the worship due to God alone, to anything that we can see. If we believe that Christ is locally present we believe what the best theologians say is not true; and if we do not believe it, Benediction is meaningless. The blessing of God is the same, whether the sacrament is used for the purpose or not.

Other objections are these: Whereas our Lord is in the sacrament for sacrifice and for Communion, "Benediction" and similar practices are not connected with either, and we cannot be sure that they have His sanction. Emphasis on His sacramental presence, apart from Communion, leads to neglect of His promise to be present wherever His people are assembled; and of the presence and power of the Holy Spirit. Benediction and similar unnecessary practices have created in many minds a strong prejudice against the reservation of the sacrament, which is often necessary for the sick and others who cannot be present at the Eucharist.

## *Chapter Eighteen*

# ABSOLUTION AND UNCTION

**254. Why should I call my priest whenever I am sick?**
If you are seriously ill you are in more danger of death than usual. Your priest can do three things for you. He can hear your

confession and give you absolution, that you may not appear before the Judgment Seat with your sins unforgiven. He can give you Communion, which will strengthen your soul and body and help you to recover or prepare for death. He can anoint you, which will help you to recover if it is God's will that you should, and if not, will make you more fit to meet death.

**255. Should we confess our sins to our priests?**

We are not bound to (unless we are guilty of very grave sins), but we are strongly advised to, for three reasons:

(1) We need all the grace that we can get. God has appointed this means of grace, and it is very foolish not to use it. I have been making my confession to a priest regularly for fifty years, so I do not speak without experience.

(2) We become much more ashamed of our sins, and are more unlikely to commit them again, if we confess them in the presence of a fellow creature (who is, of course, bound absolutely to complete secrecy) than if we confess them only in God's hearing.

(3) The skilled confessor is a physician of souls and can save us much unhappiness, and the sin from which it springs, by advising us of the right remedies for our faults.

**256. Is there a set form for private confession?**

"I confess to Almighty God, the Father, the Son, and the Holy Ghost, before the whole company of heaven and you, my father, that I have sinned exceedingly, by thought, by word, by deed, and by omission—especially that since my last confession which was [before Easter, or three months ago, or whenever it was], I have committed the following sins. . . . For these and all my other sins, which I cannot now remember, I am heartily sorry; and I earnestly desire God's pardon, and of you, my father, penance, counsel, and absolution."

**257. My religion is between God and me. Why should I ask forgiveness of a priest?**

You are entirely, disastrously, and dangerously mistaken. Your religion is not between God and you. It affects all your neighbors. Your religion teaches you to love your neighbor as yourself. If you are jealous, or bad-tempered, or cruel, or treacherous, or covetous, your neighbor will suffer. If you are a member of the Church, every sin you commit, even in the most secret thought of your heart, is an injury to the Church. The priest represents

God, and also the Church. In confessing to him you are confessing to God and to man the wrongs that you have done. God has given him authority to forgive you (St. John 20:23); see the "Form and Manner of Ordering Priests," and the words which were said to him by the bishop, "Whose sins thou dost forgive, they are forgiven" (The Book of Common Prayer).

**258. If the General Confession and Absolution are enough for forgiveness, why should we confess to a priest? Is there an easy way and a hard way?**

There is only one way, a hard way: by repentance. This must include sorrow for sin, confession, and amendment of life. God always forgives those who truly repent. But confession to a priest is a great help toward repentance (see Question 255).

**259. Is confession absolutely necessary?**

Confession to God is absolutely necessary, and we ought to make it every night before we go to bed. We all know, however, how easy it is to neglect this, or to let it become merely formal, unless we also confess to a priest from time to time. In the case of very grave sins, it is usually held that confession to a priest is necessary, because of the wrong done to the whole Church.

**260. Why should I, making my first auricular confession for a particular need, after years of private confession, be required to confess all past sins?**

"Private" and "auricular" usually mean confession to a priest in the confessional, as opposed to public confession before the congregation (common in the mission field). Here "private" seems to mean to God, without a priest. If you feel a pain and send for a physician, he may advise a complete overhaul. If he does, you will be wise to follow his advice. The skilled confessor is a spiritual physician. You are not bound to call him in, or to follow his advice, but unless he knows something of the condition of your soul, which he cannot know without a general confession, he will not know what remedy to apply to your particular need. Therefore you will be wise to follow his advice. It is useless to consult him unless you are willing to trust his knowledge and his desire to help you.

**261. Why is not the sacrament of penance a service as such in the Prayer Book?**

Because it is the Book of "Common" Prayer, which includes only public services. But in the English Prayer Book, in the order for the Visitation of the Sick, there is a form for Absolution, which has been omitted from the American Prayer Book. "Our Lord Jesus Christ, Who hath left power to His Church to absolve all sinners who truly repent and believe in Him, of His great mercy forgive thee thine offences; and by His authority committed to me I absolve thee from all thy sins, in the Name of the Father and of the Son and of the Holy Ghost. Amen."

**262. What is the personal value of sacramental confession and absolution in the counsel by the priest? May guilt sometimes inhibit a personal expression of faith?**

We must distinguish between the absolution, which any authorized priest can give, and the counsel, the value of which depends upon the skill and knowledge of the director. You may have one priest as your regular confessor and another as your director or spiritual adviser. There are people who do not allow themselves to believe, because they know that if they admitted that the claims of Jesus Christ are true they would have to reform their lives, which they are not willing to do.

**263. Why do some churches have confession and others seem to frown on it?**

I assume that "churches" here means "parishes." Some have a Catholic and others a Calvinistic tradition. It is very unwise to make your confession to a priest who has not learned how to hear confessions, has not made his own confession, and does not know what advice to give. His counsel might even be dangerous.

**264. What hope is there that the Church will recognize the great value of penance?**

The Church of England certainly does. The American Prayer Book might well restore the form of absolution in the Visitation of the Sick. Certainly every priest who is an army or naval chaplain, or has to work in a hospital or a school, should regard hearing confessions as a normal part of his work.

**265. Why is not the sacrament of confession restored openly in the Episcopal Church?**

I suppose the reason is the remains of Calvinistic prejudice and the refusal to take seriously the solemn words used at the ordination of every priest.

**266. May one go to confession to a priest outside one's own parish?**

Certainly; the words of the Prayer Book are: "Let him come

to me, or to some other Minister of God's Word" (Exhortation after the Order for Holy Communion; the English Prayer Book has "some other discreet and learned Minister of God's Word"). It is advisable to choose the holiest, wisest, and most experienced priest you can find and stick to him as your confessor.

**267. How did Holy Unction change from a means of healing to a preparation for death? Why does no one preach about it?**

The title of Extreme Unction (that is, anointing with oil) and the belief that it was a preparation for death, and that anyone who had received it, and then recovered, had done something quite unusual and hardly proper, appear to have arisen about the ninth century. All Eastern, and some Romanist, theologians object to the belief. It is psychologically dangerous, for to suggest that anyone will probably die is likely to hasten his death. Unction is intended to help the sick person to recover, and in any case to give strength and comfort to his soul (James 5:14–16; cf. 16:18). The American Prayer Book provides for a service of healing, either by anointing or by laying on of hands, which ought to be known to all members of the Episcopal Church.

**268. If oil is used (a) for healing (b) for Confirmation (c) for Ordination, Consecration, justify its use.**

The anointing of the sick for healing is based on James 5:14. Its ceremonial use, though common to many religions, is found in the Old Testament: priests and kings were anointed to symbolize their sacred calling and sanctity. The English monarch is anointed at his coronation (I Kings 1:39; II Kings 11:12). The Church from earliest times has made sacramental use of it. Anointing is done principally to separate persons or things from profane use, and for healing purposes. The oil so used is usually blessed by the bishop at his cathedral altar on Maundy Thursday.

**269. What is the "therapy of grace"?**

"Therapy" is a Greek word meaning healing, and anyone who uses it is to be suspected, for a favorite device of the charlatan, the quack, and the mystagogue is to impress his hearers with strange words when he might use plain ones. Spiritual healing is to be distinguished from the sacrament of Unction, which any priest may use. Spiritual healing is a natural gift which some people have (I Cor. 12:9, 30), not necessarily priests or even Christians. Mr. Hickson, who was famous all over the world for this gift, was a lay member of the Church. Such gifts must always be used in close collaboration with the medical profession. All who forbid resort to physicians and surgeons, as some sects do, are to be avoided as dangerous to soul and body (Ecclus. 38:1–14). The Guild of St. Raphael carries on a healing work in England, and there are also several such societies in the American Church, notably the Fellowship of St. Luke and the Order of St. Luke (see *The Episcopal Church Annual*).

**270. What is "the awfulness of something that cannot happen," as the curing of leukemia by prayer and anointing?**

It is foolish, not to say profane, to say that anything "cannot happen." God can work miracles, but we must not ask Him to do so. Setting that aside, we do not know the limits of the power of mind over matter. Many diseases, such as leprosy, formerly believed to be incurable, can now be cured. Many people have been given up as hopeless by the physicians, and have been cured by prayer and spiritual healing. I have known men who have brought about such cures (see St. Mark 8:23; James 5:16). Lately I heard of a South African native who suffered from leukemia, and who is said to have been cured, at any rate for the time being, by spiritual healing.

## Chapter Nineteen

# MARRIAGE

**271. What is Christian marriage?**

Christian marriage is the lifelong and exclusive union of one man and one woman, being Christians. If they have not been baptized, the union is still marriage, but it is not Christian. If they have been baptized after marriage, their previous union is sanctified and becomes Christian marriage, and sacramental, for Christian marriage is regarded as a sacrament of the Church. The necessary feature of this is that the couple should promise, not under compulsion but of their own free will, to enter into a lifelong and exclusive union, which only death can dissolve. If they do not intend to do this, or are under compulsion to do it, the union is not a marriage in the eyes of the Church: it is fornication and a very grave sin. There are three purposes of marriage stated in the English (but not American) Prayer Book: (1) the production of children and their education in the fear of God; (2) the control of the passions; (3) mutual society, help, and comfort, in good fortune and bad. Unions which are not permanent and indissoluble, or are not exclusive (polygamy and polyandry), as well as all use of the powers of sex outside marriage, are forbidden absolutely to members of the Church (see Eph. 5:3-5, and many other passages). The natural law requires all human beings, whether Christian or not, if they marry, to remain married until death separates them, and to have no sexual relations with anyone else (St. Mark 10:6-8). Christians are given sacramental grace to enable them to fulfill their obligations as human beings. The promise made at marriage to enter into a permanent union is fulfilled when the marriage is consummated. If for any reason it is not consummated it is not complete, and may be dissolved by the proper authority.

**272. What is the Church's position on marriage and divorce? Why?**

**273. Does the Church acknowledge divorce?**

Our Lord's teaching on this subject is quite explicit (St. Mark 10:2-12): "Whosoever shall put away his wife, and marry another, committeth adultery against her. And if a woman shall put away her husband, and be married to another, she committeth adultery" (see also St. Luke 16:18; St. Matthew 5:32, 19:3-12). It is true that in the two passages of St. Matthew we find the words "except for fornication." The best explanation of these words is that they are what in a modern book would be a footnote (a device unknown in ancient times), inserted by the Evangelist, or some early copyist, to cover the case of converts who had married within the prohibited degrees. Such marriages as those of uncle and niece were common among the Greeks, but were abhorred by the Jews and were forbidden to Christians as "fornication" (Acts 15:29). Marriages of this kind had to be dissolved when the couple were baptized. At any rate, it is quite certain that these words cannot mean that a marriage could be dissolved because one party to it had committed adultery; dissolution of marriage for this reason was allowed by the Jewish Law (Deut. 24:1–4). In our Lord's time there were two leading Rabbinic schools, that of Hillel (grandfather of Gamaliel—Acts 5:34) and that of Shammah. Shammah allowed divorce for adultery only; Hillel for many other causes. If "fornication" here had meant adultery, our Lord would have agreed with Shammah, which would have surprised nobody. But the disciples were evidently very much surprised by His teaching (St. Matthew 19:9), which shows that our Lord forbade dissolution of marriage altogether. The Church holds that marriage can be broken only by death, as the service clearly says. Anyone who "marries" again in the lifetime of a divorced partner will be living in adultery. The Church does not recognize this as marriage.

**274. Does the Episcopal Church ever allow divorced people to marry again in church?**

Divorce by itself is nowhere a bar to a fresh marriage, if the other party to the divorce is dead. It is during the lifetime of the other party that marriage is forbidden, because in the eyes of the Church both are still bound by their marriage vows, "till death us do part."

The American Episcopal Church (but no other part of the Anglican Communion) many years ago passed a canon allowing dissolution of marriage for adultery. I think this canon was passed at a time when the interpretation of the exceptive clause in St. Matthew, which I have shown to be impossible (Question 273), was widely believed to be correct. Article 20 says: "It is not lawful for the Church to ordain anything that is contrary to God's Word written, neither to expound one place of Scripture that it be repugnant to another." To interpret texts of St. Matthew in this way is to make them repugnant to St. Mark and St. Luke. It seems to me that the American Episcopal Church went beyond its powers when it passed this canon. Not even the Universal Church, still less a national Church, can alter a Divine law; in this case God's Word in the fullest sense. It is as if a state of the Union passed a law conflicting with the American Constitution, which I presume would be declared void by the Supreme Court. The Church has no Supreme Court, except for those who believe in the Pope, and even the Pope does not claim the power to dissolve a valid marriage. At any rate, the exclusively American permission to dissolve a marriage on the ground of adultery was repealed when the canon was changed in 1946.

**275. What grounds for divorce are recognized by the Episcopal Church? How can a person be divorced, married to another person, and then become a member of the Episcopal Church?**

**276. When is the marriage of divorced persons allowed, and when not? What are the exceptions?**

If by "divorce" is meant dissolution of marriage, see Questions 273, 274. A valid marriage once consummated can be dissolved only by death. The State can declare a union, which is not a Christian marriage, valid for civil purposes, such as inheritance or legitimacy. In the eyes of the Church, however, such a union is not marriage but adultery. Divorce has two other meanings: (1) The "divorces" of Henry VIII and Napoleon Bonaparte were what would now be called nullity cases; they claimed that their previous marriages were not true marriages. (2) There is also "ecclesiastical divorce," separation without the right to remarry, which is allowed by the Church as a last resort, in certain cases.

No one can become a member of the Church except by Baptism. The marriage of unbaptized persons is not Christian marriage; it may not be a true marriage, for they may, if heathen, never have intended to enter a permanent and exclusive union. If they have been divorced and one of them is later baptized, the previous marriage may be (I do not say is) no hindrance to a fresh, Christian marriage. All such cases, which may be very complicated, are for the bishop to decide.

**277. Why does not the Church take a positive stand about remarriage, and not pass the buck to the bishop?**

What is meant here by the Church? The bishop is the officer of the local Church and the judge in all marriage cases; he should have the advice of experts in canon law, but the decision is his. Neither priests nor people have any right to decide such cases. The bishop should have a Church court, and there should also be a Church court of appeal.

**278. Is the marriage of divorced persons, allowed in some dioceses, acceptable or a sin?**

It seems to me that the words of our Lord (St. Mark 10:11, 12; see Question 273) are final. It is adultery.

**279. Did our Lord intend marriage to be a permanent state or an ideal which may be missed, so that it can be asserted that the state has ceased to exist?**

Our Lord looked forward to the New Israel, the corporate body of His disciples, to govern which He was training the Apostles. He did not accept the Hebrew law about marriage (St. Mark 10:5, 6), still less those of heathen nations. He gave His Church a law to take the place of these, and stricter than either of them. What He commanded about marriage was a law for the whole community, not, like some of His teachings, an ideal for particular persons to be obeyed in the spirit, not necessarily in the letter. For marriage is always an affair of the whole community. Both Church and nation are built upon the family, of which marriage is the foundation. The notion, all too common, that marriage is only, or even mainly, a matter for the bridal couple, is disastrous both to the Church and to the nation and is not accepted by either. This is the teaching of the Church in all ages; of the Roman and Anglican Communions in particular.

The rule of the Orthodox Eastern Churches is widely misunderstood. They hold that the Church, having power to bind and loose, can dissolve a marriage for various reasons, but they do not recognize the divorces pronounced by the State. They have Church courts with a bishop as judge, which are authorized to dissolve a marriage. This divergence from the rule of the ancient Church is said to be due to the influence of Roman civil law in Byzantine times. Moreover, the Orthodox Churches have usually lived in conditions totally different from those of the modern world. The Church was the whole nation, or the whole subject nation under Moslem rule. There are always some nominal Christians who will not obey the Church's law of marriage; the more the Church is identified with the nation (as it still is in most Eastern countries) the stronger becomes the temptation to relax the law forbidding divorce.

**280. What is the teaching of the Church about birth control and about what constitutes a normal family?**

The traditional doctrine of the Church has always been that children are one of the greatest gifts of God; that to have a large family is a great privilege and a God-given responsibility (Ps. 127:3, 4) and healthy for both parents and children: that to beget and bear children is for married people a duty to their country, to the Church, and to God, to be fulfilled by bringing them up as good citizens and good Christians. Artificial prevention of conception has always been forbidden by the Church as a form of sexual perversion.

However, the Lambeth Conference of 1930, after declaring agreement with this position in general, modified it by Resolution 15: "in those cases where there is a clearly felt obligation to limit or avoid parenthood, and where there is a morally sound reason for avoiding complete abstinence." "The Conference agrees that other methods may be used provided that this is done in the light of the same Christian principles. The Conference records its strong condemnation of the use of any methods of conception-control from motives of selfishness, luxury or mere convenience." Most such resolutions are passed unanimously. This was the only one in living memory which was passed by only a majority. It was severely criticized at the time on the ground that: (a) nothing whatever can excuse such a revolting moral perversion as contraception; (b) even if in some cases it may be the lesser of two evils, it was extremely unwise to say so in public, because the press published the Resolution without the safeguards and left a general impression that the Anglican bishops had sanctioned contraception. (It might be added that it was unfair to leave the responsibility in such a matter to the conscience of the individual. Members of the Church ought to have guidance and direction in such cases.)

**281. What does the Church teach about marriage between persons of different religions? What is the status of the children of such a marriage?**

All such marriages are to be discouraged in every possible way, preferably in the earlier stages of the acquaintance. Many an unhappy marriage and many a failure of both parents to practice any form of religion or train their children in it are due to this cause.

Marriage with a Jew, or any other unbaptized person, must not take place in church without special permission from the bishop. The unbaptized person should be persuaded, if possible, to be baptized, after due instruction in the Christian religion and its duties, before the wedding.

Marriage with a Romanist presents peculiar difficulties. Rome does not recognize the marriage of its subjects as marriage unless performed by a Roman priest. If one party is not a Romanist, the couple can be married only by dispensation. This dispensation is given only on certain unfair and dishonorable conditions: as, that all the children must be brought up Romanists, that the non-Romanist parent must promise never to try to convert the Romanist (but no such promise is imposed on the Romanist spouse), and must have nothing to do with the religious education of the children. If the Romanist partner ignores the requirement of dispensation and is married in any other way, religious or secular, the Romanist clergy will tell him (or her) that the marriage is no marriage, that he is living in sin, that he ought to leave his partner if he cannot induce her (or him) to accept the conditions laid down. No Anglican priest ought to consent to celebrate such a marriage, unless and until the Romanist partner has left the Roman Communion and been formally received in the Anglican. The status of the children depends upon the parents: if they cannot agree, it is a question for the lawyers. If the children are baptized, they are Christians and members of the Church, and whoever baptized them is usually expected to take responsibility for them.

**282. What specific moral standards are required of a woman who aspires to be a priest's wife?**

There is only one moral standard for all Christians—perfection. Our Lord said, "Be ye perfect" (St. Matthew 5:48). However, the behavior of the priest and his wife is more important than that of other people; they are in the limelight, they are expected to set an example. The lady should be sure that she has a vocation to the very delicate and difficult work of a priest's wife. She must be as keen as he is about the work for God and man that he has to do, for otherwise she will probably ruin both it and him. She ought to make some study of theology and other aspects of her husband's work, but her first duty is to him, to see that he is fit and as free to do his work as she can help him to be. She is not necessarily bound to take charge of his Sunday schools or any work in his parish, but she must be careful to treat all people, whatever their class or status, in exactly the same way and to carry out all her own religious duties, both for her own sake and for the sake of her husband. On the other hand, she must remember that a priest, unlike a layman, has to put his vocation, his priesthood, even before his wife; it may be his duty, for instance, to stay on in a place that his wife finds disagreeable.

**283. Why should people be dissuaded from marrying in Advent or Lent?**

Since the fourth century the Church has forbidden its members to marry in Lent, because Lent is a penitential season unsuitable for public rejoicing. The old English canons forbade marriage between Advent and Epiphany, between Septuagesima and Low Sunday, between Rogation Sunday and Trinity Sunday. Marriage in these periods required a dispensation from the archbishop. The rules have been neglected in recent centuries, when the seasons of the Church have taken a smaller part in men's lives. The faithful may fairly be asked to avoid marriage in Lent if possible; and during the great festivals, if only not to overburden the clergy.

*Chapter Twenty*

# DEATH, JUDGMENT, HELL, AND HEAVEN (THE LAST THINGS)

**Introductory Note**

We know nothing about life beyond death, except by revelation. What is told us in Holy Scripture is necessarily symbolical; we cannot imagine living without a body or be sure that we understand the symbolism of Scripture rightly. Therefore, nearly every statement in this chapter must be read with the condition "as far as we can see."

**284. What happens to us when we die?**

**285. Develop more fully the Christian teaching about death.**

Death is the rending asunder of body and spirit. The body decays or is destroyed (as by cremation), and all that belongs to the body comes to an end. The spirit goes immediately to be judged (St. Luke 16:28; the rich man's brothers were still alive).

The judge is our Lord Jesus Christ (St. John 5:22, 27). Death is the end of our probation (II Cor. 6:2). As it is now, for human beings, death is the result and punishment of sin (Rom. 6:23). Every person will be judged according to his opportunities and how he used them (St. Luke 12:47, 48). Those who are acquitted will go into a condition of rest, which is called Paradise (a word meaning "garden" or "Abraham's bosom") (St. Luke 16:22, 23:42). Those who are acquitted at the Particular Judgment, as it is called, will not be those who have not sinned (for there are no such persons) but those who have repented of their sins; not those who have done good (for all our good deeds are by God's grace), but those who have believed in our Saviour and tried to serve Him. "By grace are ye saved through faith" (Eph. 2:8), but "faith without works is dead" (James 2:26).

**286. What happens to the unbaptized and to infants at death?**

Baptized infants, dying before they commit actual sin, are undoubtedly saved (Baptismal Service). We can say nothing about the unbaptized, whether infants or not, except that they are under the justice and mercy of God. Those who never had any chance of believing in Christ will be judged by their obedience to the natural law (St. Matthew 24:31–36).

**287. Does man live on after the body dies?**

Some philosophers have believed, with Plato, in the immortality of the soul. Kant held that we cannot prove it, but must assume it if we are to think at all. Christians believe that our Lord Jesus Christ will carry out His promise to give eternal life to those who believe in Him (I Cor. 15:12–18; St. John 3:16, 10:28, 11:26). He rose from the dead, and we too shall rise (I Cor. 15:20–23; I Thess. 4:14). Our belief that we, as His disciples, shall live forever with Him depends on our trust in His word.

**288. Shall we know our loved ones after death?**

Yes, but we do not know how. Our Lord sanctioned the belief (St. Luke 16:9, 23:43).

**289. What happens to a person between death and the final judgment?**

He enters into a state of waiting (Heb. 11:39, 40; Rev. 6:11). The parable of the rich man and Lazarus suggests that some will be at rest and others miserable, but we do not know whether this parable was meant to give us information about the future or whether it only assumed current Jewish speculation. It seems likely that those whose interests are confined to this world will not be happy when those interests no longer exist, but that those who have devoted themselves to the love of God and man will retain that love after death. In any case, their condition is temporary; the word translated "hell" in the parable is Hades, which is not to last forever (Rev. 20:14).

**290. Shall we have new bodies at death or at the final judgment? Does eternal life begin at the personal judgment or at the final judgment?**

It seems that we shall receive new bodies at the final judgment (I Cor. 15:35–58). Some think that we shall have some kind of body in the meantime, but there is no evidence for this that I know of.

Eternal life begins at our Baptism: we have it now (I John 5:11 and many other passages).

**291. Should we pray for the dead? Does the Church do so, and why?**

The Church has always prayed for the dead. The Jews did so before the time of our Lord (II Macc. 12:44). II Timothy 1:18 is probably a prayer for the dead. In any case we do not need the express authority of Scripture for a practice so universal The Church asks God to grant to the dead refreshment, light, and peace. The American Prayer Book contains the following prayers for the dead:

"We also bless thy holy Name for all thy servants departed this life in thy faith and fear; beseeching thee to give us grace so to follow their good examples, that with them we may be partakers of thy heavenly kingdom" (Prayer for the Church, in the Order of Holy Communion).

That "we, and all thy whole Church, may obtain remission of our sins, and all other benefits of his passion" (Prayer of Consecration).

"Receive him into the arms of thy mercy, into the blessed rest of everlasting peace, and into the glorious company of the saints in light" (The Commendatory Prayer in the Visitation of the Sick).

"Multiply, we beseech thee, to those who rest in Jesus, the manifold blessings of thy love" (Burial of the Dead).

Death does not separate us from the Church, and we continue to pray, both in public and in private, for all who are dead and to believe that they pray for us. This is the Communion of Saints (see Question 301).

**292. Does Holy Scripture teach that there can be no repentance after death?**

Holy Scripture teaches in many places that God gives a limited time of probation. When that time is over there is no further opportunity for repentance (see Rev. 2:5, 21, for local churches; II Cor. 6:2; St. Luke 14:12–24, 16:25; Heb. 12:17, for individuals). The end of our probation is believed to be death. Certainly we should be unspeakably foolish, if we have had opportunities of repentance before death, to suppose that we shall have any more.

**293. What is "realized eschatology"?**

It is not part of the teaching of the Church. The phrase appears to have been invented by Dr. C. H. Dodd. It means that we are now, ever since Pentecost, living in "the last days" (see I John 2:18, but cf. II Tim. 2:18).

**294. Must I die before I see any of the fruits of the Spirit in my own life?**

No; but you ought not to worry about it. If you are trying to serve God, and continue trying, they will certainly be there, whether you see them or not. You probably need the advice of a spiritual director.

**295. Who preached to the spirits in prison, Enoch or Christ? (I Peter 3:19).**

Christ, of course; Enoch, who is only a legendary figure, is not mentioned in this passage at all. The reference to Enoch is based on a conjectural emendation by Rendel Harris (described in the *Oxford Dictionary of the Christian Church* as a scholar of immense, but at times unbalanced, erudition). E. G. Selwyn (former Dean of Winchester), whose commentary deals at great length with this passage, says that Harris' conjecture is most improbable.

**296. Does Scripture tell us that men will go to Heaven when they die, as is almost universally believed? If Christ's kingdom is to be on earth, will not the saints be here on earth with Him? (St. John 14:3)**

Scripture certainly does not say so; it has never been taught

by any part of the Church; it is a relic of Calvin's heresy that
the elect will go straight to Heaven and the reprobate (the
greater part of mankind, according to Calvin) will go straight to
Hell. Few educated people still believe anything so monstrous
as Calvin's doctrine of election to Hell. As long as this world
exists men will be subject to corruption, and therefore Christ's
kingdom can never be completely fulfilled in this world. We
look for a new earth, in which sin will have ceased to exist, and
death with it (I Cor. 15:24–26; Heb. 13:14; Rev. 20:11–21:1).
Men go at death into the "intermediate state," or Hades. Romanists believe that the saints go direct to Heaven, which they identify
with Paradise, but this is not the teaching of Scripture (Rev.
6:11) or of the ancient Church. Paradise is the state of rest;
Heaven is the state of glory.

### 297. Are the dead asleep till the Resurrection, or in the abode of the dead, or in Purgatory?

The use of "sleep" for death, as a figure of speech, is common
in the Bible (Dan. 12:2; Acts 7:60; I Cor. 15:6,20). Yet the belief
that the dead are unconscious is contrary to St. Matthew 22:32;
St. Luke 16:19–31, 23:43; I Peter 3:18,19, and has been rejected
by the Church several times, as in the 40th of the Articles of
1553, the original form of our Articles.

The abode of the dead is usually called Hades, originally the
name of a Greek god, later applied to the underworld, the
house of Hades, over which he was supposed to preside. The part
of Hades assigned to the blessed dead is Paradise (St. Luke 23:43).
There is no mention of Purgatory in Scripture, and we have no
evidence that it exists. However, we may well suppose that most
of us will need cleansing from evil habits after death, and such
cleansing is compared by ancient writers to fire, on the basis of
St. Mark 9:49, I Corinthians 3:13. We must distinguish this
opinion from the Roman doctrine of Purgatory, which is held to
make satisfaction for guilt; an opinion derived from the philosopher Aristotle.

### 298. Did God die on the Cross? Explain, "My God, my God, why hast thou forsaken me?" (St. Mark 15:34)

Jesus Christ is God and Man. As God, He of course could
not die. As Man, He died on the Cross and afterward rose again.
The mysterious Fourth Word from the Cross seems to mean that

in order to suffer the whole of human pain He had, in His human nature, to feel that His Father had forsaken Him. This is part of the mystery of the Word made flesh, into which we cannot expect to penetrate.

**299. How are we to answer the argument that there is no scriptural authority for prayers for the dead?**

We do not need scriptural authority for this practice, but II Timothy 1:18 is probably a prayer for a dead person. It is not a dogma of the faith but a devout practice which is never forbidden in Scripture. There is no scriptural authority requiring us to observe Sunday (though it is mentioned), or Christmas Day, which was unknown for some centuries after the New Testament. The Church has always prayed for the dead (see Question 291).

**300. What do we mean by the resurrection of the body?**

At the General Judgment, when our Lord returns to judge the living and the dead (St. Matthew 25:31; Acts 1:11; I Thess. 4:16), we shall receive new bodies, not liable to disease, decay, or death. St. Paul says, "If the dead rise not, then is not Christ raised; and if Christ be not raised, your faith is vain" (I Cor. 15:16,17). The new body will have some mysterious relation to the old, which St. Paul likens to the relation between the corn and the seed from which it sprang. To be without a body is to be incomplete: that is the state of death, the punishment for our sins. But in order to appear before God in Heaven we must be complete, with bodies as well as spirits.

**301. What do we mean by the Communion of Saints?**

Communion means fellowship, sharing in the love and prayer of one another. "Saints" means here, as in the New Testament, all members of the Church, who are called to be holy whether they are holy yet or not. They include both the living and the dead. Even Richard Baxter, the Puritan (d. 1691) wrote:

> He wants not friends that hath Thy love,
>   And may converse and walk with Thee,
> And with Thy saints here and above,
>   With whom forever I would be.
> In the communion of saints
>   Is wisdom, safety, and delight;
> And when my heart declines and faints,
>   It's raisèd by their heat and light.
> Still we are centred all in Thee,

Members, though distant, of the Head,
In the same family we be,
 By the same faith and spirit led.
Before Thy throne we daily meet,
 As joint petitioners to Thee.
In spirit we each other greet,
 And shall again each other see.

### 302. Why is the Communion of Saints omitted from the Nicene Creed?

It was never in the Nicene Creed. It is not older than the fifth century, and is only found in Latin creeds. It appears in the Quicunque Vult, which is also of Latin origin.

### 303. What is meant by "he descended into hell"? What is the scriptural authority for it? Why do Episcopalians say it?

When our Saviour died His human spirit, like those of other men, went into the condition of spirits without bodies. This is a lower condition: therefore we say "descended," as when we say "ascended into heaven" we mean going into a higher condition. (The "highest" grade in a school need not be on the top floor.) By "hell" is here meant Hades, the condition of departed spirits. The Apostles' Creed, in which these words are found, is common to all Western Christians. The same words are found in the so-called Athanasian Creed, which is recognized by Eastern Christians. There are four passages of Scripture upon which these words are based: "To day shalt thou be with me in paradise" (St. Luke 23:43); "His [Christ's] soul was not left in hell [Hades]" (Acts 2:31); "he also descended into the lower parts of the earth" (Eph. 4:9) (this is the usual interpretation but another is possible); and, "He went and preached unto the spirits in prison" (I Peter 3:19). The last of these is the chief authority.

### 304. What is the opinion of the Church on Purgatory?

The doctrine of Purgatory, which is peculiar to the Roman Communion, has three sources:

(1) The need for souls to be cleansed from their bad habits (which may be painful, but not in a physical sense, for they will have no bodies). This is a probable opinion, held by many of the ancient writers (see Question 297).

(2) The alleged visions of St. Gregory the Great, who suffered badly from nightmares (probably due to his poor digestion)

which he took for Divine revelations. He saw souls burning in flames, and his visions passed into the traditional teaching of the medieval Latin Church, which found them extremely useful for frightening half-pagan kings, barons, and peasants into decent conduct.

(3) The notion that every sin must be paid for in this world or the next, which comes from Aristotle, and has nothing to do with the gospel.

The last two of these are what is commonly meant by the "Romish doctrine of Purgatory," rejected by the Anglican Churches in Article 22; especially as they are the basis of a colossal system of indulgences or remissions from Purgatory, which have to be paid for and by which the Roman Communion is largely financed. We do not accept any such ideas.

**305. Is Purgatory the same as Paradise?**

No. Paradise, which means a garden, is the state of rest (St. Luke 23:43; II Cor. 12:4). Purgatory, if it exists, is believed to be a condition of torment, as payment due for sin.

**306. What is the Anglican teaching on the Intermediate State?**

**307. What is the difference between the Anglican, Roman, and Nonconformist teaching on the Intermediate State?**

The Anglican tradition, based on Scripture and the ancient writers, is that the baptized pass, immediately on death, to the Particular Judgment, which divides them into the saved and the lost. Both go to Hades, but the saved go to that part of Hades called Paradise, and between them and the others there is a great gulf fixed (St. Luke 16:26). For both groups this is a temporary condition. After the General Judgment, Hades will be destroyed (Rev. 20:14), the saved will go to Heaven and the lost to Hell (St. Matthew 25:46).

The Roman teaching, if I am not mistaken, is that after the Particular Judgment the lost go to Hell (Gehenna) at once. Most of the saved go to Purgatory, which is usually described as a condition of great torment, until their sins are paid for or until they are released from Purgatory by the prayers and Masses offered by the faithful on earth. The souls in Purgatory cannot pray for themselves. The saints and martyrs and a few others go straight to Paradise, which is regarded as the same as Heaven; and those who are released from Purgatory also go there. I am told that the General Resurrection, and the final Judgment, though accepted (for it is an article of the Creed), does not fit well into the scheme (W. P. Witcutt, *Return to Reality*).

The old Calvinists believed that everyone at death went to Heaven if elect, and to Hell if not elect. They rejected the Intermediate State altogether and forbade prayers for the dead, and even prayers at funerals, as useless. What their successors believe, I am not able to say.

**308. What will happen to Jews and other non-Christians, who have not accepted Christ, and those who die unbaptized?**

They will be judged according to their obedience to the law they knew (St. Matthew 25).

**309. Explain the words Paradise, Hades, Hell, Gehenna, Sheol.**

Paradise (garden) is the abode of the blessed dead. Hades, the Greek name for the underworld, is the abode of all the dead (see Questions 305-7). Hell (the hidden place) sometimes in our Bible represents Hades (St. Luke 16:23; Rev. 20:14), as it also does in the Creed; in the Old Testament it represents Sheol. In modern English it is always used in the sense of Gehenna. Gehenna was a valley close to Jerusalem, where bonfires for the destruction of rubbish were always burning. It came to represent the state of permanent separation from God, symbolized by eternal fire (Jude 7). In the New Testament it is translated "hell" (St. Matthew 5:22, 23:15; St. Luke 12:5; James 3:6). Gehenna is regarded as the abode of the devil and his angels (St. Matthew 25:46; Rev. 20:10). Sheol was the Hebrew word for the underworld, the abode of the dead, corresponding to the Greek "Hades." It is often translated "hell" in our Bible (Job 11:8, 26:6; Ps. 9:17, 139:8, etc.; also "the grave" or "the pit" (Ps. 6:5; Ezek. 31:15; Ps. 88:4, etc.) Hebrew belief about it is clearly shown by Isaiah 38:18; it was not a place of happiness or torment but a sort of shadowy half-life. Belief in a future life hardly appears before the Book of Daniel (second century B.C.).

**310. What does the Church teach about Hell, the Intermediate State, Paradise, Purgatory, and Heaven?**

See Questions 304-7. Hell is the state of permanent separation from God. Heaven is the state of permanent union with Him, and enjoyment of the Beatific Vision (Rev. 22:1-5).

**311. Are there several stages of Hell? Is one mortal sin as bad as several?**

One mortal sin is enough to separate us from God, if it is not followed by repentance. A *course* of mortal sin is harder to repent of than a single act of mortal sin. It seems that permanent separation from God, which is the meaning of Hell, is such that nothing could be worse.

**312. What does the Church teach about the Last Judgment, the Resurrection of the Body, and the Millennium?**

For the Resurrection of the Body see Question 300. The Last, or General, Judgment, to be distinguished from the Particular Judgment, is to take place when this world is brought to an end. It is described in symbolic pictures in St. Matthew 25:31 and Revelations 20:12 (see also I Thess. 4:16; I Cor. 15:24). The theory of the Millennium is based on Revelations 20:2,3. St. Augustine thought that this obscure passage was a prophecy of the age that was to follow the conversion of the Roman Empire. It is not a satisfactory explanation, but there is no better one. It certainly does not mean a future golden age in this world; a notion which is contrary to our Lord's warning that we must always expect suffering in this world (St. Matthew 5:11; St. Mark 10:30; St. John 15:20), and which has been rejected by the Church. Since human nature will always be subjected to original sin, if a golden age were to appear, it would at once be corrupted; the golden age which we expect is in another world (Heb. 13:14; Rev. 21:1). It was because of this difficult passage (Rev. 20:2–3) that the Revelation was for a long time kept out of the Canon of Scripture. It is best to say frankly that we do not know what this passage means, and to leave it alone. Optimism about human nature, to which Americans are peculiarly liable, as the English were in the Victorian age, is connected with the Pelagianism which is the besetting error of both nations. The Christian should be neither an optimist nor a pessimist: without God we can do nothing, with His grace everything.

**313. Has the Church a hard and fast doctrine of eternal punishment?**

The Church cannot have a "hard and fast doctrine" on so mysterious a subject. In any case, punishment is not the right word. The purpose of punishment is to reform the offender; in this case no reform is possible. What we can say is that if we have free will we have the power to prefer evil to good, and to go on doing so until we cease to choose good. If we do that we cannot come into the presence of God. The appalling possibility of permanent separation from God lies before each one of us, and there is ample scriptural authority for this (St. Mark 3:29, 9:43, 14:21; St. Matthew 25:41; I Peter 4:18; Heb. 6:4, etc.). We need not believe in eternal torture, for which the only authority is Revelation 20:10 (probably from a Jewish source), and which is contrary to God's revealed character. Elsewhere the fire, not the punishment, is called eternal; and the fire is a symbol of destruction, not material fire. We dare not say that any particular person will be in Hell, or even that anyone at all will be there, but we are not to forget that any of us may be there. God condemns no one to Hell. He has done everything possible to save us. If we go there, it will be entirely our own fault. But we are forbidden by the Bible and the Church, by revelation and by reason, to believe that everybody will go to Heaven as a matter of course.

**314. What does the third chapter of Genesis teach us about original sin, the second coming of Christ, and judgment?**

See Questions 60, 72. Genesis, taken by itself, tells us nothing on these subjects. Original sin is a formula based on St. Paul's interpretation of Genesis, and on the facts of human nature which we can see for ourselves. Genesis is an earlier stage of revelation. "He shall bruise thy head, and thou shalt bruise his heel" (Gen. 3:15) is understood by the Church as a prophecy of our Saviour's death and resurrection. It has no reference to His second coming.

**315. Why should I pray to the saints? How can they read my mind? If they know all that happens on earth, how can they be happy in Heaven?**

We have no doubt at all that the saints pray for us. I knew a saintly priest who on his deathbed said to his friends, "I have always prayed for you, and I shall not stop doing so when I am no longer with you." But we do not know whether the saints can hear us if we speak to them. Scripture tells us nothing about it. The Anglican Communion does not address the saints in public worship; those who wish to address them in private are free to do so; those who do not wish it are not compelled to. In any case, we must not ask the saints for anything but their prayers; they can give us nothing else, as far as we know. According to our interpretation of Scripture, the saints are not in Heaven until after the General Resurrection (see Question 296). We do not know how much the saints are permitted to learn about what goes on here. It is possible that our troubles appear to them in a different light, like the troubles of children to grown-up people.

**316. What are we to believe about the saints, compared with Romanist teaching?**

The Roman dogmas are as follows: "There is a Purgatory, and the souls therein detained are assisted by the offering of Mass and by the prayers of the faithful. The saints reigning with Christ are to be venerated and invoked: they offer prayers to God for us, and their relics are to be venerated."

Along with this the Romanists have inherited from the Middle Ages a mass of tradition and custom, and have added to it. We do not think we ought to believe anything about the saints which is not in accordance with Scripture and true history. Some of the most popular saints, such as St. Christopher, St. Margaret, and St. Ursula, probably never existed at all. We honor and venerate all real saints (but not necessarily all who have been canonized at Rome). We think that their relics, if genuine, ought to be treated with due respect, but we doubt whether the cult of relics has any religious value, and we do not think it necessary or desirable to enclose relics in an altar or to expose them for the veneration of the faithful. We entirely reject the suggestion that God is more willing to grant our prayers than He would otherwise be if they are presented through a saint. We have no doubt that the saints pray for us, but we do not continually ask them to do so.

**317. May we ask the Blessed Virgin and the saints to pray for us?**

Yes, if you think they can hear you. Some of us are of the opinion that it is a better use of time to pray direct to God, Who has promised to hear us, and to ask Him to give us our share in the prayers of the saints.

**318. What does the Church teach about saints who are supposed to have jurisdiction over lost articles, professions, travel, etc.?**

All such ideas are remains of paganism, and are not to be taken seriously. Practices based upon them are what our Article 22 condemns as the Romish doctrine of Invocation of Saints.

## Chapter Twenty-One

# MORALS

**319. I object to confession in the services. What about all the really nice people who never commit any sins?**

Our Saviour does not call us to be "nice" but to be perfect (St. Matthew 5:48). Those who are not trying, with His help, to be perfect, are serving the devil (St. Matthew 6:24), however "nice" they may appear to be (I Sam. 16:7). No human being is free from committing sins (Rom. 3:23). Few of us pass a day without thoughts, if not words and deeds, of pride, envy, lust, sloth, or anger. The necessary first step on the road to Heaven is repentance, and the only alternative is the road to Hell. The one class for which our Saviour Himself could do nothing was the persons who thought they had never committed any sins (St. Mark 2:17; St. Luke 18:9) and were considered "nice" by their neighbors.

**320. Of what use to us is St. Thomas Aquinas in the field of moral theology?**

What St. Thomas says is always worthy of study, for he was one of the greatest and holiest thinkers of the Church. However, he lived in the thirteenth century, and many of our problems were unknown to him. His interpretation of Scripture often seems to us quite fantastic, and he knew no Greek or Hebrew, in which tongues the Bible was written. He regarded the pagan philosopher Aristotle with great veneration; but since Aristotle knew nothing of such peculiarly Christian virtues as charity and humility, St. Thomas was sometimes misled by him, and is not always to be trusted: as when he wrote that one of the joys of the blessed in Heaven was to contemplate the tortures of the damned in Hell (see also Question 524).

**321. Can you supply a list of books on Moral Theology and Ethics written by Anglicans?**

The following are the books which I have found most useful. Those marked with an asterisk are, in my opinion, the most important:

Kirk, K. E.: *Some Principles of Moral Theology**
Kirk, K. E.: *Conscience and Its Problems*
Kirk, K. E.: *The Vision of God*
Kirk, K. E.: *Ignorance, Faith and Conformity*
Hall, F. J., and Hallock, F. H.: *Moral Theology**
Green, Peter: *Problem of Right Conduct**
Mortimer, R. C.: *Elements of Moral Theology*
McAdoo, H.: *Structure of Caroline Moral Theology*
Gore, Charles: *Philosophy of the Good Life*

**322. When there are two apparently equal alternatives, how can one discern which is God's Will?**

First pray for guidance and ask others to pray for you. Then consult the wisest and most disinterested persons you know, and who know you well. Then put down in writing the arguments on each side and compare them, trying to see not what you wish to do but what is right. Then make up your mind and, having made it up, stick to it, right or wrong, unless some new element comes in which was not there before or that you did not know before. It is often better to make the wrong decision than not to be able to make a decision at all. Sometimes, but not always, the right course is to wait until God makes His Will clear.

**323. Since the Christian faith frees us from fear, why is there so much restlessness and tension when we practice it?**

I cannot answer this without knowing the circumstances. Consult your spiritual director. If the tension is in ourselves, perhaps we have not enough faith and ought to pray for more. If it is in others, perhaps they belong to that very large class of people who cannot bear to see anyone serving God better than they are willing to do themselves; as our Lord foretold: "Suppose ye that I am come to send peace on earth? I tell you, Nay; but rather division" (St. Luke 12:51).

**324. Why is it a mortal sin if I miss Mass on a Sunday or Holy Day?**

That is the Roman rule. We should put it rather differently.

It is the duty of all members of the Church who have been well taught, and have not a good reason for being absent, to be present at the Eucharist every Sunday, and at least on Christmas Day and Ascension Day, and to go to church on Good Friday (when the Eucharist is not celebrated). The Lord's Day, which has nothing to do with the Sabbath, was instituted that we might fulfill our Lord's command, "Do this in remembrance of me." The assembling of ourselves together, which we are forbidden to forsake (Heb. 10:25), can only mean the Eucharist for then there was no other Christian assembly, as far as we know. If you are absent, without some really good reason, you are committing a sin, for you are refusing our Saviour's invitation (St. Luke 14:18). Whether it is "mortal" depends on your motive. If you were to stay away deliberately, out of hatred or contempt for God or your neighbor (your priest, for instance), it might be mortal sin. But spiritual, like bodily, health depends on forming good habits. It ought to be your fixed habit to go to the Eucharist on Sunday. Every time you stay away without good reason you weaken the habit. Just as, if you eat too much, or don't take enough exercise, you weaken your body and make it more susceptible to disease, so, if you constantly commit even "venial" sins, you weaken your spiritual life, and when some sudden temptation, to which we are all liable, attacks you, you will probably fall. Therefore, don't stay away from Mass if you can avoid doing so.

**325. Are the Ten Commandments binding on Christians? If so, why do we ignore the Fourth and Seventh?**

The Ten Commandments are not only binding on Christians, but binding much more strictly (St. Matthew 5). The Fourth Commandment bids us keep all days holy; the working days by doing all that we have to do as for God's service, and the Lord's Day by taking part in the Holy Eucharist and using the rest of the day so as to serve Him best. The Seventh Commandment bids us avoid not only deeds but words and thoughts of impurity, luxury, and self-indulgence, to keep our bodies in temperance, soberness, and chastity (Office of Instruction).

**326. How can we determine whether evil thoughts are sin or temptation?**

None of us can help having evil thoughts. They become sin

only when we yield to them, take pleasure in them, or encourage them.

**327. What are the minimum requirements in discipline and life for a Christian?**

There are no minimum requirements; we are commanded to be perfect as our Father in heaven is perfect (St. Matthew 5:48). "Do all thou canst: high Heaven rejects the love, of nicely calculated less or more."

**328. How can we be optimistic and feel that the world is good when so many are hungry? Ought not our society, as Christians, do all it can to help others less fortunate?**

We are not told to be optimistic, and our society is not Christian, or only very partially so. Certainly we ought to keep the multitudes of the hungry and other unfortunate people, including those who are spiritually hungry because they have not heard the gospel, always in our minds.

**329. Is it my duty as a Christian to hurt a friend in order to defend the Christian faith?**

Do you mean to hurt his feelings, or to knock him down, or to do him a permanent injury? I cannot answer this question without knowing the circumstances. If it is your duty to defend the Christian faith, you may have to hurt many people's feelings; and it might do them a great deal of good, by making them think.

**330. How can the Church justify war?**

**331. What is the Church's theological answer to the question of pacifism?**

War is always a horrible evil, not only in itself but by the passions which it arouses and the injury that it does to the souls and bodies of multitudes for whom our Saviour died. No one ought to glorify war, to throw glamour round it, or to conceal how vile it is. But it is not the greatest of all possible evils. Therefore it may, in certain cases, be the lesser of two evils. We cannot say that Isaiah was wrong in advising Hezekiah to refuse the Assyrian demand for surrender (II Kings 19:20–34) or that Mattathias and his sons were wrong to revolt against Antiochus Epiphanes (I Macc. 2:1–28); if they had not done so, the true religion would probably have perished from the earth. Archbishop Temple held that pacifism was a heresy. The Church has always taught that self-defense is our duty; that if our country is attacked, especially by those who wish to destroy the Church, it is our duty to resist. Even complete destruction would be better than conquest by atheistic Communists, and slavery to their secret police. Further, if our country is at war and calls us to serve, we are bound to obey. It is not fair that, while others are risking their lives for our safety, we should do nothing. The English Article 37, omitted by the American Church, says: "It is lawful for Christian men, at the command of the magistrates, to wear weapons, and serve in wars." But a priest or a surgeon ought not to serve as a combatant, because he has a special vocation in which he can be much more useful. No one in wartime ought to hate the enemy; we are bound to love them and to pray for them (St. Matthew 5:44).

**332. What does the Church teach about human sterilization and insemination, and the doctors' responsibility for them?**

They are not permitted to Christians.

**333. Is it right for Christians to use contraceptives?**

No (see Question 280).

**334. What is the Church's teaching on planned parenthood and birth control?**

The Divine gift of sex is to be used by married people with moderation and self-control. They ought to have as many children as is consistent with the mother's health and strength. Those who suffer from hereditary diseases or are in any way unfit to have children ought not to marry, but to live single and chaste.

**335. Is smoking right in the sight of God? (A priest does not smoke in the sanctuary.)**

The sanctuary is reserved for the worship of God. It should not be used for any other purpose, however innocent. Like most Europeans, I cannot imagine why anyone should think smoking a sin; this notion appears to be an eccentricity of some American sects. But the smoker ought not to allow himself to become the slave of this or any other habit. He ought to be able to stop smoking at any time without discomfort, and without becoming irritable. The fast days of the Church are useful for this purpose. He ought not to smoke so heavily as to injure his health (it is now believed that cigarette smoking might induce cancer) nor to smoke in such a way as to annoy his neighbors, for many people dislike the smell intensely. He should consider whether the money he spends on smoking might not be better spent, to the glory of God and the benefit of His people.

**336. What is the Christian's relation to financial security as given by insurance, possessions, etc.?**

Nothing in this world is secure. The seeker for security should consider the parable of the Rich Fool (St. Luke 12:16–21). But the Christian is fully justified in providing, by insurance and by honest investment, against the chances of the world, for himself and his family, provided he remembers that all he has is a trust from God, to be used for His glory and the benefit of His people. He must not, then, refuse to give to those who need it, on the ground that he must have the money to make his future secure. Lay not up for yourselves treasures upon earth, but lay it up in heaven; for where your treasure is, there will your heart be also (see St. Matthew 6:19–21).

**337. May one tell senile persons lies in order to soothe them when they become agitated?**

It is always better to tell the truth, unless to do so will lead to serious harm. People who are too senile to understand what is going on round them cannot always be told the truth. This is a question to which no general answer can be given. Old people are sometimes tougher than one might think, and tend to be suspicious; if they find that you have been deceiving them, they will never again believe anything you say. People who are going to die soon ought to be told that death is near; no one ought to die unprepared, even if it means living a few days longer.

*Chapter  Twenty-Two*

# WORSHIP AND LITURGICAL CUSTOMS

**338. What is Christian worship?**

The honor, praise, and thanksgiving which is due from all human beings to Almighty God. (It was also formerly used of honor given to man, especially of the act of prostration com-

monly done before superiors in the East—Dan. 2:46; St. Matthew
15:25; St. John 9:38; Acts 10:25—usually by heathen or unin-
structed persons.) Worship of God may be private, or public
and corporate; it may be vocal or silent; it includes prayer, meditation, and contemplation.

**339. How did the custom of public prayer arise, in view of
St. Matthew 6:5–7? Was the "Our Father" meant to be a public
group prayer?**

There have always been both public and private prayers (see
I Kings 8:22; Neh. 9:5, etc., for the former; I Sam. 1:12; II Kings
20:2; Neh. 2:4; Dan. 6:10, for the latter). The ancients lived much
more in public than we do. "Our Father" might be said either
corporately or privately.

**340. What do we really pray for when we say, "Thy kingdom
come, Thy will be done on earth, as it is in heaven"?**

The words "on earth as it is in heaven" apply to each of the
three clauses before them. We pray that our own wills, and those
of all Christians and of all human beings, may obey God and do
His Will as completely as the angels do. We are not to expect
that our prayer will be completely fulfilled in this world, and
therefore we pray that God will bring this world to an end when
the time comes, and replace it with a new world, in which there
will be no more disobedience to His Will (Rev. 21:1, 22:20).

**341. What is the best explanation of "Lead us not into tempta-
tion, but deliver us from evil"?**

We pray that God will protect us when we fall into temptation.
We have to be tempted, but we pray that temptation may not
be too strong for us. "Evil" is personal here; it means the Evil
One, that is, the devil.

**342. What is the place of music in Church worship? How is it
related to individual worship?**

Music has always played a large part in the worship of God,
both public and private (Ex. 15:1; Judge. 5:1; Ps. 57:9, etc.).
The congregation ought to take part in the singing of praise to
God: especially in the Creeds, which are great acts of corporate
worship. We should also, if we can, sing in our private worship
(Acts 16:25) but without disturbing our neighbors.

**343. Why does not the Episcopal Church follow the teaching
of the ancient Church in rites and ceremonies?**

In all necessary rites and ceremonies it does, but rites and ceremonies differ in different ages and in different countries. The ancient Church did not use the same rites and ceremonies everywhere, nor do we. Climates and national habits of life differ.

**344. Why do Episcopalians have to do so much kneeling?**

The normal rule is to stand for praise (Neh. 9:5), to kneel for prayer (St. Luke 22:41; Acts 7:60, 9:40, 20:36), and to sit to listen to instruction. The Hebrew teacher sat down himself (St. Luke 4:20). The ancients also stood for prayer (as the priest does at the altar) (see Ex. 3:5, 17:9). We probably kneel too much, for no other body of Christians kneels so much as we do. At a celebration of the Holy Communion, we stand up for the Gospel (which is the universal practice, to honor the Gospel), at "Lift up your hearts" until the end of the hymn "Holy, Holy, Holy," and for "Glory be to God on high." Standing is always a proper posture for prayer, but it is not our usual custom. We should never sit for prayer, unless we are old or sick, and when we kneel we should go down on both knees, bolt upright, in the shape of an L, not of an S.

**345. What is the authority for the Episcopal Prayer Book?**

The liturgy, sacraments, and offices in the Prayer Book are for the most part those of the Universal Church. The particular "Use," or form in which they are to be used, has the authority of the General Convention, the highest authority in the Episcopal Church. In all Anglican Churches, the Province or National Church is the supreme authority in liturgical matters, within the limits set by the Church Universal in such matters as the necessary conditions of the sacraments. In the ancient Church each local Church had its own liturgy.

**346. If the clergy were more familiar with the Preface, would they be more inclined to observe the ancient practices of the Church?**

They certainly ought to study the Preface carefully.

**347. Why "bowing and scraping"?**

To "bow" is a universal sign of honor to men and reverence toward God. To "scrape" is to make an awkward bow, drawing one foot back. There is ample authority in the Bible for bowing the knees (Is. 45:23, quoted in Rom. 14:11; Eph. 3:14; Phil. 2:10, "at the name of Jesus"), the head, and in some cases the whole body, not only to God but also to man (I Sam. 24:8; II Sam. 1:2, 18:21; St. Luke 24:5). It is usual to bow to the altar, as the throne of God, on entering and leaving a church or when passing in front of it; to bow at the Name of Jesus, especially in the creeds; to put one knee to the ground at the words, "The Word was made flesh" (St. John 1:14) and "Jesus gave up the ghost" (that is, died—St. Mark 15:37, St. Matthew 27:50; St. Luke 23:46; St. John 19:30). The server, when giving anything to the priest, makes a slight bow which the priest acknowledges with another. Anyone who is censed with incense acknowledges it with a slight bow. Anyone who is being blessed kneels down or at least bows his head. All these are rules of courtesy. Such customs help to increase that reverence which we owe to God, and to any person or thing employed in worship. To object to observing them shows a lack of humility, and even of good manners (see Article 34).

**348. Why do we use two versions of the Lord's Prayer?**

The shorter one, which is probably the original one, is from St. Luke 11:2–4. The other, to which the act of praise was added very early, is from St. Matthew 6:9–13.

**349. Why were the last verses of the Venite omitted from the American Prayer Book? Why is "adorable" read in the Te Deum for "honorable"? Why is Benedictus es, Domine not in the English Prayer Book as an alternative to the Te Deum?**

I should think the last verses of the Venite were omitted from the American Prayer Book, as in the English Revised Prayer Book of 1928, through a "liberal," but quite unscriptural, objection to mentioning the wrath of God (Rom. 2:8; I Thess. 2:16; Rev. 6:16). "Adorable" is a more accurate translation of the Latin "venerandum" than "honorable"; but it spoils the rhythm of the English. "Benedictus es, Domine," which is the first part of the Benedicite, from the Song of the Three Children, has never been in the English Prayer Book; the Revised Book of 1928 uses Psalm 51 for this purpose.

**350. Why is the Te Deum put after the First Lesson rather than after the Second Lesson?**

The Te Deum is sung after the First Lesson to show that the promises of the Old Testament were fulfilled by our Saviour. The Benedictus, or Song of Zacharias, is sung after the Second

Lesson as an act of praise for the fulfillment of God's promises. It is the climax of Morning Prayer, as it was in the old service of Lauds, and should never on any pretext be omitted. The Jubilate was inserted in the Second Prayer Book to satisfy Bucer's craze for avoiding repetition. It was intended to be used only when Benedictus occurred in the Second Lesson or in the Gospel. In my opinion Jubilate, as a canticle, should be swept away; and likewise Cantate and Deus misereatur.

**351. What is the meaning of the Apostles' Creed?**

There was a tradition, rejected by modern scholars, that it was written by the twelve Apostles; each wrote one clause. In reality it is the old baptismal creed in use at Rome.

**352. What steps are being taken to enrich the liturgy?**

To enrich the liturgy always means to make it more complicated, and more difficult for simple people, unaccustomed to handling books. The Archbishops of Canterbury and York appointed in 1954 a Commission on Prayer Book Revision. It issued a report in 1957, which was considered by the Lambeth Conference, together with a similar report issued by the Church of the Province of India, Burma, Pakistan, and Ceylon. In looking forward to some future revision of the Prayer Book, the American Church has published a series of *Prayer Book Studies*, in which old and new liturgical customs and practices are weighed and considered.

**353. What is the reason for the contemplated changes in the Order for Holy Communion?**

I can see no reason for any change in the American liturgy, except that the permission to omit the Nicene Creed and the permission to use the Apostles' Creed instead of it should be withdrawn, and "Bishops, and other Ministers" should read, "Bishops, Priests, and Deacons, especially Thy servant *N.* our Bishop," which would bring the Episcopal Church into line with the usual practice of the Church in both ancient and modern times.

**354. What is a Missal used for? Is it approved by the Church?**

The Missal, strictly speaking, is the book containing the text of the Roman Mass, to be used by the priest at the altar. In the Anglican Churches the word is sometimes used for the altar book, containing the text of the Communion Service from the Prayer Book, with the proper Collects, Epistles, and Gospels. Such a book with large print is required by the priest; he need not then take the whole Prayer Book to the altar. The use of altar cards is most objectionable and ought to be abolished.

But the word "Missal" also sometimes means a book containing the Prayer Book rite, mixed up with many prayers and other formulas from the Roman liturgy. Such books are most undesirable and should be forbidden by the bishops. The "English Missal" is open to serious criticism on theological grounds, and the translations from the Latin are in very poor English. In any case, in no other part of the Church is a priest allowed to use at the altar anything but the text of the rite as authorized by the Church. If he wishes to use any private devotions, he must learn them by heart. The prayers, etc., of the Roman, or any other, Missal have no authority in the Anglican Communion.

**355. What is the meaning of signing the Cross on forehead, lips, and heart, before the reading of the Gospel? What is the origin and meaning of crossing oneself? Is the sign of the Cross allowed in Episcopal Churches?**

It is an ancient practice, signifying that we belong to Christ. It is allowed, and very common, in Anglican Churches. The reader of the Gospel crosses himself to consecrate his mind, mouth, and will for what he is going to do, and asks God to bless his reading to the benefit of the people (see Question 366).

**356. How and when did the practice of daily Communion begin?**

Acts 2:46 is interpreted by some as evidence of daily Communion in the apostolic age. There is no other evidence of it until after the Roman Empire became officially Christian in the fourth century. It is mentioned by St. Augustine, St. John Chrysostom, and others toward the end of that century, but it was not a universal custom. No one has ever been allowed to receive Communion more than once a day, except a priest who has to celebrate more than once, for he must communicate himself whenever he celebrates, otherwise the Eucharist is not valid. In the East no priest is allowed to celebrate more than once in a day in any circumstances. The daily Communion was revived in the Church of England at St. Peter's, Plymouth, by G. R. Prynne, during the cholera epidemic of 1850.

**357. How and when was the Nicene Creed changed from "We believe" to "I believe"?**

When it began, in the fourth century, to be signed by individuals as a test of orthodoxy.

**358. Why is Communion held at night only once a year, when it was celebrated at night in the Upper Room?**

The hour of celebrating was in the early morning as early as the second century. St. Augustine, in the fourth century, believed that to communicate fasting was a custom instituted by the Apostles. The Midnight Mass at Christmas was celebrated at the first moment of the day, which was considered to begin at midnight. People went to bed with the sun, rose for the midnight service, and spent the rest of the night in devotions of various kinds. The modern practice of treating this service as a very late evening Communion, after which people go to bed, is criticized on several grounds. When I was working in Dublin, the Romanists had few or no midnight Masses, because they did not want their young people on the streets at night. To spend a long day ending perhaps with a heavy supper, and then to go to Communion, appears to me to be a most unedifying practice. It is much better to spend the evening quietly, go to bed early, and come to Christmas Communion in the early morning.

**359. Why is the Second Commandment different in the Roman and Lutheran Churches from that in the Episcopal and other Protestant Churches?**

The words "Churches" and "Protestant" are here used in a most inaccurate sense. There is only one Church, of which the Roman and Anglican Communions are constituent parts. The Episcopal Church is not "Protestant" in the sense in which the sects are (see Questions 137–39). Most ancient Christian writers distinguished the Second Commandment, which forbids the worship of graven images, in honor of the true God (like the golden calves—Ex. 32:4; I Kings 12:28), from the First, which forbids the worship of false gods. This arrangement is followed by all the Eastern Churches and by the Anglican Communion; also by the sects in the tradition of Calvin. The Roman Communion unites the first two Commandments, and divides the Tenth into two; this arrangement seems to have been introduced by St. Augustine, and is followed by all Lutherans. Hence the numbering varies. What we call the Fifth Commandment, "Honor thy father and thy mother," Romanists and Lutherans call the Fourth; "Thou shalt not covet thy neighbor's house" is distinguished by them from "Thou shalt not covet thy neighbor's wife." Our arrangement is generally held to be the older.

**360. In the Nicene Creed, explain "All things visible and invisible"; "Very God"; "one Baptism." What is the background of this creed? How is it related to the Apostles' Creed?**

"All things visible and invisible" means all things whatever, whether they can be seen or not; whether they are material, like bodies or stones, or spiritual, like the souls of men, or love, fear, and honor. "Very God" means true God. "One Baptism" means that there is only one entrance into the Church, by being baptized with water in the Name of the Father, the Son, and the Holy Ghost, which conveys forgiveness of sins to those who receive it with repentance and faith or at least, in the case of infants, without any refusal to repent and believe. The Nicene Creed was the old baptismal creed of Caesarea in Palestine, to which the Council of Nicaea, 325, added the words "of one substance with the Father" to exclude those who believed that our Lord was a created being. The end of the creed, after the words "Holy Ghost," was added by the Council of Chalcedon in 451. This creed was written in Greek. The Apostles' Creed, which is the old baptismal creed of Rome with some additions, was written in Latin and is still not known in the East, whereas the Nicene Creed is universal.

**361. Has our young priest a right always to omit the Nicene Creed, the Ten Commandments, and the presentation of the alms?**

According to the American Prayer Book, the Nicene Creed must be recited on Christmas Day, Easter Day, Ascension Day, Whitsunday, and Trinity Sunday. It may be omitted on other days but only if the Apostles' Creed has been recited in Morning Prayer just before. In my opinion the Nicene Creed should never be omitted. The more we recite it the better. The Ten Commandments must be recited once a month at least. When they are omitted, the Summary of the Law and the threefold "Lord, have mercy" must take their place. (Personally, I would never use the Summary of the Law if I could help it, on the ground that it has not for modern ears the decisiveness, the "bite" of the Ten Commandments.) The priest is bound to present alms and place them on the altar.

The priest is bound by his ordination vows to obey the rubrics of the Prayer Book. Otherwise he is guilty of contumacy, conceit, and contempt for his own solemn promise. An Orthodox Eastern dignitary said to a friend of mine, "Never set up to be wiser than the Church to which you belong": words which might well be set up in letters of gold in every Anglican sacristy.

**362. What is the difference between the alms and oblations?**

It seems that originally the oblations were the money paid for church expenses, distinguished from the alms for the poor. But now they are commonly understood to mean the bread and wine, while the alms refer to all the offerings in money.

**363. Who is "he that cometh" in "Blessed is he that cometh in the Name of the Lord"? Christ or the celebrant? Is not Christ Himself the Lord?**

See St. Mark 11:9. Of course Christ is He that cometh in the Name of the Lord, that is, of God the Father. But there does not seem to be any authority in the American rite for using these words. They ought to be omitted unless the rite is altered. If it is altered, "Glory be to Thee, O Lord most high" should be changed to "Hosanna in the highest."

**364. What do we mean by "all other benefits of his passion"?**

All that we receive, besides forgiveness of sins, through the sufferings (passion) and resurrection of our Saviour: all the grace that is to make us fit for union with God.

**365. What do we mean by ablutions? What is their purpose?**

Before the priest leaves the altar after celebrating the Eucharist, he must wash the vessels with wine and water, and drink the wine and water in which he has washed them. The purpose of this ceremony is to make certain that every crumb and drop of the consecrated elements is consumed.

**366. Why is the sign of the Cross used at the end of the Creeds and in certain other places and not elsewhere? Why don't our rubrics tell us where to cross ourselves?**

The sign of the Cross is an outward token that we are Christ's soldiers and servants. It is not specifically ordered in the Anglican Churches, except at Baptism; to use it at other times is entirely a matter of personal choice. At the end of the Creeds, before the Gospel, and in certain other places, it is directed in the Romanist books, which have no authority for us. We cross ourselves after

the Creed and before the Gospel to signify that we accept the
Creed for ourselves and that we pledge ourselves to listen to the
Gospel (see Question 355).

367. Why does the priest put in salt when he blesses holy
water?

Salt has always been regarded as an emblem of purity and
cleansing (II Kings 2:21; St. Matthew 5:13). But there is no
Anglican authority for using holy water.

368. Why do we not obey our Lord's command to wash one
another's feet on Maundy Thursday?

To wash the feet of the guest was the duty of a host in our
Lord's time. It no longer has any meaning for us, since we do
not wear sandals. If we regarded this command as literally binding
we should not be distinguishing between symbols and their meaning. The command is to be understood spiritually; we are to
treat all men, especially the poor, as we would our guests.

369. Why do some prayers end with "through Jesus Christ
our Lord" and others not?

All prayers to the Father or the Holy Spirit should end with
these or similar words. When they are not said they are to be
understood. "No man cometh unto the Father, but by me" (St.
John 14:6).

370. "Provoking most justly thy wrath and indignation against
us": does this mean that we deserve God's wrath, which He
withholds because of His mercy?

Yes: and because His Son has died and risen again to reconcile
us to Him (see Question 348).

371. Why does our Church have so many different seasons
to observe?

From Advent to Trinity we praise God for the different
Mysteries of our salvation. The Sundays after Trinity have their
own moral lessons. The Holy Days commemorate the great
servants of God. Every religion has its festival days; even secular
states have their national days. We have so much for which to
praise God that we need every day in the year for it: and every
day has its own saints, though we do not commemorate them
all.

372. Why does the Church no longer publish banns?

In England the publication of banns is required by law, unless
a license from the bishop has been obtained, and the priest who

would celebrate a marriage without banns or license would be sent to prison. In the United States the publishing of banns is not generally required by civil law, but the practice is increasing. The announcement in church of a forthcoming marriage is far more Christian than an announcement in a secular newspaper. The Solemnization of Holy Matrimony is a religious service, not a social event.

**373. Why does not the Order for the Burial of the Dead provide for a sermon?**

Because the Burial Office is sufficient and a sermon at a funeral is quite unnecessary. Protestants emphasize preaching, and since few of them have any form of ordered rites and ceremonies, such as the Book of Common Prayer and the "Order for the Burial of the Dead" they feel compelled "to say something," hence a sermon at their burials. The purpose of a Christian burial is to commend the departed soul to the love and mercy of God, and to commit the body to the earth in as dignified and Christian a manner as possible, and the Church's form and manner of doing so is the same for all her children.

**374. Are fraternal bodies and organizations allowed any part in the Church's Order for the Burial of the Dead? Why?**

They have no share in the rite, because the Prayer Book does not permit it and because their services are unnecessary. Just as the Church performs all her rites and ceremonies without the assistance of fraternal orders, it allows for no such assistance at a burial. Fraternal and lodge burial services are happily dying out, because their members are busy with other matters and because the nature of their services is often unchristian and the manner of their performance unedifying. Whatever they do must be done at a time and place apart from the Church's own services.

**375. Why is the coffin closed during a funeral?**

In all her rites and ceremonies the Church insists on common decency and orderliness. As was pointed out above, the purpose of a burial is to commend the departed soul to God's care and to commit the body to the ground, not to exhibit a mortician's art or provoke inordinate outbursts of grief and confusion. The opening of a coffin at a funeral is unheard of in England, as far as I know.

**376. What is the attitude of the Episcopal Church toward cremation?**

It is allowed, and often practiced. The ashes must be decently buried and not "scattered" (which is a pagan custom). The English Church makes special provision for cremation in the rite.

**377. What is the meaning of Shrove Tuesday and Maundy Thursday?**

To shrive is to hear a penitent's confession and absolve him. Shrove Tuesday was the day when people made their confessions before Lent. Maundy Thursday is the day on which our Lord gave His commandment, "That ye love one another, as I have loved you" (St. John 15:12).

**378. Are there any rules in the Episcopal Church against the Maundy Thursday watch before the Altar of Repose?**

There appears to be no Anglican authority for it. If we are to use the Reserved Sacrament for the purpose of Communion only, such a custom is ruled out. However, this is a highly disputable question which cannot be discussed here. I should myself be opposed to any such custom, as tending to encourage the false belief that our Lord is locally present in the consecrated elements or that He is there for any purpose other than for sacrifice and Communion (see Question 253).

*Chapter Twenty-Three*

# RELIGIOUS COMMUNITIES

**379. Tell us about religious orders.**

The "religious life" is a special vocation to give one's life wholly to God, without the distractions of family and property. Those who receive this call from God are accepted into a community, or order. No one can be sure that he or she has received this call unless and until it has been approved by such a community, recognized and regulated by the Church; for to enter such a life without such approval is dangerous and should never be attempted. There is a large number of religious orders in the Anglican Communion throughout the world. The *Episcopal Church Annual 1959* lists eleven for men and fifteen for women. Most orders are "active," engaged in teaching, nursing, parish work, etc. A few are "contemplative," giving themselves wholly to prayer; vocations to the contemplative life are rare among us. The principal duty of every order, active or contemplative, is the regular daily recitation of the Hours of Prayer. The word "convent" is applied to the house of any order, but now more usually to those for women. Members of religious orders are first received as "postulants"; during this period they may leave at any time. The next stage is to be "clothed" as a novice, by a formal service. The novitiate may last from one to three years. If the novice still wishes to remain, and is acceptable to the community, he or she is "professed," and takes the three vows of poverty, chastity, and obedience. Poverty means that the man or woman has no private property. It is usual for him or her to have the capital put in trust and to give the interest on it to the community. Celibacy means to abstain from marriage and to live a chaste and single life. Obedience means to observe the Rule of the Community, approved by the bishop or higher Church authority, and to obey the superior in accordance with the rule. The superior is elected by the community, for a period or for life.

**380. Explain the vocation of the religious, and the need for more of them.**

The purpose of a religious order is to live the Christian life more perfectly than it can be lived in the outside world. No one should venture to enter this life unless he or she is certain in his or her own mind that it is God's Will, and that there is no other motive. For this reason no one should take the vows except in an approved religious order. The Religious Orders have always been of great use to the Church. The conversion of the British Isles, and of many other European countries, was due entirely to monks and nuns. But these orders are also liable to various special dangers and need to be controlled strictly. Each community has a visitor, normally the bishop of the diocese or some bishop or priest appointed by him, whose function is to see that the rule is kept, to examine the community at least once a year, and to interview every member in private, in case there is any ground for complaint.

**381. Can a person who has taken life vows ever return to the world?**

The vows of a religious community are either "simple," that is, for a period, usually with a declaration of intention to remain for life, or "solemn," until death. There must be a power of dispensation, because no one is infallible, and there are cases of mistaken vocation. In the Roman Communion, all vows may be "dispensed" by the Pope; in the Anglican Communion, either by the bishop of the diocese or by the metropolitan (archbishop) of the province. A celebrated case of dispensation from vows was that of Erasmus, who was given a dispensation by the Pope. Priests who are members of orders are automatically dispensed from their vows if they are consecrated bishops, their vows are modified or retained unless by special permission.

## Chapter Twenty-Four

# FASTING

**382. How does the Church expect its members to practice fasting and abstinence?**

**383. Does the Church ask its members to observe Friday? How?**

**384. Why the Friday fast?**

We are required to fast in order that we may be better able to control our bodily desires. Friday is appointed as a fasting day in memory of our Saviour's death on the Cross; it is a Good Friday in every week, as the Lord's Day is an Easter Day in every week. We are not given fixed rules, because we are expected to be capable of making them for ourselves. We ought to mark fast days by not doing something harmless, which we like doing, in order that we may be able to do without it. What we do will differ according to our habits, tastes, and conditions; but whatever we do, it should be something, if possible, that is not noticed by our neighbors (St. Matthew 6:16–18). Our Lord said, "when ye fast," showing that He assumed fasting to be a duty. The traditional rule to abstain from meat dates from a time when all fish was salted. It is not fasting to eat delicate fish or vegetable dishes. Habits, to abstain from which on fast days might be a suitable rule for some people, are: chewing gum, eating sweets, taking sugar in tea or coffee, smoking, going to the movies, listening to the radio, or watching television. Some people might get up earlier, go to bed earlier, avoid dances or other entertainments (so far as these things can be done without annoying others or even telling them the reason for so doing). A very good way of fasting is to spend more time in prayer or other devotional exercises. To devote some time to visiting the sick or aged, to give some hard-pressed woman a few hours off by doing her household tasks for her, to perform any act of self-sacrifice for others, as a regular habit, and as thanksgiving to our Lord, is true fasting.

**385. Where can we find Anglican rules for fasting Communion, Holy Days of Obligation, Confession, etc.?**

The Anglican Churches treat their members as grown-up persons, who are expected to make such rules for themselves. The custom of fasting Communion is to receive Communion before eating or drinking anything else that day, in honor of our Lord's Body and Blood. If for any reason you cannot do this, get as near to it as you can. Christmas Day, Good Friday, and Ascension Day should be observed by all Christians as far as possible. If you can go to church on Holy Days, do so. Priests, I think, are bound to communicate on all such days if possible. As to confession to a priest, you are advised to make such a rule as suits you and stick to it (see Questions 254–65).

**386. Why is there so much diversity in fasting, and why so many different attitudes toward divorce?**

As to fasting, see Questions 382–85. Marriage while a divorced partner is alive is called adultery by our Lord. Neither the Church nor any member of it is free to disregard His command (see Questions 273–74).

**387. What Anglican authority is there for keeping the traditional abstinence from flesh meat on Friday?**

The American Prayer Book gives Ash Wednesday and Good Friday as fast days; and the forty days of Lent, the Ember Days at the four seasons, and all Fridays except Christmas Day, the Epiphany, and any Friday falling between them as days of abstinence (I do not know why Fridays in Eastertide should be fast days) (see Questions 382–84).

**388. Why do we not abstain from flesh meat all the days of Lent, as well as Fridays?**

Well, why don't you? There is no rule against doing so. But if it is inconvenient to your neighbors there are several other ways of fasting besides abstaining from meat (see Questions 382–84).

**389. What constitutes a Good Friday or Ash Wednesday fast?**

If you cannot abstain from food all day (which the young and strong could do), at least abstain from one meal, and do not eat anything very pleasant at the others. But it is much more important to go to all the services in your church on those days and to spend as much time as you can in private devotion.

**390. What is the difference between fasting and abstinence?**

Fasting is going without food. Abstinence is eating less food or a less pleasant kind of food. If you eat no dinner you fast. If you eat fish or dry bread instead of meat you practice abstinence. This is the ancient and universal distinction. The Prayer Book, however, does not distinguish sharply between them, but leaves it for us to decide for ourselves. "The Scriptures bid us fast; the Church says, now" (George Herbert).

**391. Why do we fast? Give historical references.**

**392. State, simply and clearly, the Prayer Book's instructions on fasting and abstinence.**

**393. What is our personal duty on days of fasting and abstinence, and on Holy Days?**

See Questions 382–84. If you are able to go to church, especially to the Holy Communion, on all Holy Days, you ought to do so. They were intended to be kept exactly like Sundays. But in the modern secular and industrial world only a few people have the opportunity.

**394. How strict is the Church about fasting before Communion? Should a young priest refuse the sacrament to those who do not fast?**

Whether to observe the ancient and universal custom of fasting before Communion must be decided by everyone for himself. No priest has any right to refuse the sacrament to anyone on such a ground. If he does, you ought to complain to the bishop.

**395. How did Lent develop in the Church?**

The direction to keep Lent is first found in the canons of the First Council of Nicaea, 325. The Greeks fasted for seven weeks, but not on Saturday (except Easter Eve) or Sunday. The Latins fasted for six weeks, but not on Sunday. In both cases the fast lasted for thirty-six days. The Latins added Ash Wednesday and the three days after it in the seventh century.

**396. What are the customs of the Church for observing Lent?**

Customs of observing or keeping Lent have varied down through the centuries, and they still vary in different parts of the world. General Lenten customs are these: marriages are not solemnized (not that the Church frowns on marriages at any time, but on the gaiety that inevitably accompanies them); card parties, dances, etc., are not given or attended; church attendance is increased; a Lenten "rule of life" is adopted; the richer foods are avoided; gala affairs are not attended; television interest is restricted, etc. Church members have not only an obligation to respect and follow Lenten customs but also a duty to supply the proper example to any friends and neighbors who may not even know that Lent has arrived, or is about to arrive, or what it means and implies.

**397. What is the history of Passion Sunday?**

It is an old name for the Fifth Sunday in Lent, because it is the beginning of Passiontide and the first we hear of our Lord's suffering, or passion.

**398. What is the origin and meaning of Ember Days?**

Ember is a corruption of *quatuor tempora*, the four seasons. They were originally pagan feasts of seedtime and harvest, but are now used as days of prayer and fasting for those about to be ordained. They are said to be traced to the third century.

*Chapter Twenty-Five*

# ORNAMENTS OF THE CHURCH AND ITS MINISTERS

**399. Why must a priest dress up like a Christmas tree and insist on being called "Father"?**

Apparently what is meant is the Eucharistic vestments, which are a survival of the dress of the ancient Greeks. The alb (of which the surplice is one development) represents the cloak, and the chasuble the "coat" of New Testament times (St. Matthew 5:40). It is a universal custom that those who perform special functions should wear special garments. The Eucharistic vestments are worn in the Roman as well as in the Anglican Communion, in the Church of Sweden and by many Lutherans, and in a different form by the Eastern Churches. They link the Church of today with other ages and others lands and are a great help to the priest who wears them, by reminding him of the importance of what he is doing. "Father" is a term of respect and affection traditionally given by the laity to the clergy. A priest is the spiritual father of his parish and the one person to whom the people in their sin and sorrow may turn for comfort and advice. He should be called by an intimate, but not flippant, title. The reluctance to address a priest as "father" possibly arises from the misunderstanding of the term "Protestant" in the legal title of the American Church and the failure to appreciate the Church's Catholic nature. No one need call a priest "Father" unless he wants to, and no priest with any humility or common sense would insist on it. (*Never* call him "Reverend.")

**400. What is the origin of, and reason for, robes in Church services? Why is the clerical collar worn?**

See Question 398. The choir habit (surplice, scarf, and hood) is the uniform of the Anglican clergy for all services which are not sacramental. The surplice (*super pelliceum*) is an alb with wide sleeves, to be worn with the fur cassocks needed in unheated medieval churches. The black scarf, or tippet, peculiar to the Anglican clergy, shows that its wearer has been ordained, and it is the only sign of distinction in church between cleric and layman (such as choirman or server). The hood is the mark of a university degree, but a "literate's" hood of plain black stuff may be worn by nongraduates. It has been the universal practice of the Church since about the fifth century that the clergy should be distinguished by their clothes, both in church and on the street. Their distinctive dress helps both them and others to remember who and what they are, and Whom they represent. The clerical collar is a nineteenth-century invention, and is a sufficient sign that its wearer is a minister of religion.

**401. Why do we have altars, crosses, and candles in the church?**

The altar, or holy table, where the Holy Eucharist is offered, is the most important thing, and the one necessary thing, in a church. Without an altar it would not be a church. Large churches have several altars for convenience. The cross, or crucifix, reminds us of our Lord's death on the Cross. The candles signify that He is the light of the world. The two candles on the altar represent the two natures of Christ, the Godhead and the Manhood. Other candles are sometimes added round the altar for glory and beauty.

**402. What is the origin of the rule that women should wear hats in church?**

It is based on I Corinthians 11:5. St. Paul told the Corinthians that their women ought to be veiled at the public assemblies, which was no doubt necessary for women in such a city as ancient Corinth, as it was for Moslem women everywhere until lately.

**403. Need a woman always wear a hat in church?**

She should follow the local custom and avoid causing comment. It is a good practice, if only to remind women that they are in God's house. A man removes his hat for the same respectful reason.

**404. Why has the circle round the cross become common lately?**

The ancient Irish crosses had this form. It has no particular significance.

**405. Why do our rubrics not tell us when to cross ourselves and genuflect?**

Because they are matters of personal devotion and discretion.

**406. What are the prescribed, preferred, or traditional colors to paint the interior of a church?**

None is prescribed. The matter is one of taste, local custom, and common sense.

**407. What does the Church teach about wearing medals with the likeness of saints?**

There is no harm in it provided the wearer does not suppose that wearing such a medal will benefit him in any way, which is grossly superstitious. Put your trust in God, and not in charms.

**408. What is the Sanctus bell?**

A bell rung during the Sanctus ("Holy, Holy, Holy") to tell

the people what is about to happen. Since the Mass was said in Latin and in a low voice, and the view of the altar often obstructed by a rood screen (such as in Westminster Abbey), the people could not otherwise know what was about to take place. Bells are often rung on joyful occasions.

**409. Why do girls wear white veils at their Confirmation?**

In order that they may all be dressed alike, may not be distracted by looking at one another, and to permit the bishop to place his hands upon their head. Confirmation veils are usually provided by the parish and returned after the service.

**410. Should flowers be on the altar all the year round, or left off in Advent and Lent?**

Flowers are seldom placed on the mensa (table part) of the altar itself. Customs vary in time and place, but it is a general practice not to use flowers on the altar during Advent and Lent by way of accenting the penitential character of those seasons.

**411. Why are palms given on Palm Sunday?**

To remind us of the palms spread before our Lord when He rode into Jerusalem in triumph (St. John 12:13).

**412. What is the purpose of the ring in marriage? Justify the use of two rings.**

The ring signifies that the marriage vows are endless and are binding until death. A second ring for the bridegroom is a foreign custom not known in our tradition and its use is not provided by the Book of Common Prayer.

**413. When should stoles be worn? Are there special preaching stoles?**

The stole, which signifies the yoke of Christ (St. Matthew 11:29), is one of the Eucharistic vestments, and is worn only during the administration of sacraments. It has nothing to do with preaching. It is worn by the celebrant and his assistants at the Eucharist (but not by the reader of the Epistle); by the priest or deacon at Baptism and by the priest who is hearing confessions and anointing the sick; by the bishop when confirming and ordaining. For other services the priest and deacon should wear choir habit (surplice, hood, and scarf) but not stole. The black scarf, or tippet, is much broader than the stole, and is worn over both shoulders by deacons as well as priests, whereas the deacon's stole is worn over the left shoulder only.

**414. Should crosses in church be draped in Passiontide?**

All crosses, crucifixes, and pictures should be draped in veils during Passiontide. The general American custom is to use purple from Passion Sunday to Maundy Thursday, when the color of the veils is changed to white. On Good Friday the altar is usually stripped bare, and any irremovable crosses, etc., are draped in black. In England crosses are covered in white veils from the beginning of Lent till Maundy Thursday, when they are taken down and the church left bare.

**415. What is the historical background for the Christus Rex now often used?**

Until about the twelfth century Christ on the Cross was always represented as robed and crowned. (The Feast of Christ the King was instituted by Pope Pius XI in 1925. It has no authority in Anglican Churches, and there is no need for it: for the Kingship of Christ is observed on Ascension Day. I have evidence to show that the purpose of the Pope was to teach that, since Christ is King of all things, all the secular life of men, all politics, economics, education, etc., ought to be subject to the Pope as Vicar of Christ, a doctrine which is not acceptable to us.)

## Chapter Twenty-Six

# ANGLICAN TEACHING

See also Questions 127–41.

**416. Explain clearly the belief of the Episcopal Church.**

The belief of the Episcopal Church, as of all Anglican Churches, is based upon Holy Scripture, as it is interpreted by the Universal Church and in particular as it is defined in the doctrinal decisions of the first four General Councils, Nicaea (325), Constantinople (381), Ephesus (431), and Chalcedon (451). The Nicene Creed and the Quicunque Vult are a summary of these definitions. The Anglican Churches maintain the sacraments and the ministry of the ancient Church and interpret Scripture by the critical methods of the best modern scholars who are believing and practicing members of the Church. Their teaching is briefly summarized in what is called the Lambeth Quadrilateral: the Holy Scriptures of the Old and New Testaments, the Apostles' and Nicene Creeds, the sacraments of Baptism and the Eucharist, and the apostolic ministry of Bishops, Priests, and Deacons.

**417. If the Anglican Communion has no theology but the faith of the Undivided Church, where is this to be found? How can one know what is of faith and what is not?**

The theology of the Anglican Communion is the same as the faith of the Undivided Church, but it is a modern theology, for it takes into account the discoveries of modern science and criticism. "Every scribe which is instructed unto the kingdom of heaven . . . bringeth forth out of his treasure things new and old" (St. Matthew 13:52). The Offices of Instruction, the Creeds, the Church Catechism, and the rest of the Prayer Book; the dogmas of the first Four Councils (for those of the fifth and sixth hardly affect us today); those of the Thirty-Nine Articles which are concerned with doctrine. Nothing is "of faith" that cannot be proved from Scripture; but it is for the Church, not the individual, to decide what can be proved from Scripture, for no prophecy of Scripture is of private interpretation (II Peter 1:20).

**418. What does the Anglican Communion regard as necessary to believe, and where is it to be found? Is it necessary to believe the Articles of Religion?**

**419. How binding are the Thirty-Nine Articles?**

See Question 417. The Thirty-Nine Articles, rightly understood (for which some historical and technical knowledge is required), are an admirable statement of the Anglican position as it was understood four centuries ago. They do not cover modern problems. They are not in any way binding on the laity, and the clergy give only general assent to them: that is, we are not bound to accept every word of them nor to believe anything which cannot be proved from Scripture (Article 20). For instance, we are not bound by statements in the Homilies (Article 35), some of which are historically absurd.

**420. What is the ethos of the Anglican Communion?**

The Oxford English Dictionary says that an "ethos" is the prevalent tone of sentiment of a community. It is agreed that the Anglican Communion is distinguished by great emphasis on the public and private reading of Scripture in the mother tongue, and on the moral claims of the Christian religion on all members of the Church. It allows great freedom to the individual to think and to say what he chooses; it tries to look at all sides of every question and is unwilling to punish anyone for false belief; it dislikes any kind of fanaticism or superstition; but it maintains its continuity firmly and is very conservative in practice. Like the English nation out of which it sprang, it is not fond of logical thought or of basing action upon it; and it prefers to be guided by custom and intuition rather than by law.

**421. As the Lambeth Conference has no legislative power, may a bishop admit members of sects to Communion, under Resolution 12.A. 11. of the 1920 Lambeth Conference?**

If the National or Provincial Synod (in America, the General Convention) has ratified this resolution, a bishop may act upon it, but he must observe the safeguards attached to the Resolution. It was made with reference to the peculiar conditions of South India. Anyone admitted to Communion under this Resolution must declare that he accepts the authority of Scripture, that he believes every clause of the Creeds, that he has been baptized (of which he must produce proof) and believes in Baptism and the Eucharist, and that he accepts the three orders of the ministry in principle, and recognizes the authority of the Anglican bishops. The Resolution seems to apply only to members of congregations concerned in a scheme for union. I doubt whether many such cases are likely to occur.

**422. Can anything be done to reverse the declaration of the Lambeth Conference of 1920 that all the baptized are members of the Church?**

I do not think that anything can be done or ought to be done. The reference is to the pamphlet *Who Are Members of the Church?* in which Darwell Stone and P. W. Puller sought to show by evidence from early writers that a person baptized in heresy or schism is not a member of the Church unless and until he is received formally into communion with it. I knew the two learned authors well, and Father Puller wrote to me criticizing what I had written on this very subject. I still think that in every part of the Church today those who have been baptized outside its communion are recognized as members in some sense. The ancient writers, and Stone and Puller with them, seem to me not to have recognized sufficiently two important distinctions: The first is that there are different degrees of membership. To be baptized makes a man one sort of member; to be confirmed, a second; to be a regular communicant, a third. There are also the baptized who have never been practicing members, lapsed communicants, persons excommunicated; persons baptized irregularly (as by ministers of the sects), and so on. They all have to be treated differently. For instance, all except the excommunicated may be married and buried with the rites of the Church, which is not allowed to the unbaptized, because they are not members. Secondly, there is a distinction between the external and internal effects of a sacrament. Baptism, even if irregular, makes one a member of the Church (though only in the lowest degree, if it is not followed by Confirmation). If, however, Baptism (in the case of an adult) is received without repentance and faith the spiritual gifts which it bestows seem likely to be dormant. If anyone is baptized in a sect that denies that Baptism conveys the New Birth and forgiveness of sins, his baptism is recognized all the same, and if he is received into full communion with the Church later, he cannot be baptized again; but until then he is likely to lose part of the internal effect of Baptism, because of his ignorance.

Therefore I think that the Lambeth Conference was right. Certainly this is now the practice of the Anglican Communion and I understand of the other Catholic Communions also. A person baptized outside the fellowship of the Church is not a full member of it; but he is for some purposes a member, and if he becomes a full member he cannot be baptized again.

**423. Can anything be done to induce the bishops to consult assessors before making statements at Lambeth?**

I think some do. However, it would certainly be advisable for those bishops who are not themselves theologians to bring theologians with them.

**424. What is the history of the lay reader? Why is he not in minor orders?**

The lay reader is a layman who is licensed to read sermons and certain services. He has not, or ought not to have, any share in administering the sacraments. The office is not older than the nineteenth century and is partly caused by a shortage of priests. The ancient minor orders are those of subdeacon (which Rome regards as in some ways a major order), acolyte, reader, doorkeeper, and exorcist. None of them was in the least like the order of lay readers. They belonged to liturgical arrangements which we do not now possess any longer. Even in the Roman Communion they are only a survival and are normally received all together in the seminary.

## Chapter Twenty-Seven

## CHURCH ORDER

**425. Why is there not more liaison between different Anglican Churches?**

**426. Why does not the American Episcopal Church join forces with the Church of England in Europe, Africa, and the West Indies?**

There is a great deal of cooperation and it is growing rapidly; for instance, the Archbishop of Canterbury has now an American bishop on his personal staff. Paris, Rome, and Florence, in all of which there are large British and American colonies, are the only cities in Europe where there is both an English and an American chaplaincy. In other cities the two Churches arrange it so that there shall be only one chaplaincy. Liberia, Puerto Rico, etc., are under the jurisdiction of the General Convention and cannot be under the Archbishop of West Africa or of the West Indies. Recently a conference of the Anglican bishops in Southeast Asia met at Manila in the American jurisdiction.

**427. Why does the Episcopal Church, alone among Anglican Churches, have no archbishops?**

It is not alone. The Chinese and Japanese Churches have Presiding Bishops. The Scottish Church has a Primus who is not an archbishop. The Scottish bishops swear obedience, not to the Primus, but to the Synod. There were no archbishops in Scotland before 1472, or after 1695, and their history between these dates was unfortunate. In the United States the framers of the Episcopal Church's Constitution and Canons seem to have thought the title of archbishop was too much akin to monarchy.

**428. What is the origin of "'Very Reverend," "Right Reverend," "Most Reverend"? Why is not the Presiding Bishop called Most Reverend?**

These titles appear to date from the seventeenth century. Archdeacons are called Venerable; deans and provosts, Very Reverend; bishops, Right Reverend; archbishops and other chief bishops, including the presiding bishops, and also for a special reason the Bishop of Meath in Ireland, are called Most Reverend. Primate is a higher title than archbishop and means the chief among several archbishops, as in Canada and Australia. The Archbishops of Canterbury, York, Armagh, and Dublin are all Primates; but not the Archbishop of Wales, or Cape Town, or West or Central Africa. The Archbishop of Lyons is Primate of France; the Archbishop of Toledo, Primate of Spain.

**429. What machinery is there for disciplining the clergy?**

This is a difficult question, because discipline ought to be imposed equally on all members of the Church, both clerical and lay. Since the seventeenth century our laity has refused to submit to ecclesiastical penalties, while insisting on regulation of the clergy, and most ecclesiastical offenses (apart from moral ones) are such as only the clergy can commit. In the American Episcopal Church, bishops and priests can be tried for heresy in the Church courts provided by the Canons, with certain safeguards, and there is a Court of Appeal. In England every diocese has a Consistory Court, in which the judge is the chancellor, an eminent lawyer representing the bishop. Above this there are the Provincial Courts of Canterbury (the Court of Arches) and York. English law gives every subject a right of appeal to the crown, for the diocesan and provincial courts are the Queen's courts, as the civil courts are. The crown is represented in this case, under an Act of 1834, by the Judicial Committee of the

Privy Council, which is an entirely secular court. There is widespread refusal to recognize the decisions of this court on doctrine and worship; but as they are held to be binding on the provincial and diocesan courts, these courts do not possess general confidence. Hitherto no attempt to overcome this difficulty has been successful.

**430. Why do our priests give so much time to administration that materialism overrides spiritual needs?**

This is a very old difficulty (Acts 6:1). It appears that some bishops and priests are more at home with administrative than with spiritual and theological duties; that the administration must be carried out and, if the clergy do not do it, someone else will have to be paid to do it; that the clergy are often unwilling (and not altogether without reason) to hand over to the laity all administration and the power that goes with it.

**431. Are there mystics in the American Church? How do they affect the general thinking of the Church?**

If there are not, it is a serious weakness. I am not mystical, but the Church must make provision for those who are, or they will be tempted to fall into the errors of theosophy or some other kind of non-Christian mysticism.

**432. What is the role of the layman in the Episcopal Church?**

A layman is not just a man who has not been ordained. He is a member of the "laos," the chosen people of God. His duty is to do all he can, according to his capacity and opportunities, to promote the work of the Church, under the direction of the bishop and his clergy. The first duty of the priest is the leadership of the worship of God and the administration of the Word and sacraments. The layman, if he is competent, trained, and authorized, can do much to help the clergy even in this: by serving at the altar, reading the lessons, singing in the choir, playing the organ, teaching in Sunday schools, etc. Laymen, if trained and competent, orthodox and loyal, may be licensed by the bishop to take services which are not sacramental and to preach. The layman has his share in the government of the Church, and no important change, even in doctrine and worship, ought to be made without the consent of the laity. The decisive voice in all matters of Church services and all parish affairs must be that of the parish priest, subject to the control of the bishop;

the decisive voice in all matters of doctrine is that of the House of Bishops, within the limits set by the Bible, the decrees of the General Councils, the universally accepted conditions of the validity of sacraments, and the general Anglican tradition.

**433. Why do we not have more definite instruction for those who wish to join the Church?**

Nobody can "join the Church." He is received into the Church by Baptism; but it is God Who of His goodness receives him and Who gives the wish to be received. Such a person, if an adult, or a boy or girl who is not a baby, ought to be most carefully prepared for Baptism, and it is the obligation of the parish priest to see that he is so prepared; Confirmation and First Communion should follow Baptism, either immediately or as soon as possible. If he has been baptized or confirmed in some other church or in some sect, he should be formally received into the Church, either by the form for the reception of one privately baptized (if he has not been confirmed), at which he should have godparents, or by an authorized rite for the reception of converts (if he has been confirmed in the Roman Communion). Members of the Eastern Churches should not be accepted except, with the permission of their own bishop, for some special reason. Members of the Polish National Catholic Church or of the Old Catholic Churches in Europe should be received as already members, precisely as if they came from the Church of England or some other Anglican Church, but they will probably need some teaching about our forms and methods of worship.

**434. What is the difference between a parish and a mission?**

A parish is self-supporting, whereas a mission is supported entirely or partly either by the diocese or by the parish to which it is attached. In England, and indeed throughout Europe, a parish is an area with fixed boundaries, and the parish priest or minister is responsible for the pastoral care of everyone living within those boundaries; even if they are of a different denomination he is expected to know and help them if required. I understand that parishes in the United States are not of this kind.

**435. What are the values of a cathedral over a parish church? Why should a parish church be made a cathedral? Is a cathedral an expression of Christianity?**

The cathedral in any diocese is the bishop's church, the place where his "cathedra," or seat, is placed. Some cathedrals are quite small, but in most historic European cities, as in London, the cathedral is the largest and most beautiful building in the city, because it is the chief place for the worship of God. The relation of the cathedral to the parish churches is rather like the relation of the head office of a business to the branch offices. The cathedral is the place where the services are rendered as beautifully as they can be, for the glory God and for a model to the parishes (though the services in the cathedral need not be so congregational as those of the parishes). It is, or should be, served by a staff of priests with diocesan functions, and should have no parish of its own. The chief members of the staff (called the "Chapter") were formerly, and in some cathedrals are still, the dean, who was the chairman and ruler, the precentor, who was responsible for all liturgical and musical arrangements, for the servers, the choir, and the organ; the chancellor, who controlled the cathedral school, the seminary for ordinands and all teaching work in the diocese, and might also be the bishop's theological adviser; and the treasurer, who was responsible for the finances. These formed the Chapter and were expected to be present every day at the Chapter services. The cathedral should also have a diocesan missioner, responsible for organizing missions and retreats; a library available for the clergy and laity; and a staff of experts in all aspects of Church life. Every day prayers are offered for one of the parishes by name. Diocesan festivals and synods are held there; pilgrimages are organized from the parishes to it. Ordinations are usually held there.

**436. What is the jurisdictional position of the Anglican Communion outside the British Isles?**

In England, the Channel Islands, and the Isle of Man the Church has, besides its ecclesiastical jurisdiction, civil jurisdiction derived from the crown; elsewhere only ecclesiastical jurisdiction. Jurisdiction in this sense is the right to act within a certain area or for certain persons within that area. In Wales and Scotland we claim to be, as in England, the Catholic Church of the country; all Christians living there, except members of foreign churches, belong to our jurisdiction, whether they recognize it or not. On the continent of Europe and in countries where there are ancient Churches, such as Syria, Palestine, Egypt, and Ethiopia, the English and American Churches do not claim to serve any but their own people. Our chaplaincies exist to serve and help Anglican residents, to promote friendly relations, as far as possible, with the Christians of the country and other residents, and in some countries to evangelize Jews and Moslems. They do for the Church what embassies and consulates do for their country. In new countries, such as the United States, and in countries which have never been Christian, such as India and China, no Church can justly claim exclusive jurisdiction, and the Anglican Communion has as much right as any other part of the Church to be there, to minister to its own people and to all who are willing to accept its services, and to take its full share in the life of the community.

**437. How many communicants are there in the whole Anglican Communion?**

Nobody knows. It is not worth while to spend time and money in compiling statistics; for in spiritual matters statistics are of little value. The number has been estimated as thirty-five or even forty million.

**438. Am I right to attend regularly a church twenty-five miles away, if I don't like the teaching and practice of the local church?**

It is a question for your own judgment. If you live twenty-five miles away you can hardly expect the priest to bring you the sacraments when you are ill; you cannot do much for the daily life of that parish; you have also to consider, if you have children or other dependents, whether they are likely to continue regular attendance at so distant a church. It seems to me that such practice can be justified only by exceptional conditions.

**439. Why does not the Anglican Communion speak with authority on matters of faith to its member churches?**

The resolutions of the Lambeth Conference, which are usually unanimous, do speak with some authority. If you mean, why are not directions given in matters of faith, the large Churches have no right to dictate to the small ones; and the American Church in particular has always opposed any approach toward a centralized authority. The most binding authority is that which is reached by universal agreement, as all history shows.

**440. Give clear and decisive arguments about tithing.**

The American Church practices this much better than the English Church.[1]

**441. Why are the Offices of Instruction and the Church Catechism so seldom used in the Episcopal Church?**

When I was working in a parish all our teaching was based on the Catechism. In Sunday school we taught nothing else. But apparently Americans have widely accepted the modern educational fad that children ought not to learn much by heart. I am quite sure they are wrong. Children have been given good memories, and the more they learn the Catechism and the best parts of the Bible by heart the better. Even if they do not understand it, they will later.

[1] A leaflet, *Something about Tithing*, prepared by an American priest, is worth repeating here:

The Jews tithe; so do the Mormons and the Seventh-day Adventists. . . . It is simply trying to play fair with God. It is testing the vitality of your Creed by the reality of your sharing. It is putting your religion on as sound a basis as your patriotism by taxing your income for your Church as you tax it for your State.

It is taking 10% of your gross income and setting that aside as a basic minimum for objects to which you can conscientiously contribute in God's Name and for His sake, and not for any personal or private benefit. After the 10% you begin to give!

Tithing is fair to everybody: it distributes the load, or rather, it lifts the subject to the level where it belongs; it tries everybody's faith by the acid test of "What is it worth to you?" It brings us face to face with our Crucified Lord and makes us answer the question: "How much would I sacrifice for Him?"

To the argument that tithing is legalistic, or that it is an old Jewish law, St. Paul would reply, "If by the Law such giving abounded, by Grace it should much more abound." Jesus said that if we were not faithful in the use of money, how could He entrust to us spiritual riches?

God's sanctuary is stained by the ghastly hypocrisy of our casual contributions that have no significant relation to our income. The stain comes from spending on our own bodies and starving the Body of Christ, so that it sits by the wayside begging instead of striding across the world on its ministries of Grace.

Giving to the Church is a spiritual matter. One way in which you may show your love for God, for His Church, and for your fellow man is by "old-fashioned" tithing.

We do not tithe because the Church needs money (which it always does), but simply because we love God. When a person loves God, he naturally wants to tithe; he would not think of doing less. If you do not tithe, it could be a warning that your love for God is weak and that repentance and a deeper conversion is needed for the welfare of your soul.

Many people on all income levels *do* tithe; people whose obligations and costs of living are just as high as yours. God would not have asked us to tithe if tithing were impossible.

**442. Why has not the Episcopal Church the centralized authority of Rome?**

Because we do not believe in centralized authority. The Roman system is a dictatorship, and we do not believe in dictatorships. The authority of this particular dictatorship is founded on claims which are historically baseless. It is because we reject these claims and that kind of authority, because we expect to be treated as free adults and not as children, that we are Anglicans and not Romanists.

**443. How far is the American Church bound by English canon law?**

Canon law, unlike statute law, ceases to have any force when it has long been universally disregarded. The English Canons of 1604 are largely obsolete even in England, and can hardly be considered binding in the United States. Whether the whole body of medieval Latin Canons, which is still in force in England as far as it is applicable to modern conditions and not contrary to English statute law, is still in force in the United States appears to be a question about which the experts differ.

**444. Why does not the General Convention legislate for more uniformity in worship?**

Many people do not think that more uniformity is desirable; those who do think so only wish to make others conform to what they themselves practice. No legislation on this subject is likely to win a majority, and even if it did, many people would not obey it, and there is no means of enforcing it. The only way to secure greater uniformity is by general agreement to obey the rules. These rules might, indeed, be more explicit; the Episcopal Church has removed the Ornaments Rubric and put nothing in its place.

**445. Why do most Episcopalians fail to grasp the truth of the Church?**

Because they are not taught, or because they do not listen when they are taught, or because they are affected by the religious atmosphere of the sects. The sermon should normally be an instruction rather than a moral essay or an emotional appeal, for it is often the only means of teaching.

**446. Is not the training of priests in seminaries about divorce, etc., the same? Why is there so much difference?**

RELATIONS WITH OTHER CHRISTIANS    185

I should think that there is divergence of teaching in the semi-naries. In my experience on the staffs of theological colleges (in England the word "seminary" is applied only to Romanist col-leges), which is considerable, students do not always accept or practice what they were taught in college. It is the duty of the bishops to enforce the law and to punish those who break it.

**447. Consecrated Churchwoman wants to know why priests are allowed to deny the Resurrection and Ascension in a church claiming to be Catholic.**

I should think that the bishops do not do their duty; the orthodox priests do not refuse to have anything to do with heretics; and the laity do not refuse to receive ministrations from such men. It often does more harm than good to bring heretics to trial, because they get so much notoriety, but there are other ways of dealing with them. (No one can be consecrated except a bishop; the lady is using the wrong word.)

**448. Is the title "Father in God" reserved for the diocesan bishop?**

It may also be applied to his coadjutor or suffragan (assistant) bishop. (In England there is a difference between the suffragan bishop, appointed by the crown, and the assistant bishop, appointed by the diocesan.)

**449. Are all the clergy rectors?**

Certainly not. A rector is the priest in charge of a parish. There are also bishops, deans, canons, chaplains of many kinds, mission-aries, professors in colleges and seminaries, members of religious orders, assistant curates, and many others.


*Chapter Twenty-Eight*

# RELATIONS WITH OTHER CHRISTIANS

See also Chapter 13.

**450. Where does the Anglican Communion fit into the Na-tional Council of the Churches of Christ in the U.S.A.?**

The National Council, as the American branch of the World Council of Churches, is a valuable and almost necessary institution, provided it does not go beyond its proper purpose. (Its title is misleading, because most of its members are not churches but sects. Still this cannot be avoided.) Christian leaders ought to get together, know one another, and act together, as far as they can, in moral, political, and social questions. Governments will sometimes listen to a deputation that represents many different kinds of Christians when they would not pay attention to separate denominations. But certain cautions ought to be observed by all who take part in the National Council of Churches. It has no spiritual or theological authority. It is not a Church and has no right to speak in the name of the Church; most of the communities represented in it are independent of the Church. It should not be made a means of open intercommunion: members of the Church should take no part in any such action, and if they do, should be officially repudiated and deprived of any right to represent the Church. The World Council of Churches does not represent more than about a third of Christendom. The Roman Communion, which is by far the largest Christian body, both in the United States and in the world, takes no part in it. The Eastern Orthodox Communion is very poorly represented in it, and the great majority of Orthodox people, who are under the control of Communist governments, not at all. Many fundamentalists also refuse to take any part in it and have a rival International Council of their own.

Any attempt to treat the National Council of Churches, or the World Council of which it is a part, as "Pan-Protestant" should be strongly opposed. The Anglican Communion ought to have no place in any organization which includes only heirs of the Reformation, but as long as the Eastern Churches are there, even on a small scale, we ought to be there too.

**451. What is the policy of the Church on cooperation with non-Anglicans in Church matters?**

It differs greatly in different dioceses and countries. In one English diocese the cathedral and the leading parish church follow entirely different policies. It is desirable to cooperate with those who are not in communion with us, as far as we can without compromising our principles (as by premature intercommunion) and without encouraging the belief that it does not matter to what church or sect you belong. There is only one Church and everybody ought to be a full member of it (see Chap. 10).

**452. What is the attitude of the Anglican Communion toward Reformation and Post-Reformation Churches?**

The religious societies founded during the Reformation and after it are not churches but sects, for they have no institutional continuity with the original Church. Their members, if baptized, are fellow members with us of the Catholic Church; but as societies they are independent of it.

**453. How shall I deal with a Romanist (Anglican until his marriage) who cannot believe Romanist practices and is nothing, though his wife and family are faithful Romanists?**

Persuade him, if possible, to return to the Anglican Communion, which he ought never to have left. The reason why he became a Romanist was a bad one. The only justifiable reason for becoming a Romanist is that one is convinced, on grounds of reason and with no other motive, that the Roman Communion and no other is the true Church and that all its claims and dogmas are true.

**454. Ought we not to study one another's historical, rather than doctrinal, differences?**

The study of the two cannot be separated. It is always doctrine that separates us; but we cannot understand the differences of doctrine without knowing how they began and developed.

**455. What chance is there for the Episcopal Church to unite with other Christian churches?**

(I assume that "churches" here, though used incorrectly, is meant to include sects.) I should say practically none, at least not in the immediate future. Reunion with Rome is impossible; it would require a miracle. Reunion with the Orthodox Churches, in any case very difficult, seems to be impossible as long as most of them are controlled by Communist governments. The same applies to the Armenian Church. Reunion with the Church of the East (Assyrian) is perhaps possible (since there are no fundamental differences) but not easy. The Philippine Independent Church ought to be in full communion with the Episcopal Church. The sects have a very different conception of the

Church, and union with any of them is unlikely for many years. We cannot unite unless we are agreed on the meaning of "church" and the meaning of "union."

**456. How can an Anglican parish take part constructively in the Ecumenical Movement?**

It is impossible to give a general answer to this question. No one should take any part in relations with other churches or with the sects, who is not thoroughly instructed and convinced about the position of the Church to which he belongs. Otherwise he will do more harm than good. Careful study of the doctrines at issue, discussion groups with the object of understanding, not of converting, one another, cooperation in moral and social work, are all good. There are many pitfalls, and many things are taken for granted by one side which are startling to the other. To give an instance known to me, most members of the sects assume that the Blessed Virgin Mary was the mother of a large family; an idea intensely shocking to all who have been trained in Catholic tradition (see Question 99). Members of some sects think smoking wicked (see Question 335); others, that even the most ordinary acts of reverence are idolatrous. In relations with other Christians we have to learn not to be shocked easily.

*Chapter Twenty-Nine*

# DIFFERENCES OF CHURCHMANSHIP

**457. What is the ultimate aim of the Anglo-Catholics? Reunion with Rome? What conditions would they force on Evangelicals or Dissenters? What is the least they would require for ecumenical status?**

The Anglo-Catholics, like the Evangelicals, are not a single united group: they differ sharply from one another. Only what has been called the "lunatic fringe" desire reunion with Rome, except on conditions that Rome could not conceivably grant.

Probably all Anglo-Catholics would like to see the whole Anglican Communion believing and practicing the Catholic religion; heartily accepting the creeds and obeying the Christian marriage laws; taking part in the Eucharist on all Sundays and great festivals, communicating reverently and frequently, practicing voluntary confession to a priest, and taking their full share in the conversion of non-Christians, at home and abroad. They all desire union with the Eastern Orthodox Churches, and the return of the sects to the faith and practice of the Church. I cannot answer questions about what would happen *if* . . .

I do not think Anglo-Catholics in general wish to impose any belief or practice on anyone by force.

**458. Why do ritual and Church history get more discussion than the problem of making God through Christ an integral part of our lives?**

All Christians who take their religion seriously believe that they ought not only to devote their personal lives to God but also to try to make their corporate life and that of all other men obedient to Him. However, this is not a subject for public discussion. It is always the minor, not the major, matters that are disputed in the newspapers. We do not argue publicly about the things nearest our hearts. Sometimes what appears to be unimportant is discussed warmly, because we all know that it stands for something vital that we do not care to mention. This is the reason for controversy about vestments and ornaments.

**459. Can the difference of practice in fasting, genuflecting, etc., be bridged as it drives people away?**

Such people must learn that we are not all made alike. The Church is Catholic, that is, for all men, and we must all learn to tolerate in minor matters the freedom we claim for ourselves. Why should anyone refuse to do his duty to God in His Church because someone else's notion of reverence differs from his own?

**460. Is an Episcopalian who believes the Anglican Catholic faith an Episcopalian or an Anglican Catholic?**

Both. Every Episcopalian is an Anglican Catholic, that is, a Catholic in communion with the See of Canterbury and the Anglican bishops. Every Anglican is a Catholic, and if he is in the United States he is an Episcopalian. You might as well ask whether the patriotic Texan is a Texan or an American citizen!

**461. Is not the Book of Common Prayer a Catholic book? Why not let our people know this?**

Why not indeed? "I believe one Catholic and Apostolic Church."

**462. Why do the clergy have different opinions and substitute them for what has been held from the earliest times?**

Such an accusation requires evidence. If you refer to articles of the Creed, your remedy is a prosecution for heresy; if that is impossible, go to another parish. If you refer to personal opinions, I suggest that not everything which has been long held is true: for instance, we now know facts about the authorship and date of Old Testament books which were not known to the Apostles.

**463. Why do people (not in the Church) shy away from the word "Catholic"? Why do people in the Church shy away from what "Catholic" means in worship and practice?**

Because, in both cases, they have been taught to fear and hate the power and the errors of Rome and do not know how to distinguish between what is Roman and what is Catholic.

**464. Why are there so many differences in the teaching, forms, and ceremonies of the Church even in one diocese? I do not think they strengthen the Church.**

There are different traditions in the Anglican Communion, and they express themselves in methods of worship. We cannot expect those brought up in different traditions to believe or behave in precisely the same way, but we are all bound to obey the Prayer Book, and by the rule of charity to avoid irritating one another by unnecessary divergence, especially in unimportant things.

**465. How can we present a united front when priests differ so much on what is necessary for themselves and for the laity?**

By universal observance of the rules in the Prayer Book. What the priest thinks necessary for himself is a matter for his own conscience. He has no right to insist that something is necessary for his people unless he can prove it by the Bible, as interpreted by the formularies of the Episcopal Church.

**466. Define "high church" and "low church" and give arguments for and against each.**

These phrases are used with different meanings at different periods, in different countries, and by different people. It is therefore impossible to define them strictly. The majority of Church members are neither "high" nor "low" but are influenced by both in different proportions. The words "Catholic," "Evangelical," and "Liberal" are now more commonly and more accurately used to describe different tendencies in the Church. All of the groups described are sharply divided among themselves. In many ways they supplement one another, and the Church could not afford to do without any of them. There are liberal "Catholics" and liberal Evangelicals, conservative "Catholics" and conservative Evangelicals, "Catholic" Evangelicals and Evangelical "Catholics" (which have not the same meaning). Broadly speaking, the "Catholic," or High Churchman, emphasizes belief in the Church as a sacramental and supranational society, values all the institutions which are inherited from the ancient and medieval Church, and regards Church services as first of all an offering to God. The Evangelical emphasizes the evangelistic side of the work of the Church and the values of the Reformation, especially Justification by Faith and reconciliation with God by the precious Blood of Christ, and tends to regard the purpose of Church services as first of all preaching and the conversion of the people. The Liberal emphasizes the moral and intellectual elements in the Christian religion, which he tends to regard as a form of individual and political morality. Each group has an eccentric fringe of extremists, by which it ought not to be judged. The "high church" eccentric fringe treats the Anglican Communion as a rather odd form of Romanism; the evangelical eccentric fringe as a Puritan sect which happens to have bishops; the liberal eccentric fringe as a form of German philosophy, or a secular morality almost stripped of definite belief.

**467. Why are priests allowed to repudiate articles of the Creed, and the Real Presence?**

They are not allowed to repudiate articles of the Creed. They are bound to recite the Creed, and if they do so without believing it they are lying to God and man and must take the consequences. Prosecutions for heresy are very difficult: but the faithful should refuse to attend the services held by anyone who is known to deny any part of the Creed. The Real Presence is not a dogma, but a rather ambiguous statement of the mystery of the Eucharist. Anglican doctrine is not rigid on this subject, but no priest ought to repudiate the language of the Prayer Book and of the Articles.

**468. Why do college professors and textbooks give a different historical background from that of the Church?**

Professors and writers of textbooks are often uninterested in, and ignorant of, the theological bearing of historical events. Others have been brought up in the Whig and Puritan tradition represented by Macaulay and cannot be expected to give due weight to the Catholic claims of the Anglican Communion. Romanist textbooks take another and entirely different viewpoint, especially if the authors are Irish. It is almost impossible to write the history of some periods without being biased or dull.

**469. Why are Episcopalians who are not Anglo-Catholics against the High Church?**

There may be several reasons. Many people with narrow minds dislike intensely anything to which they are not accustomed, especially in religion. To some people, such harmless ornaments as vestments and incense, which are well inside the Anglican tradition, are associated with Romanism. Some Anglo-Catholic priests (and lay persons) are foolish enough to use Romanist terminology, or terminology which is thought to be Romanist, to people who are not accustomed to it; to copy purely Roman practices, and in other ways to arouse unnecessary prejudice. A more profound reason is that the Catholic religion imposes obligations which those who are accustomed to a laxer religion feel is a reproach to them. The Catholic feels bound to go to the Eucharist on Sunday, communicate fasting, confess his sins to a priest, observe fast days, avoid sectarian worship, and obey strict marriage laws. In these matters the Anglican who is conscious of being Catholic feels bound by his conscience as truly as the Roman Catholic is bound by the rules of his Church. Many persons cannot bear that anyone should be more religious than they are willing to be themselves.

**470. Why do some of the clergy in ——— object to the permission of traditional Catholic teaching and worship?**

"Traditional" is sometimes used for Romanist; the practices of Romanists are not always ancient. Probably these priests oppose what is not in accordance with their own tradition. Anglican teaching and practice ought to be strictly in accordance with the Prayer Book and with genuine Anglican tradition, neither modern Romanist nor Puritan.

**471. Why do we need more "high" churches?**

As long as the Catholic religion is faithfully taught and practiced with charity toward all and the Gospel is preached to those outside, without putting stumbling blocks in their way, it matters little how much ceremonial is used.

**472. Why do missionary churches seem more Catholic than many churches in the United States?**

They have more elaborate services (not necessarily more Catholic) because they do not have to make allowance for Puritan prejudice; and because natives of tropical countries like highly ornate services.

**473. Which is right, the High or the Low Church concept, teaching, and practice in the Episcopal Church?**

The traditional teaching of the Anglican Communion is High Church, and goes back to Hooker, Andrewes, and Laud. I do not think that the Anglican position can be defended on any other ground or that there is today any rival system of doctrine and worship. The old Evangelicals had such a system, but it was destroyed, for all reasonable men, by modern biblical criticism and by the rejection by modern consciences of the unscriptural doctrine of penal substitution. But the High Churchmen are not always right, because they sometimes tend to follow Romanist teaching and practice; to teach doctrines for which there is no evidence, and to follow customs which have no Anglican authority.

**474. Why does the Episcopal Church have such different forms of worship?**

We are bound to use the forms of worship prescribed in the Prayer Book. There are different traditions about how they should be used, and different types of congregations have different needs. As long as the Prayer Book is obeyed as strictly as possible, no one has any right to complain. There are also modern needs which were not thought of when the Prayer Book was drawn up. If clergy and laity alike would behave with loyalty, charity, and common sense, there need be no difficulty. We are members of one family, and we must make allowances for differences of temperament and upbringing.

**475. Is the presence of "low" and "high" churches a hindrance to the Ecumenical Movement among Protestant Churches in the United States?**

The only Church in the United States which can be called

Protestant is the Episcopal Church. The others are sects and not churches (see Questions 162, 163). If the Ecumenical Movement were in any way Pan-Protestant, we ought to have as little to do with it as possible: but it is intended to include all Christians, no matter what their relation to the Reformation may be. It is true that the presence of "low church" traditions in the Anglican Communion is the most serious obstacle to reunion of the Anglican Churches and the Eastern Orthodox Churches. On the other hand, the "high church" tradition in the Anglican Communion is the only point of contact that many members of the sects have with the Catholic religion. The sons and grandsons of those who have joined the Evangelical end of the Anglican Communion have often been led to fuller Catholic belief and practice by using the Prayer Book, without thereby losing the Evangelical emphasis on personal religion and study of the Bible, of which some of the older parts of Christendom stand in need.

**476. Why is there so much feeling about variations in Churchmanship?**

Those for whom the religion of Christ is more important than anything else naturally feel strongly about religious differences, a fact which puzzles and irritates those to whom religion means little or nothing. If anyone is afraid that the truth (or what he supposes to be the truth) is being threatened, his fear may easily lead him to hatred and bigotry, which are contrary to every form of the religion of Christ (St. John 13:34, 35; I Cor. 13:4-7).

**477. Does the difference between "low" and "high" Church practice hinder the progress of the Anglican Communion in the United States or throughout the world?**

To some extent it does; especially when either school of thought extends practices peculiar to itself without considering the effect on those of another school of thought. The Anglo-Catholic cult of the Reserved Sacrament as a center of worship and the exaggerated devotion to the Blessed Virgin offend Evangelicals; the Evangelical carelessness about liturgical details, and still more their practice of intercommunion (unauthorized) with the sects, offend all High Churchmen. None of these practices are at all necessary, or justified by Anglican tradition. However, all schools of thought are now growing together.

**478. Why do some Episcopalians deny that they are Catholics?**

Probably because they have never been taught that Catholic does not mean Romanist. Every time they recite the Creed they declare that they believe in the Catholic Church: every time they join in the Prayer for All Sorts and Conditions of Men they pray for the good estate of the Catholic Church, which implies that they themselves belong to it.

**479. What is the Broad Church Movement? Is it influenced by theosophy?**

It is not a movement, but a temperament. The Broad Churchman is the heir of the rationalists of the eighteenth century. He is interested in morals and social reform, but not in doctrine or evangelism. He tends to regard man as a mind to be persuaded, rather than as a soul to be saved, and he is anxious that the Church shall not do anything which would exclude those whose scientific training makes them unwilling to accept miracles. He is often inclined to take a radical view of biblical criticism, to pay great attention to the latest theories from Germany, and to reject the authority of the Church, which he regards as a merely human society. Broad Churchmen are of value as a counterweight to superstition, but they have no gospel for the poor. Theosophy is a form of Hinduism adapted for Europe and America, admirably described by an Indian friend of mine as "Buddhism gone rancid." Those attracted to it are usually second-rate mystics, whereas the Broad Churchman tends to be a rationalist.

**480. How have the variations in practice come about?**

To answer this fully would take too long. The Tractarians and their followers a century ago sought to make their people understand the doctrine of the Church and sacraments, which they had revived after long neglect, by reforming the services of the Church. Some of them unwisely copied Romanist practice, for they did not always face the question of the authority for what they did or understand how great a difference there is between modern Romanist customs, closely connected with the doctrinal and devotional system of the Jesuits, and the practice of the English Church just before the Reformation, to which the rubrics of the English Prayer Book refer. Many changes are due to the ignorance and self-will of particular priests of different schools of thought; and some have been exaggerated by party prejudice.

**481. Why are priests called "ministers" by the public?**

In England they scarcely ever are. The probable reason is that most Americans are accustomed to the ministers of the sects; they think that the Episcopal Church is "Protestant" and that its ministers are more like those of the sects than those of the Romanists. The Romanists encourage this belief. Our priests are ministers and are so called in the Prayer Book, but they are also priests, as the ministers of the sects are not and do not claim to be.

*Chapter Thirty*

# CANONIZATION AND OTHER MATTERS

**482. What is the Anglican belief about the saints? Have we any means of canonizing new ones?**

See Questions 315–16. The English Convocations in 1661 formally canonized King Charles the Martyr and appointed a collect, epistle, and gospel for the day of his martyrdom (January 30). About eight churches were dedicated to his name (and others recently). The South African Church has canonized the Martyrs of Uganda and Bernard Mzeka, who was martyred in Rhodesia. In the United States the General Convention has the power to canonize.

**483. Why has no one been made a saint in our Church for about four hundred years?**

See Question 482. The Church of England is cautious, but a commission, appointed by the Archbishops of Canterbury and York, has just reported on this subject. Other provinces, such as Scotland and South Africa, are not so cautious.

**484. What is the procedure for canonizing saints in the Episcopal Church?**

The General Convention could do it. However, as the Episcopal Church has no saints in its Calendar except those in the New Testament, canonization of new ones seems to be premature.

**485. Who determines who our saints are?**

The National and Provincial Synod. Some missionary dioceses have their own lists.

### 486. Why does not the Church build more churches and hospitals?

It is always building churches, where there is need for them and money to pay for them. Except for special purposes (as St. Luke's Hospital in London, for the clergy and their families), hospitals are usually built by the State. The Church builds hospitals in countries where the State does not provide them.

### 487. What is a good readable complete history of the Anglican Communion?

I do not think there is such a history of all the Anglican Churches. Dr. Moorman's is the most recent history of the Church of England; another is by Dr. S. C. Carpenter.

### 488. Why is it hard to interest priests in unchurched groups?

Perhaps because some priests who are not trained for evangelism and are not attracted by it find themselves fully occupied with pastoral and administrative work. In English dioceses we have a canon missioner, who is responsible for organizing evangelistic work throughout the diocese.

### 489. Do most Anglicans face the problem raised by Father Huddleston? Was he recalled because he embarrassed his order?

The color problem is especially difficult in South Africa because of the policy of the South African government. In England we have only the beginnings of it, chiefly in a few big towns. Several black priests of various races have served in English parishes without any difficulty. The suggestion that Fr. Huddleston embarrassed his order has been officially denied. He has much greater freedom and publicity in England than he would have in South Africa; he draws great crowds everywhere, and nearly everybody sympathizes with him.

### 490. Why do many priests not visit their people?

Perhaps because they are too lazy or too shy. Some perhaps think, mistakenly, that they are following a Protestant example. Perhaps the people do not encourage their priests to visit and do not call them when needed.

### 491. How many editions of the Prayer Book have there been? Who decides what changes are to be made?

The first in 1549 (Edward VI); the second in 1552 (Edward VI); the third in 1559 (Elizabeth I); the fourth in 1604 (James I); the fifth in 1661 (Charles II). A sixth was passed by the English

Convocations in 1927, but was rejected by the House of Commons. However, it is very widely used in England and overseas. Other Anglican Churches have their own versions of the Prayer Book. The first American Prayer Book was issued in 1789; the second in 1892; the third and present book in 1928. The National or Provincial Synod revises the Prayer Book when required. In England, because the Prayer Book is part of the Act of Uniformity (1662) it can be revised only with the consent of Parliament.

**492. What are the acknowledged typographical mistakes in the Prayer Book?**

I do not know whether there are any, and I do not think the matter has any importance.

*Chapter Thirty-One*

# PERSONAL PROBLEMS

**492a. Please give some simple teaching about prayer.**

To answer such a question would require a whole book. Prayer is the way by which we come to God, as grace is the way in which He comes to us. We cannot pray without His grace, which comes into our hearts as the incense falls on the burning charcoal in the censer and produces prayer as the incense produces sweet-smelling smoke. "Let my prayer be set forth in thy sight as the incense" (Ps. 141:2).

Prayer may be vocal or silent. Vocal prayer may be praise, thanksgiving, petition (for ourselves), or intercession (for others). All four of these ought to find a place in all our private prayers, as in our public ones. When we ask God for something we do not try to persuade Him, for He knows what we and our friends need better than we do. We lay our wills alongside His, unite our desires to His Will, and, as it were, swim with the stream of His love. We offer all our prayers "for Jesus Christ's sake"; we are not to pray in any other way, for "No man cometh unto the Father, but by me" (St. John 14:6). Silent prayer is the act of meditation; we take a subject, such as a passage of Scripture, pray over it, turn it over in our minds, try to learn what God means it to teach us, and then form some resolution upon it, which we ask God to help us to keep. Before any vocal prayer, public or private, we ought to be quite still for a minute or so, to realize the presence of God. It is because we neglect this simple rule that we find it often so hard to attend to our prayers. We ought always to pray night and morning, and at night include self-examination and confession of our sins during the day. We ought also to make a meditation every day, even if only for five minutes. We should have a list of people for whom we pray; some daily, some weekly, some monthly. Every fresh event in our lives, and every fresh person with whom we are in regular contact, should find a place in our prayers. We cannot hate anyone for whom we constantly pray.

**493. I was confirmed two years ago and I still cannot overcome my faults.**

Did you expect to? The conquest of our faults will take our whole life, and probably more. Take them one by one. Set yourself, with God's help (for by yourself you can do nothing), to resist and get rid of your worst and most besetting sin. When you think you have conquered that (but don't be too sure), set to work on another. Get a skilled spiritual director and ask his advice, as you would consult a physician about pain in the body. You may be attacking a particular fault in the wrong way. Give the priest your confidence and do what he advises.

**494. I tried in vain to persuade a friend to go to church. My rector, being asked to call, bade me remember the economy of Christ. What did he mean?**

He ought to have expressed himself more clearly, but I think he meant that our Lord chooses His own time to approach a soul. In this case the time may not have been ripe. Our Lord promised to make St. Peter a fisher of men. The art of bringing souls to Him requires, like fishing, great patience. Certainly you were not meant to cease praying for that person; perhaps you had not prayed long enough or someone else, not you or even your rector, was the chosen instrument for that purpose. St. Peter could not have done the work of St. Paul.

**495. What is the purpose of a retreat?**

To be alone with God for a few days, to listen to what He

wishes to say to us, and for that to maintain *complete silence* (except of course in case of emergency, or to ask the help of the conductor of the retreat). Each day of the retreat begins with Holy Communion, in addition to Morning and Evening Prayer. An annual retreat of three or four days should be part of the regular life of every devout Christian.

**496. What should be our attitude toward science?**

The truth discovered through natural science comes, as all truth comes, from God. There can be no real contradiction between religious and scientific truth. If they appear to us to be contrary to each other, probably we have failed to understand one or the other, or both, as has often happened before. Everyone ought to know something about different sciences and the scientific method, for otherwise he will not be able to understand the world in which God has placed him. The passion for objective and impartial truth, which most scientists take for granted, deserves our admiration and imitation.

**497. What should a communicant do when he finds that he does not fully appreciate the Holy Communion?**

Continue to communicate regularly, make careful preparation and thanksgiving, make quite sure, by self-examination, that his failure to appreciate does not arise from unrepented sin or lack of love. He might do well to make his confession to a skilled director of souls. In any case, he must not worry about himself. We are commanded to "do this"; we are not commanded to appreciate it. All the masters of the spiritual life warn us that the will, and not the feelings, is what matters. If you do not appreciate the great privilege of receiving the Body and Blood of Christ, but still go on obeying His command as well as you can, you are all the more pleasing to Him.

**498. What should one do to prepare for death?**

First, forgive with your whole heart anyone who has in any way injured you. If you are not on speaking terms with anyone, do all you can to put an end to the quarrel. Pay all your debts: restore anything that you have wrongfully taken from anyone or of which you have cheated anyone. Apologize for any wrong you may have committed; if it was public, apologize publicly. Then make your will, if you have not already made it; dispose of all your property in such a way as to cause no family quarrels and to give the least possible trouble to your heirs and executors, and bequeath a due proportion for the service of God. Complete all obligations which are not fulfilled. Then send for a priest, make your confession to him, and receive Holy Communion. If you are ill, or death is expected soon, ask him to anoint you with holy oil: the chief purpose of this is your recovery, but it will also strengthen your soul for the crisis of death. Put aside all thoughts of this world, as far as possible, and give as much time and strength as you can to prayer and spiritual reading: if the illness is prolonged, receive Holy Communion as often as you can. If you have children or dependents, give them your blessing. Ask all your friends to pray for you, ask your parish priest to request the congregation to pray for you, and beg some religious community that specializes in such prayers to put your name on its list.

**499. Cannot mind reading be recognized as communion of saints in which helpful thought is exchanged?**

No. Very little is known about "mind reading." If the people to whom you refer are still alive, it is much better to exchange thoughts by speech and writing. If they are dead, both the Bible and the Church forbid any attempt to communicate with them (Ex. 22:18; Lev. 19:31; Deut. 18:10; I Sam. 28:3; II Kings 21:6). The reason for this is that if it is possible to get into touch with spirits outside the body (which many people deny), the spirits with which we might get in touch are certainly *not* the spirits of the dead but devils who pretend to be spirits of the dead in order to lead us away from God and destroy our souls. *It cannot be too strongly emphasized that any attempt to get in touch with the spirits of the dead is futile, dangerous, and wicked.*

**500. What is the real power of prayer?**

The almighty power of God, Who has promised to grant our prayers, but does not always grant them in the way that we expect.

**501. Is prayer for others a Christian responsibility?**

Of course it is (Rom. 12:12; Eph. 6:18, 19; II Thess. 3:1; James 5:16, 17). We have been given the power and privilege of prayer: it is our duty to use it to the utmost of our power (see Question 492).

**502. Is the Church's claim on a man's time, talents, etc., con-**

fined to regular worship and response to the individual needs of parishioners?

No. I presume that this question refers to the laity, for clearly it is not true of the clergy. All that we have is given us by God to be used for His glory. The layman must be guided by his own conscience. If he has time, talents, or money, and opportunity to use them for the promotion and extension of the Kingdom of God, of which the Church is the principal instrument, it is his duty to do so.

**503. Why is not more stress laid on the duty of godparents?**

In modern conditions, godparents cannot do much for their godchildren while the parents are alive except pray for them. If the parents die before the children are grown up, the godparents become responsible for seeing that they are brought up in the Church. During the lifetime of the parents, however, whether they do their duty by the children or not, the godparents can hardly interfere.

**504. Can't I let my children grow up and choose for themselves?**

You can, but if you do you will be grossly neglecting your duty to them and to God, Who entrusted them to your care. You can also turn them out into the street to look after themselves and choose whether they will live or die, but if you do, no one will say a word in your defense. The assumption behind your question seems to be that religion is a thing which one may choose or refuse, like a taste or hobby. In reality, the glory and service of God is the purpose for which we are put into this world. You have no more right to refuse a child the knowledge which alone will make him happy or useful in this world and the next than you have to neglect to feed or clothe him or to send him to school. There are not a number of different religions between which we are to choose. There is only one true religion, the Gospel of Jesus Christ, which we are free to accept or reject, just as we can go on living or kill ourselves; but if we reject life, or cause anyone else to reject it, we shall have to bear the consequences.

**505. Are not many Church members hypocrites who worship God on Sunday and please themselves the rest of the week?**

Are you one of them? If not, what right have you to ask such a question, which shows a lack of that charity without which whatever virtue you claim is useless? "Why beholdest thou the mote that is in thy brother's eye, but considerest not the beam that is in thine own eye? Thou hypocrite, first cast out the beam out of thine own eye; and then shalt thou see clearly to cast out the mote out of thy brother's eye" (St. Matthew 7:3, 5).

**506. Why do Episcopalian congregations have to be so cold and wanting in cordiality?**

It is true that many of us have much to learn in this respect. But, many people are reserved by temperament and do not open out easily to strangers. Anything like "heartiness" is as hateful to some people as it is natural to others. It is the duty of the clergy and church officers to get to know all their congregations, especially those who are young or lonely, and introduce them to suitable friends if they are needed.

**507. What can we do to stir the souls of men in our congregations?**

This question seems to come from a priest. Live as nearly as you can by the commandments of our Lord. Get to know your people, visit them regularly, pray for them continually, and let them know that you do and that you really have their interests at heart. And cultivate endless patience.

**508. What shall I do when after Absolution I go on doing the same things?**

This is a well-known spiritual disease, for which you should consult a skilled director of souls. Much depends on the kind of sins that you keep on doing. There are some grave sins of the flesh, from which, if the penitent cannot free himself at first, he is advised to go to confession again every time he commits them. You should, if possible, avoid the time, place, or persons that are most likely to lead you into temptation.

**509. Must we repent before being forgiven? Must we forgive those who do not repent, such as an unfaithful husband who glories in his unfaithfulness?**

We certainly must repent or we shall not be forgiven. "Except ye repent, ye shall all likewise perish" (St. Luke 13:3). You must pray for your husband's repentance and be ready to forgive him as soon as he begins to repent. However, as long as he persists in adultery you ought not to live with him as his wife. You should,

after consulting an experienced priest who knows the circumstances, get a legal separation—not a divorce, for that would only
set him free to treat someone else as he is treating you, and would
not set you free, because the Church, by Divine command, does
not recognize the right of the State to dissolve a marriage. You
married him for better or for worse, and whatever he does he
is still your husband as long as you are both alive.

**510. Are we wrong if we fail to worship God every Sunday
through pressing material demands?**

God does not expect us to neglect necessary duties or to do
what is impossible; but we must not make our duties an excuse
unless they are really necessary.

**511. Why are some parishes unfriendly and lacking in spiritual
growth?**

Perhaps because those who think so do not pray enough for
their priest and his people.

**512. How is a Christian student to witness for Christ in his
college campus?**

He should observe strictly all his religious duties, never talking
about religion without necessity, but making no secret of his
belief and practice. He should do his work as diligently as he
can, for that is what he is there for. He should take his full share
in the social life of the college and be as kind, friendly, and
sociable as he can, without interfering with his work. He should
be especially friendly to the lonely and unpopular. He should
show his displeasure at any profane or dirty language and refuse
to take part in any form of gambling or in any entertainment
inconsistent with his religion. He should be prudent in his use
of alcoholic drinks, which, even in moderate quantities, weaken
self-control; he will be wise to abstain entirely from anything
stronger than beer or wine. He should be particularly discreet
in his relations with the other sex. He should be most careful to
pay all his bills promptly, to avoid any unnecessary expenses, and
to keep a close guard over his tongue.

**513. How should we be able to distinguish a Christian student
from a non-Christian?**

Everybody who has been baptized is a Christian. The student
who practices the Christian religion should be known by his
regular attendance at his religious duties, his conscientiousness in
everything that he does or undertakes to do, and his kindness

and good will toward all his neighbors, even if they do not treat him well. Psalm 15 is a good guide.

**514. How can I bring the good news to friends who are mentally disturbed or who ignore all organized religion?**

Pray for them regularly and earnestly, win their confidence, and watch for your opportunity.

**515. What makes a prayer circle valid? How many should there be?**

The word "valid" has no meaning here. That is "valid" which is recognized by the community, whether Church or State; as when we speak of a valid marriage or a valid will. What you appear to mean is, what sort of prayer circle is most effective? I should say one in which all the members without exception are in dead earnest. There should not be less than three members or more, perhaps, than twelve (the number of the Apostles).

**516. How am I to seek a spiritual director?**

Consult the wisest priest you know. If you do not know one likely to help you, write to the Society of St. John the Evangelist at Boston, Massachusetts, or to the Holy Cross Fathers at West Park, New York.

**517. What help and advice can I get for renewed faith in sacraments?**

See Question 516.

**518. Which need the clergy more, "outsiders" or "insiders"?**

"Outsiders," because they do not know where to obtain grace. "Insiders" have the Bible and the sacraments. Some priests are more competent and have more experience in evangelistic work for "outsiders"; others, in pastoral work for "insiders." "There are diversities of gifts, but the same Spirit" (I Cor. 12:4).

*Chapter Thirty-Two*

## MISCELLANEOUS MATTERS

**519. How can I answer Russellites (Jehovah's Witnesses) and Seventh-day Adventists, who object to saluting the flag, inoculation, and blood transfusion?**

It is useless to argue with members of these sects, because they have not the capacity to reason. All these practices are voluntary, so that there is no need to argue. If you refer to parents who refuse to allow their children at school to salute the flag or benefit by inoculation or blood transfusion, they must be told firmly that these rules are made for the benefit of the great majority of the children and must be obeyed. If they do not wish their children to observe the rules they must take them away from the school and educate them at their own expense.

**520. How can I help to restore the faith of students who have lost it through Communist infiltration?**

This is altogether outside my experience. I think you should win their confidence, avoid argument with them, but pray constantly for them. Make yourself familiar with the Communist case and the answer to it, and know the Christian religion as thoroughly as you can, for they probably don't know much about it. Don't be drawn into an argument, but be ready to show that what they have been told about the Christian religion is not true.

**521. Does any sincere Anglican or Romanist continue in sin that grace may abound?**

I should not think so; I can only say with St. Paul, God forbid (Rom. 6:2).

**522. What is vicarious suffering of the Church for individual Christians, non-Christians, or lapsed Christians?**

There is no such thing. Our Saviour made, by His one oblation of Himself once offered, a full, perfect, and sufficient sacrifice, oblation, and satisfaction for the sins of the whole world (see Article 31, first sentence). However, we are all members one of another; when one member suffers all suffer with him.

**523. How can a lay person who has gifts of physical or psychical healing best function in the Body of Christ?**

Consult the Guild of St. Raphael. He should do nothing without the approval of the diocesan bishop.

**524. What is the relation of reason to revelation?**

This is an immense question which can only be touched on here. Revelation is the way in which God has given us knowledge of Himself and of His plan for us. Reason also is given us by God; it is the way in which knowledge in general is reached by our minds. By reason we are enabled to understand the meaning of revelation; by revelation our reason is enlightened with the knowledge of God. Since both come from God, they cannot be contrary to each other. They may appear for a time to contradict each other, but if we wait patiently we shall sooner or later find that we have misunderstood one or the other, or both. The greatest Christian thinkers have always spoken highly of the Divine gift of reason; to attack or despise it is a sure sign of pride, folly, and false thinking.

**525. Why do so few vestrymen make use of business or professional experience to promote the Church's mission?**

I can only say that I do not think the suggestion is true.

**526. What is the difference between Christian propaganda, such as that issued by the Episcopal Book Club, and "brain washing"?**

Presumably the inquirer has not been "brain-washed," any more than I have, and therefore we are not in a position to know. No one is "brain-washed" voluntarily; it is a form of compulsory propaganda imposed by the Communists. Christian propaganda is never, or should not be, forced on any grown-up person. (Children have to be taught religion, like any other subject, by compulsion; for they have not the experience to learn for themselves what they ought to know, and until their reason is fully developed they must learn to obey lawful authority.) The arguments for the Christian religion are addressed to the reason, and hearers are encouraged, if capable of judging, to read the other side. On the other hand, the Communist method, if I am not mistaken, is to repeat constantly the same jargon until the hearers, who are forbidden to hear the other side, are hypnotized into believing it to be true. Christianity has been accepted by many nations of their own free will. Communism has never been accepted by any nation except under armed compulsion. Marxian communism is a religion of class hatred: Christianity is a religion of universal love. The gospel of Karl Marx is false; the Gospel of Jesus Christ is true.

# INDEX

(The reference numbers here given are to numbered questions, not to pages.)

Chrysostom, St. John, Bishop of
  Constantinople, 97
Clement, St., Bishop of Rome, 181
Colenso, John William, heretical
  bishop, 124
Communion, part of Church, Chap.
  10 (intro.), 156
Communion: admission to, 169; daily,
  356; perseverance and, 497; sacra-
  ment of, 219–52
communion of saints, 291, 301
Confession, sacramental, 254–65, 385
Confirmation, 200–202, 211–18
Councils, General, 135, and the
  Orthodox, 142; list of, 416
cremation, 376
Cross, sign of the, 355, 366
crosses, veiling of, 396, 464
Curwen, Hugh, Archbishop of
  Dublin, 161
Cyril, St., Bishop of Jerusalem, 237

Daniel, Book of, 56, 309
death, 24–26; Christian meaning of,
  284–300; preparation for, 498; see
  also Burial of the Dead
De Dominis, Marcantonio, Archbishop of Split, 161
denomination, 128
devil: created good, 6; in Gehenna,
  309; nature of, 15; opportunity of,
  237; serpent in Genesis a type of,
  74; service to, 204
discipline of clergy, 429, 447

economy of Christ, 494
Edward VI, 156
Elizabeth I, 156
England: Church courts in, 449; his-
  tory of Church in, 156
Epiphanius, St., Archbishop of
  Cyprus, 97
Episcopalian, 426–27, 460; see also
  Anglican
Erasmus, 381
eternity, 1
Eucharist (see Communion, sacra-
  ment of)
evil, not created by God, 1, 6
Evangelicals, 466

faith, 94

Fall of Man, 38, 60, 72
fast days, 382–97
fasting Communion, 232, 236, 280
feast days, 371, 393
foreknowledge, Divine, 88, 90
free will, 13, 86, 204
Fundamentalist International, 450
funerals, 373–75

Gandhi, 81
Gehenna, 309
gladiators, 120
GOD, 1–7; see also JESUS CHRIST,
  SPIRIT, TRINITY
godparents, 503
Golden Rule, 108
grace, 78–85; see also sacraments
Gregory the Great, St., Bishop of
  Rome, 304

Hades, 297, 303
Hall, Frederick, American theologian, 88, 321
Hall, Joseph, Bishop of Norwich, 97
hats, women's, 402–3, 409
healing, spiritual, 267–70, 523; health,
  71
Hell, 309–13; see also Gehenna,
  Hades, Sheol
Henry VIII, 156
Hinduism, 18
holy water, 367
hospitals, 486
hours of prayer, 379, 495
Huddleston, Fr. Trevor, 489
hypnosis, self-, 16

Ignatius, St., Bishop of Antioch, 181,
  185
Ignatius Loyola, St., 71
image of GOD, 58
Immaculate Conception, 99
immersion, baptismal, 209
immortality, 287
Incarnation, 28–29
incense, 492
individualist heresy, 101–3, 111, 117,
  126, 214, 504
insurance, 336
intention, 154
intinction (in Holy Communion),
  240